"John Feinstein maintains that the best of all golf stories come from Q School, and he's certain to go right on maintaining that up until he writes a book about the British Open. Actually, Feinstein makes a good case for his contention, and *Tales from Q School* is full of stories that will probably make most of the people who read the book grateful that they're not trying to make a living on the golf course."
— Bill Littlefield, *Only a Game,* National Public Radio

"Veteran sports writer John Feinstein went through the six rounds that comprise the PGA Tour Qualifying Tournament, which golfers must survive to qualify to play on the PGA Tour. His account shows all the pain, frustration, and elation that define golf." — Allen Pierleoni, *Sacramento Bee*

"*Tales from Q School* returns to the format that made *A Good Walk Spoiled* a bestseller.... [Feinstein] fills the pages with anecdotes from present, former, and hopeful Tour stars.... Readers will see glimpses of themselves in these professional golfers as they face the mounting pressure, enjoy a jubilant celebration, or are brought to their knees in one of the game's many humbling moments."
— Jennifer DeCamp, *St. Petersburg Times*

"Every golf fan (and Feinstein fan) should read *Tales from Q School*.... Feinstein takes readers inside the lives and dreams and nightmares of pro golfers young and old. Inside Tommy Tolles's nine-hole nightmare (now, that's a good week spoiled) and inside Brett Wetterich's dream come true. They finished one shot apart—and about $3 million apart in earnings. *Tales from Q School* is full of those stories, and some of the best are about golfers you've never heard of and probably never will. Unless you read the book."
— Bryan French, *Fort Worth Star-Telegram*

"Feinstein's story is not one of verdant courses and green jackets, but rather of those other 'greens': the ones where the putts don't fall; the one that is fatal inexperience; the one that describes the sickly pallor of nausea; the one that speaks to envy. Some may prefer the next chapter in Tiger's tale. But to me this is an equally captivating yarn. And one to which I can more readily relate." —msnbc.com

"Fantastic. It really leaves you with a sense of how incredibly difficult it is to make it to the tour. It is also one of the more humorous golf books on the market. Funny stories are sprinkled about and there are plenty of underdogs to root for. I highly recommend it for golf lovers." —golface.wordpress.com

"John Feinstein has rightly been acclaimed as one of America's best sports writers.... He has to find and create drama where the big, on-stage drama has already taken place in public and is already known to the fan. At this task, discovering the stories behind the flash, he has no peer. In *Tales from Q School*, however, Feinstein faces another problem entirely: How to make us care about a bunch of golfers who—for the most part—nobody knows at all. He has succeeded so brilliantly that *Tales from Q School* becomes the very best of tension-fraught adventures, with some episodes literally hair-raising in intensity." —Lawrence Henry, *American Spectator*

"If you want a closer look into the stress and torture which come with what is known in golf circles as the toughest tournament in the world, this is a must read.... The book is the latest in a series of great ones from John Feinstein."
—Dennis Miller, *Inside Bay Area*

Tales from Q School

Tales from Q School

INSIDE GOLF'S FIFTH MAJOR

John Feinstein

BACK BAY BOOKS
Little, Brown and Company
New York   Boston   London

Back Bay Books / Little, Brown and Company
Hachette Book Group USA
237 Park Avenue, New York, NY 10017
Visit our Web site at www.HachetteBookGroupUSA.com

Originally published by Little, Brown and Company, May 2007
First Back Bay paperback edition, June 2008

Back Bay Books is an imprint of Little, Brown and Company. The Back Bay Books name and logo are trademarks of Hachette Book Group USA, Inc.

Library of Congress Cataloging-in-Publication Data
Feinstein, John.
  Tales from Q school : inside golf's fifth major / John Feinstein. — 1st ed.
    p. cm.
  ISBN 978-0-316-01430-4 (hc) / 978-0-316-01432-8 (pb)
  1. Golf — Tournaments — United States.   2. PGA Tour (Association).
  I. Title.
  GV970.F458 2006
  796.352'660973 — dc22   2006031380

10   9   8   7   6   5   4   3   2   1

RRD-IN

Printed in the United States of America

This is dedicated to the memory of absent loved ones:

Tom Mickle

Hymie Perlo

Red Auerbach

Vivian Richman

Dad

CONTENTS

Tales from Q School

INTRODUCTION

In 1995, when *A Good Walk Spoiled* was published, I was thrilled by how many readers seemed to get caught up in the lives of the players about whom I had written.

What fascinated me was that most of the comments I received about the book weren't about the sections on Greg Norman, Nick Faldo, or even Nick Price, Paul Azinger, or Davis Love III — all stars who generously shared both time and thoughts with me during my research.

The names that came up most often in conversation were Paul Goydos, Brian Henninger, and Jeff (not John) Cook. All were PGA Tour rookies in 1993 when I began my research; all had to go back to Qualifying School at the end of that year. Goydos got his card back that December and has remained on the tour ever since, winning the Bay Hill Invitational in 1996 before injuries and a divorce clouded his career. He began 2007 with a stunning victory at the Sony Open in Hawaii, capping a remarkable comeback. Henninger missed getting his card by one shot at the end of '93 but won the Deposit Guaranty Golf Classic in 1994. He has bounced from the PGA Tour to the Nationwide Tour and back the past few years and found himself back at Q School in the fall of 2005.

Jeff Cook's story may be the one that most clearly defines how cruel a world professional golf can be. He arrived at the 17th hole on the final day of the '93 Q School at PGA West sitting squarely on "the number"—the score that, even though there are no scoreboards at Q School, everyone somehow knows will be needed to qualify for the PGA Tour. After a twenty-minute wait on the tee, Cook hit a perfect six-iron to an island green that flew right over the flag and was probably no more than six inches from sucking back to the pin, which would have set up a possible birdie, an easy par. Instead, the ball just hung on the top shelf of the green, leaving a brutal downhill birdie putt that he rolled four feet past the cup. He missed coming back by about an inch, and that inch was the difference between getting his card back and not getting it back. He had one final chance at the difficult 18th hole, but his 20-foot birdie putt swerved just low of the hole, making it official: he had finished one shot outside the number.

He never played on the PGA Tour again.

After several more years on the Nike Tour, Cook realized his time had passed and made the hard decision to become a weekend golfer. He was hired by Mizuno as a club rep, which allows him to make a good living and spend three days a week at tour sites, still hanging out with old friends.

Whenever I see him, usually standing on the range at a tour event, we talk about the "old days" and laugh about things that happened during Jeff's one full year on the tour, frequently retelling the story about the day Jeff was paired with Tom Watson in the third round in Los Angeles and caught himself wondering what Watson would think of his putting stroke as he lined up a birdie attempt on number one. Three putts later, he walked off the green with a bogey and noticed that Watson was standing with his back turned to the green, practicing his putting stroke. It was then that Jeff realized there was only one putting stroke Watson had any interest in, and it wasn't Jeff's.

"You know, I feel like I'm very lucky," Jeff often says. "There are a lot of guys who are like me: pretty good players, but, for one reason or another, they aren't going to be able to get out here and be consistent money winners. They're going to play the Nationwide [formerly known as the Ben Hogan, the Nike, and the Buy.com Tour] and make some kind of living, or play the Hooters [Tour] or mini-tours until they run out of time and money. I think I knew when it was my time. I never got to the point where I hated doing it but kept on because there was nothing else I could do. That's why I'm lucky."

Cook, who grew up in Indiana and graduated from Indiana University, still dreams of someday being the golf coach at his alma mater. But for now, he enjoys his life, and he doesn't wake up every morning wondering if his golf dreams are nothing more than fantasies.

"If nothing else, I can say I did get there," he said. "I was a full-fledged PGA Tour player. I wish it had lasted longer, but who doesn't? I think every athlete faces the question at some point about when it's time to quit. It's especially hard in golf because there *are* stories about guys who flail around for years and then find it. Look at Tom Lehman.

"But for every Tom Lehman, there are a thousand guys out there thinking they're Tom Lehman. The problem is, only one of them—if that—is going to be right."

IN THE BACK OF my mind, I always wanted to go back to Q School. In the years after *A Good Walk Spoiled,* Q School became a sort of cult story among golf fans and the media. The Golf Channel began televising the finals in 1996, and PGA Tour Productions put together an annual one-hour documentary that aired on NBC. David Gould wrote a book called *Q School Confidential* that focused on the 1998 finals but was more about Q School history and lore than one particular year at Q School.

When I went to PGA West for the 1993 Q School finals,

three other print reporters were there. In 2005, in addition to the Golf Channel, there were at least thirty writers on the premises of the Orange County National Golf Center and Lodge in Winter Garden, Florida. That isn't exactly a Masters turnout, but it does reflect a quantum leap in interest.

In spite of the growth in coverage and interest, most people who follow golf still think the six-round finals that are on television are Q School. In fact, the case can be made that the finals are now the least pressurized aspect of Q School, because everyone in the finals knows he will have some kind of job playing golf the next year. If he isn't one of the thirty players (and ties — those tied for the last available spot) who make it to the PGA Tour, he will have, at the very least, some status on the triple-A Nationwide Tour. When the Nationwide Tour began in 1990 (as the Ben Hogan Tour), the average weekly purse was $100,000. Now it is closer to $550,000. That is still less than 15 percent of what PGA Tour golfers play for each week, but enough for some players to make a living.

That doesn't mean there isn't heartbreak at the finals. Every year, there are players who come up a shot or two short, often for a bizarre or hard-to-envision reason. Almost anyone who has followed golf for more than fifteen minutes has seen Joe Daley's two-foot putt on the 17th hole at PGA West (the same hole that brought Jeff Cook grief) in 2000 go right in the middle of the hole and then, somehow, pop back out, as if someone had pressed a spring underneath the cup.

"To me that's the quintessential Q School moment," said Casey Martin, the disabled player who successfully took the PGA Tour to the Supreme Court so that he could use a golf cart in tournaments. "I still remember seeing that happen and thinking to myself, 'There are two days left in this thing, but he's going to miss by one shot.' Sure enough, that's what happened. That's Q School right there."

Martin knows about Q School. He went through it eight times, made the finals four times, but was never successful making the PGA Tour via the finals. His only year on tour, 2000, was the result of a 14th-place finish on the Nike Tour. In those days, the top 15 players on the Nike got PGA Tour cards. Nowadays, the top 20 players on that tour, currently sponsored by Nationwide Insurance, make the PGA Tour.

The presence of the Nationwide 20 has cut the number of spots available at Q School. Once, 50 players and ties received tour cards. Now it is 30 and ties — this at a time when about 1,200 players sign up each year, even though the fee to play rose from $100 in 1965 to $4,500 in 2005, with a bump to $5,000 for those who would have to play first stage in 2006. The first year of Q School, 49 players showed up, and 17 cards were issued. But that was a long time ago in golf history.

What makes Q School so fascinating is the breadth of stories. In 2005, the 1,205 players who signed up to play ranged from Larry Mize, the 1987 Masters champion, to a guy whose *low* round at first stage was an 89. There was one woman in the field, Isabelle Beisiegel, who played for the second straight year and finished last at her first-stage site. And there were all sorts of names familiar to golf fans. When Paul Azinger decided not to play, Mize was the only major champion in the field, but there were past PGA Tour winners, veterans trying to hang on, and, of course, youngsters attempting to make it to "the big tour" for the first time.

Casey Martin was one of those who played in 2005 — for the last time. After watching his game go south for several years, he decided to make one final effort to get back to the tour. He worked hard throughout the summer before showing up to play his first stage in Rancho Murieta, California.

The chances of getting from first stage to second stage to the finals and the PGA Tour are pretty close to 100-to-1. Martin knew all that. He also knew that his game wasn't nearly what it once was. But, like a lot of players, he wanted one more shot. He failed to make it through first stage, missing by six shots. Unlike some players who never figure it out, he knew it was time to move on.

"Put it this way, it didn't come as a shock to me," Martin said. "I know for some guys, walking away is impossible—especially if you've ever had success. You just *know* you're on the verge of a breakthrough. Guys say, 'I'm hitting it great, but I can't make any putts.' Well, last I looked, putting is part of the game. There's always a reason. At some point, you have to look in the mirror and say, 'The reason is that I'm not good enough.' That's not easy for anybody."

Never is that more apparent than at Q School. It is toughest to watch players who have been good enough at some point, because they can make the case that they aren't fooling themselves. They know they have the ability to play on the tour.

"It's the finding it again that's so tough," said Stephen Gangluff, who played on the PGA Tour in 2002 but bounced all the way back to playing first stage in 2005. "I feel as if I have these demons following me around sometimes. I know there's a good player locked up somewhere inside me, but I've got to find a way to chase the demons and let that player out."

One of my more vivid memories from researching this book is of Gangluff sprawled in a chair outside the locker room at the Tournament Players Club (TPC) Tampa Bay, having just shot 75 in the third round of first stage to knock himself out of contention. He couldn't leave the course because the approach of Hurricane Wilma had forced the schedule to be moved up so that the final round would start an hour after the third round began. It was too hot to pound balls on the range, and what was the point anyway? He couldn't bring himself to walk into the dining room and sit with other players who were rehashing their rounds and preparing for the last 18 holes. And he was too much of a professional to do the easy thing and withdraw from the tournament so he could get the hell out of there.

So he sat in that chair, staring into space, hoping, no doubt, that he would wake up at home in bed and find that it had all been a bad dream. Instead, with no chance at all to qualify, he got out of the chair and ground out a 67 in the last round — an effort that still left him six shots and twenty-one players outside the number.

You have to hope that there are happier days ahead for someone like Gangluff — and for many other players I encountered along the way. Q School is filled with sad stories, because, let's face it, most of the players who enter aren't going to make it to the PGA Tour when they hand out the cards in December. In fact, most of the players who enter Q School will never make it to the tour. Only about one-third of them will ever make it to the finals, and about half will never make it out of first stage.

Think about that for a moment. There are no bad players at the second stage of Q School. You might be able to fake your way into first stage — although the tour has cracked down on frauds in recent years — but you can't fake your way through first stage and into second.

Most of those who sign up for first stage are superb players. There are more than 30 million golfers in the United States. Perhaps 2,000 can legitimately think about trying to make a living playing the game. Maybe 500 of those players are good enough to play somewhere — PGA Tour, Nationwide Tour, NGA/Hooters Tour, or the mini-tours — and pay their bills. Half of that number are good enough to play regularly on the PGA Tour or the Nationwide on a steady basis, and, of course, only a handful end up becoming millionaires and owning their own airplanes.

And in case you haven't been paying close attention, there's only *one* Tiger Woods.

Even among that tiny gaggle good enough to make it to the PGA Tour, there is absolutely no guarantee of continued success. Each year, most of the players who make it through Q School to the tour find themselves back at Q School the following year. At the end of 2005, eleven of the thirty-five players who had earned their cards at the 2004 Q School finished in the top 125 on the money list to retain full privileges for 2006. Three—Sean O'Hair, Lucas Glover, and Jason Bohn—won tournaments, guaranteeing themselves exemptions through 2007.

It isn't the least bit uncommon for ex–tour players like Martin and Gangluff to find themselves back at first stage and failing to make it through. Mike Grob, another ex–tour player, did make it through the same first stage that Gangluff failed in Tampa, but he did so carrying his own bag because he didn't want to pay for a caddy for the week. And second stage? The six sites where second stage events are held each year may be the six most tension-filled golf venues in the world. The number of quality players forced to play second stage is staggering. The players in the 2005 second stage included multiple PGA Tour winners. Larry Mize, Bill Glasson, Steve Stricker, Dan Forsman, Brian Henninger, and Blaine McCallister, as well as more than a dozen others who had won at least one PGA Tour event.

Success in professional golf is more fleeting than in just about any other sport. When a successful pitcher like Steve Blass suddenly can't throw strikes anymore and sees his career flame out, it is such a big story that thirty years later, any pitcher with a sudden case of wildness is referred to as having "Blass disease," and everyone in baseball knows exactly what that means.

In golf, very good players get some form of "Blass disease" all the time. Some get the yips with their putter, others with their driver. Still others simply can't score anymore. Most of the time, there's no explanation for what makes golfers fall to earth. They all *think* there's an explanation—a swing change, an equipment change, an instructor change—but if it were that simple, they would all straighten themselves out and be back on top in no time.

Some do find the answer. Steve Stricker, who has won three times on the tour and almost won the PGA Championship in 1998, couldn't make it through the 2005 Q School finals. But he got a sponsor exemption into the Shell Houston Open in April 2006, shot a final-round 65 to finish third, and began to play like the young star he had once been. He finished in a tie for sixth place at the U.S. Open and had made more than $1 million halfway through the 2006 season. He would not have to go back to Q School at the end of 2006. "I hope I never have to go again," he said.

Q School is not a place anyone wants to go back to, but most players will tell you they're glad they had the experience at least once. "Think about this," said Steve Pate, a six-time winner on the tour who has been back to Q School several times in recent years. "Have you ever encountered any player who told you he *didn't* have a Q School story?"

The answer to that is no, unless you count Tiger Woods, Phil Mickelson, Justin Leonard, and, more recently, Ryan Moore, all current players who were so good coming out of college that they managed to avoid Q School. A number of top foreign players also have been able to steer around it.

But just about everyone else who has joined the tour since 1965 has been there, and they all have stories to tell—some funny, some sad, many both. There were 1,205 entrants in the 2005 Q School, and every one of them had a story to tell. Time and space have limited me to a relative handful of those stories, but watching all three stages and hearing stories about Q Schools present and past was a remarkable experience.

There has been some talk among golf people that Q School's

time has passed, that with the growing importance of the Nationwide Tour, it should be the sole proving ground for the PGA Tour. After all, they argue, a full year of golf played on a competitive tour proves more about a player than one, two, or three weeks of Q School in the late fall.

That may be true. But Q School should continue to be part of the PGA Tour. As heartbreaking as it can be, it also produces the most unlikely and uplifting stories one is likely to encounter anywhere in golf. Ask anyone who has watched the last round of a major championship up close and the last round of Q School up close which one has more human drama, and the answer will always be the same: Q School. And if you, like me, happened to be fortunate enough to be standing next to Jay Haas on the final day of the 2005 Q School while he watched his son Bill line up a four-foot birdie putt that would either put him on the PGA Tour or leave him one shot away, you wouldn't even have to think twice about your answer.

Watching Jay Haas watch Bill Haas is the kind of moment you can only see at Q School.

The Fifth Major.

1

Dreams (and Nightmares) Come True

THE DREAM IS ALWAYS THE SAME. It starts with Tommy Tolles standing on the ninth tee of the Panther Lake course at Orange County National Golf Center and Lodge on a windy Monday afternoon in December. He has a three-wood in his hands and is wondering: "Is eleven the number? Could it slide to ten? Maybe it will go to 12. Do I really need a three-wood? The hole is playing downwind, and the fairways are baked from the wind and lack of rain. A par might very well be all I need." For a moment, he wishes that instead of his pal Jamie Rowland, he had a tour caddy on his bag. Nothing against Rowland, who had walked 18 grueling holes every day for six days just to try to help Tolles, but this is one of those times when talking to someone who has been through this sort of golf-trauma would be helpful.

Tolles finally gets over the ball, three-wood in his hands. He takes the club back, and he can hear from the sound as he follows through that he has caught the ball flush, that, in golf lingo, he's hit it right on the screws. The ball screams straight down the middle of the fairway, several yards to the right of where Tolles was aiming. The left rough, he knew, was safe; he could get the ball on the green from there. But there was water on the right.

The ball drifts a little bit right, and Tolles feels his heart pounding. It hits the ground and bounces—hard—to the right. It is bouncing in the direction of the water, and because the fairway is so burned-out, there's nothing to slow it down. It gets closer and closer. By now Tolles knows what is going to happen. It disappears into the lake. "No!" Tolles wants to scream. It can't be in the water. Only it is, and he knows, at that moment, that all his work to get back onto the PGA Tour has been for naught.

He wakes up, drenched in sweat. Even sleeping on top of the covers, he's covered in sweat.

That isn't the worst part, though. The worst part is knowing he is going to have the dream again.

And again.

IT IS LIKE THAT every single year at what is now officially called the PGA Tour Qualifying Tournament, although to everyone connected with golf, it is known simply as "Q School." Once upon a time, there was a "school" aspect to the event, with players forced to sit in classrooms to learn rules, etiquette, and teaching techniques, since, once upon a time, all golf pros were expected to be teachers as well as players.

Every year at Q School, there are stories of heartbreak. At the 2005 Q School finals, Tolles was one of those stories. An accomplished player who has finished as high as 16th on the PGA Tour money list, Tolles was trying to fight his way back onto the tour after years of swing changes and frustration had landed him in golf's minor leagues. He had struggled for almost five and a half rounds, staying on the fringes of contention more because of smarts and experience than because of the way he was hitting the ball.

"I had pretty much given up hope to get back to the tour midway through the last day," he said later. "I was just trying to make sure I had full Nationwide [the tour's highest minor league] status. Then I birdied 18 [he had started his round on the 10th tee] and hit a four-iron to four feet on number one. Suddenly, it clicked in. Two hours later, I'm on the ninth tee, and I've birdied six of nine holes and I'm right there with that three-wood in my hands."

Which is where the dream of returning to the tour ended and the recurring nightmare began. After his ball found the water, he double-bogeyed the hole. His wife in tears, Tolles was finished except for the dream that would not go away.

For Grant Waite, another accomplished veteran, there was no need to rally late, no reason to believe that the week would end up as anything other than a ticket back to the place where he had happily made his living for most of a dozen years. He had steadily played his way into a comfortable position, well inside the number that would put him back on the PGA Tour. With nine holes to play, he was 16 under par for the event, which, he figured, put him in about 10th place. Among the 165 players who had made it to the Q School finals, the top 30 (and ties) would make it to the 2006 tour. There are no scoreboards on the golf course at Q School, but the players always have a sense of what the number needed to make the top 30 is going to be. With the wind blowing steadily and the golf course playing hard, Waite and everyone else knew that the number that day would be around 10 or 11 under par.

Sixteen under, after a very solid 32 on the front nine, certainly felt comfortable. But then Waite somehow four-putted the 10th hole for a double bogey, and he suddenly felt a little shaky. Another bogey and then another, and now he had no control over his golf swing or his emotions. It took him 42 shots to maneuver his way around the back nine, and when he finally holed out on 18, his hands were shaking and his face was chalk white. He wasn't so much angry as stunned. His wife, Lea, who had walked every hole with him for six days, was in a state of shock, too.

"People simply don't understand what this is like unless they've gone through it," she had said earlier in the week. "There's no tension in sports quite like this tension."

Her husband agreed. "You aren't asked to do anything at Q School as a golfer that you aren't capable of doing," he said. "But you have to do it *this week*. Not next week, not last week, *this* week. There's no appeal, no way to get a second chance. And there's very little margin for error. Too many guys playing for too few spots. You can't count on playing well for six straight days, but you have to make sure your bad days aren't really bad. One over, two over, you can survive. You just can't throw in a six-over or seven-under day."

Waite had followed the script perfectly the first five days, hanging close to par the first two days when he was fighting his swing, then playing the next three rounds at 13 under par with one round to play. "The key now," he said late on the penultimate afternoon, "is to not think about any number, just go out and play well tomorrow."

Easily said. Not so easily executed. What is more difficult in life than not thinking? Especially when you tell yourself not to think?

For nine holes on that final day, Waite didn't think. But the instant he double-bogeyed the 10th hole, he started thinking. The result was that he came up one shot short—or, more accurately, one shot long—of where he needed to be. Thirty-two players finished 108 holes of golf in 422 or fewer shots. Waite was one of ten players, including Dan Forsman, a five-time winner on the PGA Tour, who needed 423 shots. In many cases, that 423rd shot was less than a foot long, a tap-in that the player knew would doom him to a tour where the total prize money each week is far less than the weekly winner's share on the PGA Tour. When the 2006 PGA Tour opened in January, the purse for the first full-field event of the year was $5.1 million, with the winner getting $918,000. When the Nationwide Tour began play in Panama in February, the purse was $550,000, with the winner receiving $99,000. The leading money winner on the Nationwide Tour in 2005 was Troy Matteson, who made $495,009. There were 151 players who earned more than that on the PGA Tour—including 79 who made more than $1 million in prize money for the year.

The PGA Tour is a dream world of big-money contracts for equipment and endorsements; courtesy cars and courtesy phones; people standing by to grant your every wish, whether it is a shopping spree for your wife or luxury box seats to a ball game. The Nationwide Tour is real life: searching for cheap airfares or driving from event to event; looking for the best rate the Fairfield Inn or Hampton Inn or Holiday Inn can give you. It is playing in front of hundreds instead of thousands. It is being shocked by how much it costs to refuel your car versus how much it costs to refuel your plane.

It is 423 shots instead of 422.

"It hurts, it really hurts," Dan Forsman said. "I think it hurts more when you've known what life is like on the PGA Tour. To say we don't get spoiled would be silly. We do get spoiled—bigtime. Then you put everything you have into getting yourself back there, heart and soul for six days, and you come up an inch or two short. It's tough to take."

Like Tolles, Forsman had rallied late on the final day, making three birdies on the final nine of the week to get to 10 under par. "When you've done this for as long as I have, you have a feel for what the number is going to be," he said. "You don't need a scoreboard. You can tell by the weather conditions, by the condition of the golf course. Your gut just tells you. Some guys think they know the number. In my gut, I *knew* the number was going to be 11—just *knew* it. I came to the last hole needing a birdie to get to 11. I was between nine and pitching wedge for my second shot and finally hit the wedge. It came up about 20 feet short. I knew exactly what was at stake. The putt just didn't break as much as I thought. It stayed a few inches outside the hole. That was how much I missed getting my job back by—three, four inches. I'm not sure I can remember feeling quite as crushed as I did at that moment."

Months later, Forsman's voice was soft and sad as he remembered that day. "In March I got to play at Bay Hill [a PGA Tour event in Orlando]. One day, I'm not sure why, I drove out to Orange County and just kind of walked around. I can't even tell you why I did it. Maybe I was looking for some kind of closure with what had happened in December. I just remember feeling a kind of melancholy walking around out there again, remembering shots—good and bad—from that week. I had a chance once to win the Masters on Sunday, and hit it in the water at 12 and finished seventh. That hurt. But this was different. I'm forty-seven years old. I can hear that clock ticking. I know time is going to run out on me—soon. I just want the chance to play against the best players on a week-to-week basis again before that clock runs out."

Everyone hears the clock—the old, the middle-aged, the young. When you miss at Q School, people pat you on the back, say "Good playing; you'll get 'em next year," and you don't want to hear it. Next year is never guaranteed in golf, except for an elite handful who have won major titles and climbed so far up the ladder they seemingly can't fall down. Tiger Woods, Phil Mickelson, Vijay Singh, Ernie Els, Fred Couples, and Jim Furyk are at that level. There may be a few others: Retief Goosen, Davis Love III, José María Olazábal, and David Toms are probably safe for the rest of their careers.

That's a short list. In 2004 and 2005, Larry Mize—whose 140-foot chip-in to beat Greg Norman in a play-off at the 1987 Masters is one of the most replayed and remembered shots in golf history—found himself back at Q School trying to regain fully exempt status on the tour. In 2006 two-time U.S. Open champion Lee Janzen kept his exempt status only by invoking a one-time exception granted to those in the top 50 on the all-time tour money list. By the end of 2006 he, like Mize, was back at Q School. Paul Azinger, the 1993 PGA champion and a Ryder Cup hero on numerous occasions, entered Q School in 2005, then decided part-time status on the tour was enough for him when combined with his work for ABC. Azinger would have preferred totally exempt status but decided in the end it wasn't worth the torture of Q School.

"You do wonder if you aren't pushing the envelope a little bit when you are paired with guys who call you 'Mr. Mize,'" Larry Mize said, laughing, as he hit balls on the range one afternoon. "One day after we got through playing, one of the kids in my group said to me, 'Mr. Mize, I just have to ask you about the shot at Augusta.' Actually, I kind of enjoy that. I never mind replaying that for people, because it was such a great moment for me. But then I realized later that the kid who asked me about it, who is now a peer I'm trying to compete with, was four years old when that shot happened. Now *that's* a little bit freaky."

Mize is forty-eight. Like Forsman and Waite (who is forty-two), he has some access to the PGA Tour as a "past champion"— someone who has won at least once on the tour during his career. It wasn't that long ago that a player in that category might get into twenty tournaments a year, but changes in the rules, designed to give younger players more opportunity to play, have made it tougher. For Mize, as a major champion, there might be fifteen chances a year to play. Forsman and Waite aren't likely to get that many opportunities. Waite, who first lost his full-time playing privileges in 2002 after ten years on the tour—including a victory in 1993 and a dramatic one-shot loss to Tiger Woods in Canada in 2001—spent a couple of years in the netherworld of "wanderers." He tried to get into PGA Tour events wherever and whenever he could, and when he couldn't, he played on the Nationwide Tour.

"At some point, you have to accept the fact that, like it or not, your golf game at this moment is only worthy of the Nationwide," he said. "That's tough to take when you've been on the PGA Tour for a while, but once you accept it, you have a better chance to find your game on the Nationwide." Waite had done that in 2005, playing in twenty Nationwide tournaments and only six PGA Tour events. Even so, it hadn't been easy for him. He had made only nine cuts and finished 96th on the money list. "It's a different world on that tour in so many ways," he said. "You're playing against young guys, who can hit it 50 yards past you and are focused on one thing: making the top 20 on the money list for the year so they can get onto the PGA Tour the next year without going to Q School. You see the kids on the Nationwide, and you realize that they're *you* fifteen or twenty years ago—fearless, excited to be there, and playing without any doubts at all." He smiled. "I would love to feel that way again, but I know I'm not going to."

Waite wasn't talking specifically about Peter Tomasulo when he described the young guns on the Nationwide Tour, but he might have been. Tomasulo was twenty-four and had been a professional for a little more than a year. He had gone from a barely recruited, barely scholarshipped (books only) freshman at the University of California to an all-American as a senior. He had started 2005 without status on any golf tour and had ended it in 35th place on the Nationwide Tour money list after winning the Alberta Classic, which gave him full status on the Nationwide. Tomasulo had come to Q School without any fears or any doubts. He knew that it was going to be just another step on his journey to the PGA Tour.

"My year had just been on an up escalator from the start," he said. "I'd gone from trying to make it onto the Canadian Tour to playing well on that tour to making it to the Nationwide Tour to finishing fourth in the Nationwide Tour Championship to get the 35th spot on the money list." That finish was crucial to To-masulo because it meant he didn't have to go to the second stage of Q School. Each year, there are three stages of Q School. A small cadre of players — those who finish between 126th and 150th on the PGA Tour money list and those who finish between 21st and 35th on the Nationwide Tour money list — are exempt from the first two stages. A somewhat larger group — past PGA Tour winners, anyone on the PGA Tour during that year, and those who finish between 36th and 70th on the Nationwide list — are exempt from first stage. Everyone else goes to one of fourteen first-stage sites around the country. In 2005 there were 1,205 Q School entries. Those who started at first stage had to ante up $4,500 to play. Once upon a time, the fee was $200, but inflation and the tour's desire to scare off those who might want to enter just to say they played in Q School have sent the price soaring in recent years. If the fee is a deterrent, no one has noticed a drop-off in entries because of it.

Tomasulo was exempt until the third and final stage. Like Waite, he appeared to be in perfect position going into the final day. He was at 11 under par, right on the number, when he began his round. He was at 12 under par with nine holes to play on that last afternoon, and he didn't have a shred of doubt about what was going to happen at the end of the day. But he got an awful break on the 10th hole, when his second shot to the par-five, a perfect layup, somehow landed squarely on top of a loose divot and stayed right there. "All the years I've played golf, that's never happened to me," he said later. "I had no idea how to play the shot. I ended up chunking it into the rough in front of the green, and the next thing I know, I've made a bogey instead of the birdie I was sure I was going to make. That was the first time I got a little nervous. In fact, it was the first time that the thought 'I wonder what the number will be?' crossed my mind. Until then, I wasn't even thinking about the number; I was just trying to make as many birdies as I could so I'd finish as high up on the final list as possible. Once that thought came into my head, I couldn't get it out no matter how hard I tried not to think about it."

Tomasulo bogeyed the next two holes but managed to right himself long enough to squeeze out a couple of tough pars and then birdie the 16th hole. He was at 10 under, convinced like everyone else that was probably one off the number. "But I had 18 left," he said. "A downwind, downhill par-five that I could easily reach in two. I knew I just had to get off the 17th with a par and then go after birdie on the 18th."

Maybe it was the twenty-minute wait on the tee — there is nothing in the world slower than the last round at Q School — or maybe it was the gusty wind or the difficult pin placement on the small back shelf of the water-protected green. Or maybe it was just nerves. Tomasulo selected an eight-iron, not wanting to come up short. Then he watched in horror as the ball drifted left of where he had aimed, took one big hop, and spun into a back bunker. "When I saw it go in there, my knees just about buckled," he said. "I'd seen other guys play out of there during the week, and I knew how tough a shot it was. But I had to try and get it close."

Trying to hit a perfect second shot to give himself a chance to save par, Tomasulo instead squirted the ball out of the bunker, and it ran straight across the green, almost rolling into the water. From there he made a double-bogey five and walked off the green knowing he wasn't going to be on the PGA Tour in 2006. "As I was watching my second shot run across the green, the thought went through my head, 'Oh, my God, you aren't making it. *Oh, my God, you aren't making it!*'" Tomasulo said. "It was a hollow feeling that went right to my knees. I just couldn't believe it."

The toughest part may have been having to play the 18th hole knowing that he had no chance — unless he could somehow hole out from the fairway for a miraculous double-eagle two. The two men he was playing with, Brett Wetterich and B. J. Staten, had managed to hang on to finish at 11 under, meaning they would be going to the PGA Tour, while Tomasulo went back to the Nationwide. "The worst part of the whole day was probably shaking hands with them on the 18th green and telling them congratulations," Tomasulo said. "Not because they weren't good guys, but because they had done what I couldn't do, and it hurt — it just really hurt."

He smiled. "I have no memory at all of what I said. I just hope I wasn't rude."

Tomasulo wasn't rude. Staten remembers him saying congratulations, but he also remembers the look on his face. "It may have been the happiest moment of my life," he said. "But shaking hands with Peter, I felt awful. I knew just how close I'd come to being exactly where he was."

Even if Tomasulo had been rude, chances are good neither Staten nor Wetterich would have noticed or cared at that moment. Tomasulo was in shock; they were in ecstasy. The three of them had spent more than five hours that day grinding toward the same goal. In the end, Wetterich and Staten had been able to lunge across the finish line. Tomasulo had come up a few steps short.

Because Staten had never made it to the tour before and was one of ten players who had survived all three stages to get his tour card, he was surrounded by both well-wishers and media after he signed his scorecard. Tomasulo stood a few yards away with his caddy. He appeared to be staring at Staten, as if torturing himself by watching the celebration. "It wasn't anything like that at all," he said. "I know I stood there for a while, because I didn't have the energy to walk back to the clubhouse. It was as if all the life had drained out of my body. But I don't remember anything about it. I don't even remember seeing B. J. or anyone around him. I didn't see anything. I didn't hear anything."

Staten's memory of those few moments isn't much better than Tomasulo's. "I know I was happy, and I remember a lot of people being there," he said. "But if you ask me any details—who said what to me, what I said to anyone—I don't remember much at all. It's all very hazy."

That's what Q School does to people. It leaves them dazed—with joy; with utter dejection. A small cadre are invited to a PGA Tour–sponsored party that night to welcome them to the tour. The rest go back to hotel rooms to pack their bags and wait till next year. If, by some chance, one of the nonqualifiers were to wander into the party for the qualifiers—perhaps to congratulate a friend—a tour official would very politely but firmly ask him to leave.

When Q School is over, you are either invited to the party or not. There is no in between.

2

Forty Years Ago...

THE ARGUMENT CAN BE MADE that there are more legendary tales attached to the PGA Tour's Qualifying School than to any other event in golf. This may explain why players refer to it as the fifth major.

The Q School's history isn't very long, dating back only to 1965. That was 105 years after the first British Open — or, as it is known in Europe, the Open Championship — was played and 70 years after the first U.S. Open was held. The PGA Championship was first played in 1916, and the Masters, the baby among the four majors, began in 1934. Each of them has had more than its share of memorable moments, and most of those moments have been chronicled in print, on film or tape, or orally. Golf fans have heard so much about Gene Sarazen's double eagle at the 15th hole in the 1935 Masters that most of them are probably convinced they witnessed it. Is there anyone who has ever touched a golf club — *looked* at a golf club — who hasn't seen the video of Tom Watson's chip-in at Pebble Beach in 1982, Larry Mize's miracle at Augusta in 1987, Tiger Woods's chip-in on the 16th green at the Masters in 2005, or Jack Nicklaus's march up the 18th fairway at St. Andrews during his last British Open, also in 2005?

That's just a small sampling, of course.

"The difference between moments like that and Q School is that when golfers get together—pros, I mean—they tell Q School stories," said Steve Pate, a six-time PGA Tour winner and recent Q School returnee. "You don't sit around and talk about Watson or Mize; you sit around and talk about Joe Daley's putt popping up out of the cup at PGA West or Cliff Kresge stepping backward to line up a putt and falling into the water. Or you tell your own stories, because everyone—I mean everyone—has them. If you're a golfer, you have a Q School story, with very few exceptions."

Tiger Woods is one of those exceptions. He won in his fourth tournament as a pro and has been exempt ever since. Phil Mickelson won a tournament while still in college, so he was already exempt when he turned pro in 1992 and never had to deal with Q School. Justin Leonard and Ryan Moore each earned enough money playing on sponsor exemptions (in 1994 and 2004, respectively) after graduating from college to avoid having to go to Q School to earn playing privileges. A number of top foreign players earned playing privileges in the United States through their success overseas: Greg Norman, Nick Price, Nick Faldo, and Vijay Singh, to name a few. Everyone else who has joined the tour since 1965 has been through Q School. Most have been more than once. All describe it as a difficult, if not torturous, experience. And yet all of them say that they're glad they did it—at least once.

"It's a rite of passage if you're a professional golfer," said Tom Watson, who finished fifth in the 1971 Q School and never looked back. "I'm not going to go so far as saying that I feel sorry for Tiger or Phil or Justin or anyone else who skips Q School completely. But I will say that I think they missed something. My memories of that week are as vivid as anything I've ever done in golf, including the majors that I've won. I remember every round, and I remember going back to the hotel every night, eating dinner by myself, and thinking about what I had to do the next day. I remember thinking I was in great shape the last day and then double-bogeying the 10th hole and having a panic attack for a moment, thinking, 'Oh, my God, am I going to blow this?' And I remember the incredible feeling of satisfaction when it was over, when I'd made it. It was thirty-five years ago, but all those feelings are still tangible now."

Very few people claim to enjoy Q School, although younger players approach it far more optimistically than older ones do. "I remember the first time I went to Q School, I was excited about it," said Dan Forsman, who first made it to the tour in 1982, the same year he turned pro. "When I had to go back twenty-two years later, I was bummed—and a little bit scared. The quality of player was so much higher than when I was a kid, it was almost intimidating at first. I had to remind myself that I was still a pretty good player. It wasn't all that easy."

But regardless of how difficult it may be or how disappointing it can be just to have to be there, most are like Watson. They see Q School as part of the journey. For some it is a continuing part of the journey. In 2006 Michael Allen played in the finals for the thirteenth time in eighteen years and was successful for the ninth time in getting back to the tour. Allen, who is now forty-eight, has never won on the tour and has succeeded only twice in keeping his playing status for consecutive years without a return to Q School. "I just put it on my calendar as if it's another tournament," he said, laughing. "I try to look at it as a golfing vacation."

Some of the best Q School stories appear to be apocryphal. Almost everyone tells the one about the guy who walked onto the first tee on the first day, heard the starter call his name, and raced off the tee so he could get sick in the bushes nearby. No one can name the player or the year, but everyone swears it happened. In 2000 Joe Daley did tap in a two-foot putt on the 17th hole at PGA West on the fourth day of the six-day competition. He then watched in horror as the ball somehow bounced back out of the cup. Naturally, he ended up missing his card by one shot. Cliff Kresge did step off an island green and into a lake while trying to line up a putt.

Peter Jacobsen, who won his first event on the tour in 1980 and his last in 2003, had to go to Q School only once, in the fall of 1976. Like everyone else, he remembers the pressure and the nerves, and the feeling of relief when he wobbled home on a frigid final day in Brownsville, Texas, to get his card on the number. He also remembers the guy who threatened to shoot him.

"I don't even know his name, because it turned out he was using an assumed name," Jacobsen said, beginning the story that he always starts by saying, "I'm not making this up."

"The first two days I was paired with this guy who simply could not play dead. He was awful, clearly someone who shouldn't have been allowed to play but had somehow gotten in under the radar. This was before they had stage qualifying. It was just one stage, so there was no way for him to have been weeded out earlier. Well, I don't think the guy broke 90 the first day. If he did, it was only because he cheated. I mean, really cheated—moving balls in the rough, things like that. When the day was over, I just had to say something to the rules guys, because I thought the guy was dangerous—to me, to everyone—plus he was cheating. I guess they went and did a little homework, because the next morning they walk up to the guy and say, 'You're going to have to leave.' He asks why, and they say, 'Well, for one thing, we found out you played last year under a different name, and we sent you a letter saying you couldn't come back this year because you were noncompetitive. For another, your fellow competitors caught you cheating out there yesterday on more than one occasion. So we're disqualifying you.'

"I'm standing there watching all this. The guy looks at the officials, then looks at me and says, 'Okay, then, I believe I'm just going to go out to my pickup and get my shotgun.' He wasn't smiling when he said it. I don't know if the officials called the police, but I spent the next couple of days looking over my shoulder a lot."

There are plenty of Q School stories about guys who couldn't play, which is one reason the rules for getting into even first stage are far stricter now than they once were. A player has to be a professional and has to show some evidence that he has played competitive golf someplace in order for his application to be accepted. "A truly bad player can make life miserable for the guys he's paired with," explained Steve Carman, the Q School's tournament director for the past seven years. "It really isn't fair to ask someone who has paid $4,500 to play for his life to play with someone who can't break 90. It doesn't happen nearly as often as it used to, but we still get one or two every year who slip through the cracks."

Most of the time, the horror stories are self-inflicted—the kind of stories that make players cringe rather than laugh. Many involve guys who simply couldn't make it to the clubhouse on the final day or had one awful moment—à la Tommy Tolles or Peter Tomasulo—on the last few holes. Some are funny because they have happy endings, such as the time in 1983 when Jeff Sluman's caddy showed up on the first tee with the wrong golf bag, or the moment years later when Shaun Micheel thought he had made the tour by tying with nine others for 37th place. Micheel thought that the low forty players and ties made the tour. So when he heard the announcement, "All players at six under par please report to the 10th tee for the play-off," he panicked, thinking he had to play off to get onto the tour. Micheel was the most relieved man on earth when he learned that the play-off was simply to determine in what order the ten players would be ranked when they began playing on the tour in January. "I was so relieved, I birdied the first hole and got number 37," he remembered, laughing.

The story that everyone knows but almost no one wants to bring up involves Jaxon Brigman. In 1999, after five years on the Nike Tour (now the Nationwide Tour), it looked as if Brigman's time had finally come. On the last day of the finals, played that year at Doral Golf and Country Club in Miami, Brigman played the round of his life, shooting 65, to make the tour right on the number. Elated, he walked into the scorer's tent, signed his scorecard, and left to join friends and family and let the celebration begin. He was standing near the scoreboard, with the widest smile of his life on his face, when Steve Carman approached. "Of all the things I've ever done in golf as a rules official, this had to be the toughest," Carman said.

"Jaxon," Carman said softly. "I need you to look at this card for me."

Carman still remembers the look on Brigman's face—even before he said another word. Brigman looked at the card and, an instant later, was prone on the ground, crying. At all golf tournaments, a player's official scorecard is kept by another player in his group. Nowadays, there is also a walking scorer who keeps track of all scores in the group as a backup, and each player keeps his own score unofficially. That day, Brigman's card was kept by Jay Hobby, who had made certain to circle each birdie so that it would be easier for Brigman to track how far under par he was: seven circles and no squares (for bogeys) would make it pretty clear that he was seven under par. Most players make some kind of mark on the scorecard to make clear any score that isn't a par.

Hobby had circled all of Brigman's birdies, including the one he had made at the par-four 13th hole. The problem was, he had written down a 4 and circled it instead of recording a 3. Especially in the crucible of the last day of Q School, it isn't surprising that someone could make that kind of mistake. When Brigman had gone into the scorer's tent, he had simply counted the seven circles and written down 65 as his score—which was what he had shot, even though the hole-by-hole numbers added up to 66. Then he had signed his card without asking the walking scorer to go through her card and confirm his score. When the scorekeeper at the scoreboard went through the card, he noticed the discrepancy and took the card to Carman. When Carman added up the numbers Brigman had signed for, he felt sick to his stomach, but he knew he had no choice but to take the card to Brigman.

"The only sliver of good in the whole thing was that he initially thought he was completely disqualified—which would have meant he didn't even have a spot on the Nationwide the next year," Carman said. "That would only have happened if he had signed for a score lower than his actual score. I told him that he wasn't disqualified but that his official score had to be the 66 that the numbers added up to on the scorecard."

That left him one shot above the cut line for the tour. It meant returning to the Nationwide Tour for a fifth year instead of being a rookie on the PGA Tour. It also meant becoming the poster child for sad-but-true Q School tales.

A year later, forced to play second stage, Brigman was in a four-way tie for the final three spots. Today, all four players would have advanced to the finals; there are no play-offs for a final qualifying position at first or second stage. Back then, however, they played off. Brigman made a bogey and was the one player among the four who didn't advance. "After seeing that, I decided it was time to get rid of the play-offs," Carman said. "If you shoot the number over four days, you should move on. We have the flexibility to handle a few extra players—whether it's at second stage or at finals. I just hated the idea that a player could go 72 holes and then be in a position where one poor swing—or, even worse, a lucky shot by someone else—made him wait another year for his next chance."

Q School has changed a lot since 1965. At the first School, forty-nine players showed up in Palm Beach Gardens, Florida, to play the PGA National Golf Club. They didn't even know how many spots they were playing for, because the event was brand-new. As it turned out, seventeen players qualified for the 1966 tour. "Qualifying" had a very different meaning then than it does now. At that time, only the top 60 money winners at the end of each year were guaranteed spots in every tournament during the next twelve months. Everyone else had to take part in Monday qualifiers, which filled out each week's tournament field. Players who had to qualify were known as "rabbits," because they were constantly hopping from city to city hoping to get into the next week's field. For the rabbits, making the cut on Friday was critical because everyone who made the cut was automatically in the next week's field without having to qualify.

That system, referred to now as "the non-exempt tour," remained in place until 1982, when Commissioner Deane Beman, pushed by the rank and file players on tour, created the "all-exempt tour." Now, the top 125 players on the money list are exempt for the following year, along with any tournament winners from the previous year who failed to make the top 125 and a number of players who received medical exemptions because of injuries. The Nationwide Tour, which was created in 1990 as a developmental tour, now sends its top 20 money winners to the PGA Tour the following year. Because the number of players who make the tour off the Nationwide list has grown (it was originally only five), the number of players who make the tour out of Q School—once as high as fifty players and ties—has shrunk to the current thirty and ties. Ranking on both the Nationwide list and the Q School list is important because players from both groups fall below the top 125 money winners, the tournament winners, and the medically exempt players in the pecking order for spots in tournaments. Early in the year, when everyone wants to play and tournament fields are smaller, the bottom half of the Q Schoolers frequently have trouble getting to play.

By the time the all-exempt tour was born, Q School had gone through many incarnations. In the fall of 1968, there were two Q Schools—one run, like the first three, by the PGA of America, and the other put on by the Association of Professional Golfers (the category then used within the PGA to describe tour players). That was at the height of the battle between the PGA of America and the tour players for control of the tour. Eventually, the players were allowed to break off and form the PGA Tour. Until then, those who wanted to play on the tour had to go through the same testing as teaching pros who were members of the PGA of America (all pros were PGA members). The late 1960s were not that far removed from the days when most tour players also worked as club pros. As late as 1955, Jack Fleck, a club pro by trade, won the U.S. Open, beating Ben Hogan in a play-off. For most of his career, Hogan was the pro at La Quinta Country Club in Palm Springs, California (although one suspects he didn't do a lot of teaching or spend a lot of time doing inventory).

The split between the PGA of America and the PGA Tour—to this day, people frequently refer incorrectly to the PGA Tour as the PGA—made perfect sense because the lifestyle of a pro on tour could not be more different than that of a pro working in a golf shop: a touring pro's life is consumed by trying to improve his golf game; a teaching pro's life is consumed by trying to improve *others'* golf games. For many years, however, Q School contained a classroom element. In the early years, when it was still an eight-round event, the classroom portion came smack in the middle of Q School. In the later years, it came after the golf had been played and was required only for those who qualified for tour cards.

From 1969 to 1971, there were two Q Schools a year, the thought being that players shouldn't have to wait a full year to try to qualify for the tour. There was more flexibility in terms of handing out cards in those days, because a card only gave a player rabbit status—the ability to enter Monday qualifiers. The holy grail was making the top 60 on the money list, because it got you out of the Monday qualifiers. Those who didn't make the top 60 had to earn at least $5,000 in prize money each year to avoid going back to Q School. That wasn't an overwhelming amount of money, but it wasn't as easy as it might sound. Purses were a fraction of what they are now, and making the cut didn't guarantee a player a check. Seventy players and ties made the cut each week, then as now, but only between forty-five and sixty actually got paid. Some players perfected the dubious skill of making it through the Monday qualifier and through the cut, but then failed to cash a check. That meant they had played five rounds of golf (plus a practice round), had paid their expenses for the week, and yet hadn't earned a nickel. Today's players would find that totally unacceptable.

Tom Watson played well in his rookie year, 1972, when he was a rabbit, making $30,413 in thirty-two tournaments. That was good enough for 74th on the money list. (In 2005, just for comparison purposes, J. L. Lewis finished 74th on the money list and made $1,031,159.) It kept him safely away from Q School but meant he had to start 1973 still playing on Mondays. Watson was the son of a successful Kansas City insurance agent and had a degree in psychology from Stanford. "I remember telling my dad when I was a senior that I wanted to at least try the tour because I wanted to find out if I was good enough to play out there," he said. "In the back of my mind, I was going to give it two or three years, and if I hadn't established myself by then, I'd go back to Kansas City and probably go to work with my dad."

To Watson, establishing himself meant getting out of Mondays. By the end of 1973, he had done that by finishing 35th on the money list. From there, he never looked back, going on to become the number one player in the world while winning eight majors.

Watson's approach — make it or go home — was fairly typical in the 1960s and 1970s. That's because there really wasn't any viable fallback position. The PGA Tour did establish a satellite tour in the mid-'70s, and there were some semi-organized mini-tours where players could play, but there really was no way to make a living playing golf unless you were on the PGA Tour. Overseas tours were just starting to pay decent purses, but the idea of going overseas to play golf rarely occurred to players. Most were like Watson: two or three years of the PGA Tour or bust. And if it was bust, go look for a job.

Now it's entirely different. Although the money on the Nationwide Tour is a fraction of the money on the PGA Tour, it is both a way to make a reasonable living (fifty-six players earned more than $100,000 in 2005) and a potential route to the PGA Tour. There are now tours all over the world that pay players well, and there are mini-tours all over the United States that pay well enough to allow a player to hang on to the dream for a few more years. "You don't get rich, that's for sure," said Garrett Frank, who has been playing mini-tours for close to a decade. "But you can make enough to live on and keep playing golf."

In many ways, Frank is symbolic of how different golf is today than when Q School was launched. He grew up in Ohio, a good athlete who played all sports well. "In some ways, I was too good for my own good because I never worked all that hard," he said. "I actually worked harder at basketball than golf, because golf came easily to me."

Frank played for four years at the University of Akron, still not taking the sport all that seriously. His father had made a good living selling hearing aids, and Frank got his master's degree in audiology. He worked for a year as an audiologist, then decided this wasn't meant to be his life's work. "I just didn't think I wanted to spend forty or fifty years digging wax out of old people's ears," he said. "I'm not putting it down, and I know it's important work. It just wasn't for me."

Still a very good amateur player, he turned pro at the end of 1999 and gave himself five years to work at his game and make it to the PGA Tour. He moved to Florida, made some money by investing in real estate, and began playing mini-tours. He failed to make it through the first stage of Q School at the end of 2000, then made it successfully through first stage each of the next four years. In 2003 he was paired the last day of second stage with Gary Nicklaus, with whom he had played on the mini-tours. One of those mini-tours was the Golden Bear Tour, named for Gary's father, Jack, and sponsored by his company.

"I'd never really played in front of a gallery before," Frank said. "We had about a hundred people following us. It was different, but it was a lot of fun." Among the spectators were Jack Nicklaus and his wife, Barbara.

"That's the closest I've come to getting through," Frank said. "I played well that day. I think I shot three under for the round, and I had good looks at three putts coming in. If I'd been able to make them, I'd have gotten through. Burned the edge on all of them and finished one over. The number was one under, so I missed by two. Somehow, Jack thought I'd finished one under and made it. He came over and congratulated me and told me he really liked the way I played. I was thrilled he said that, but a little embarrassed I had to tell him I hadn't made it. I could tell he felt badly about the mistake."

Frank went back to the mini-tours. He was still playing there in 2006, even though his self-imposed five-year deadline had passed. He had gone home at the end of 2004 intending to work with his father. By New Year's, though, the itch was back. "I knew my friends were down there in Florida playing," he said. "The weather was awful. I wasn't doing what I wanted to do. I still wanted to play golf. I had made decent money in '04 [about $50,000, offset by $18,000 in entry fees], and I still thought I could get better."

He made a little bit less money in '05 but still put up the $4,500 entry fee for the 2005 Q School, to give it one more go. "I'm thirty-three," he said, stretching in the locker room before starting his final round of first stage. "I know I can't keep trying forever, but it's hard to walk away."

ONCE THE PGA OF AMERICA and the PGA Tour split, Q School continued to evolve. After three years of biannual qualifiers with twenty-five spots open in each, the tour decided to go back to an annual event with fifty spots. That lasted until 1976, when the decision was made to go back to two qualifiers a year. In the spring of 1977, the qualifier at Pinehurst had 408 entrants. That was when the regional qualifiers were begun, or what is now known as second stage. In 1982, when the all-exempt tour was created, the tour went back to an annual qualifying event, which has been the case ever since. In 1986, with the number of entrants continuing to grow, first stage was established, making it a three-step process to get to the tour for those with no prior status.

The birth of the Ben Hogan (now Nationwide) Tour in 1990 changed the face of golf for those going up and down the ladder of the game. The new tour gave players who made it to the final stage but didn't get a PGA Tour card a place to play for the next year, with prize money that began with purses of $100,000 a week and has now risen to an average of $550,000 a week. No one gets rich on the Nationwide Tour, but players can make a living while keeping their dreams of playing on the PGA Tour alive. Fifty players and ties come out of Q School each year with fully exempt status on the Nationwide Tour. The remaining players—usually about half the field—have what is called conditional status, meaning they get into tournaments on a space-available basis. Most will get into enough tournaments during the year to have a chance to make a mark.

What that means, quite simply, is that getting to the finals nowadays means you have some kind of job playing golf for the next twelve months. That's why, for most players, second stage has become as much of a crucible as the finals were prior to 1990. "It isn't as if you feel relaxed playing in the finals," said David Sutherland, who has played on both the PGA Tour and the Nationwide Tour during the past fifteen years. "But you do know there's a safety net there if you don't make it to the big tour. I think there are some younger guys who, their first or second time in the finals, they aren't even thinking that much about making the PGA Tour. They just want to be sure they get a good number on the Nationwide Tour." He smiled. "Some of those guys are probably the ones who play well because they don't feel the kind of pressure we older guys [Sutherland is forty] feel. Second stage is a completely different deal. There, almost everybody is playing for a job. No one wants to go back to mini-tours, paying to play, just trying to keep your head above water for another year so you can get another shot at Q School."

Of course, Q School is no longer the only route to the tour now that the top 20 on the Nationwide money list go straight to the PGA Tour. In fact, that is now considered the better way to get to the tour, because it is a reward for playing well for an entire year as opposed to playing well for one week. Every year, after the last round of the Nationwide Tour Championship, when the money list is finalized, there is a card presentation ceremony in which PGA Tour commissioner Tim Finchem presents the new "class" with their PGA Tour cards for the next year. There is no such ceremony on the last day of Q School.

Q School does have the feel of a tournament now, especially the finals, which have been televised by the Golf Channel since 1996. There is roping around the golf courses to give the players some distance from the handful of spectators who come out to watch, and the leaders each day are usually asked to do some postround interviews. There's prize money, although not enough to make it really matter.

"Put it this way, if you have a chance to play for that prize money or stay home that week and watch, you'd much rather stay home and watch," said Brian Henninger, a two-time winner on the PGA Tour who has been forced to go back to Q School in recent years and has played the Nationwide Tour for most of the past four years. "But there's no question the tour has tried to make you feel more comfortable, at least when you make the finals. It does feel more like a real golf tournament than when I first started playing in the early '90s."

A lot of that can be traced to Arvin Ginn, a veteran rules official who was put in charge of Q School in the late 1980s. Ginn didn't think it was right that Q School was treated almost as a punishment for players. As if going back to Q School wasn't purgatory enough, players also had to deal with second-rate golf courses in fourth-rate shape and no amenities at all. Ginn pressed the tour to try harder to find good golf courses for all stages and to have the tour assign as many of its full-time rules officials to the events as possible. In the past, prior to the finals, almost all the officials working Q School were local officials supplied by the PGA of America and local PGAs. Ginn also came up with the idea of making the final week a qualifier for both the PGA Tour and the Nationwide Tour. He thought it would be cruel and unfair to require those who didn't make the PGA Tour to go through yet another qualifier for the Nationwide.

When Ginn retired as a full-time official in 1999, the Q School mantle was passed to Steve Carman, a computer whiz who had worked in a hospital setting up computer systems before being hired to do a similar job at the tour. He had decided he didn't want to sit around an office programming computers and had gone through all the various tests required to become a rules official. He had worked with Ginn on Q School and had come to respect its importance for everyone involved. Since Q School finals are always held the week after Thanksgiving, Carman spends the holiday at the finals site making sure everything is in place for the players, many of whom will show up on the weekend to begin playing practice rounds before the start of play the following Wednesday.

"You know how tough a week it's going to be for everyone," Carman said. "You know most guys are going to walk away disappointed. I just want to be sure they don't have any hassles to deal with beyond what they have to go through by being in the event."

Carman and his staff do everything they can to have the golf courses in the best possible shape and to handle all the logistics for the players: there are plenty of range balls to go around, the pin placements are fair, and any question can be answered in an instant. But there's only so much you can do.

Donnie Hammond still holds the record for the greatest margin of victory at the Q School finals: he won by 14 shots in 1982, the first year players were qualifying for spots on the all-exempt tour. Hammond won twice on the PGA Tour and became eligible for the Champions Tour in April 2007, when he turned fifty. He went back to Q School in 2005 because he wanted to have full status during his last full year on the PGA Tour. "I want to pick and choose my spots," he said during a second stage held at Lake

Jovita Golf and Country Club in Dade City, Florida. "I don't want to be waiting around finding out which eight or ten or twelve tournaments I might get into. There are some events, like the Memorial and the Colonial, I'd like to go back to once more."

Still, the pressure on Hammond at second stage wasn't anywhere close to what it was on those who had no status, right? Hammond laughed. "There isn't a minute during Q School that you're awake that you don't feel uncomfortable," he said. "And you don't sleep very well either."

As Kelly Gibson, another tour veteran back at second stage, put it, "I've seen the pressures of Q School make a grown man cry."

Who have you seen cry at Q School? Gibson was asked.

Gibson smiled. "Me," he said. "And I'm not making it up."

Indeed, very few Q School stories are made up. There's really no need.

3

In the Beginning

To MOST OF THE GOLFING PUBLIC, Q School is something that takes place each year in December over a six-day period in either Florida or California. Some may know that there's a second stage that takes place in November, although very few people understand that those second-stage events take place at six different sites around the country. Even fewer know that Q School actually begins in October with first-stage qualifiers at fourteen different sites over a period of three weeks. In fact, in 2005 Steve Carman decided to add a fourth stage—tentatively called the preliminary stage—that was meant to be a prequalifier for players who could not show evidence that they were qualified to play in the first stage.

According to the entry form, a player had to play in the preliminary stage if he hadn't taken part in Q School for the past three years and couldn't provide evidence that he had played "successfully" in at least two tournaments—either sanctioned by the PGA of America or a recognized mini-tour or state open—that were at least 36 holes long. If a player was an amateur, he had to show that he had played reasonably well in two college events, two tournaments sanctioned by the U.S. Golf Association (USGA), or two state, regional, or metropolitan championships. The tournaments had to be stroke play, and being club champion or having won a member-guest somewhere didn't do the player any good.

A player also had to take part in the preliminary stage if he received a "noncompetitive" letter from any tour around the world or any national federation. Such a letter is sent to any player who participates in Q School and plays, well, noncompetitively. "Generally speaking, if someone plays four rounds and doesn't come close to breaking 80, they're going to get a letter," Carman said. "They can certainly write back with an explanation of some kind, but in all likelihood they're going to have to show proof that their play was an aberration before they can enter first stage again."

In 2005 the tour had about 400 players in its noncompetitive file. That, along with the growing number of entrants despite the higher entry fee, led Carman to create the preliminary stage. It was planned for two sites in September, and Carman expected between 100 and 150 players to participate. As it turned out, though, there were fewer than 50 entries, and the preliminary stage was put on hold until 2006.

"We've tried a lot of things to make sure that we don't have guys who simply don't belong," Carman said. "Most of the guys in first stage these days are good players, guys who have a legitimate chance, if they play well, to at least make second stage. But we still run into the occasional player who has somehow faked his way in or, in some cases, might have been a reasonably good player once upon a time but just isn't good enough now. We figured by adding the preliminary stage, we might scare some guys off. I guess, based on the entries, we did — at least for one year."

In 2005 a total of 1,205 players entered the PGA Tour Qualifying Tournament. Forty-two of those players met at least one of the six criteria that allowed them to go straight to the finals.

1. Any player who had finished between 126th and 150th on the 2005 PGA Tour money list.

2. Any nonmembers who had earned enough money to finish at least 150th on the money list. (This category rarely came into play. When it did, it usually involved someone who had graduated from college in the spring, turned pro, and, playing on special exemptions, made as much money as the 150th player on the money list but not as much as the 125th player. If a player made as much as the 125th player on the list, he went straight to the PGA Tour. In 2005 Ryan Moore, the 2004 U.S. Amateur champion, made it straight to the 2006 tour by earning $686,250 in twelve events after turning pro. That would have placed him 117th on the money list if he had been a tour member and put him $60,000 clear of Nick Price, who finished 125th on the list.)

3. Any player on a medical exemption whose earnings in 2004 (assuming he was healthy at the time) would have put him between 126th and 150th on the money list.

4. Any player who had finished between 22nd and 36th on the 2005 Nationwide Tour money list.

5. Any player who had finished in the top ten on the money list of a major foreign tour (e.g., the European, Australasia, or Japan tour).

6. Any player in the top 50 of the World Golf Ranking. (It is highly unlikely that any such player would need to go to Q School. The only time it might occur would be if someone who played strictly on an overseas tour decided he wanted to play full-time in the United States.)

Among those who were exempt into the finals were past tournament winners Notah Begay (who had won four times on tour), Neal Lancaster, J. P. Hayes, David Peoples, Tom Scherrer, Ian Leggatt, Frank Lickliter, and Garrett Willis. Also on that list was Bob May, who had never won on the tour but was vividly remembered by most golf fans because of his final-day duel with Tiger Woods in the 2000 PGA Championship, which Woods finally won in a play-off. May had undergone major back surgery in 2004, and Q School would be his first tournament since the surgery. Other notable names who would go straight to the finals were Bill Haas (the twenty-three-year-old son of longtime tour star Jay Haas), who had finished 23rd on the Nationwide money list, and Joe Daley, who had not made it back to the PGA Tour since his two-footer had somehow bounced out of the hole in Palm Springs. Daley, who hadn't turned pro until he was thirty-two (he'd worked as a credit manager in a bank until then), was forty-five and running out of time. He had finished 24th on the Nationwide money list.

There were nine ways to get out of playing first stage.

1. Any member of the PGA Tour in 2005.
2. Any player who had won a tournament on the Nationwide Tour since 2000.
3. The top ten finishers in the PGA Club Professional Championship who chose to enter Q School (down to a floor of 25th place). (Most didn't have time to leave their jobs to do so.)
4. Any player who had made a cut at one of the four major championships or the Players Championship. (The PGA Tour is clearly trying to put the Players in the same category as the four majors.)
5. Any player from a major foreign tour who had finished between 4th and 10th among those entered from his tour.
6. Any player who had made at least fifty cuts on the PGA Tour.
7. Any player who had finished 37th through 71st on the 2005 Nationwide money list.

8. Any player ranked 51st through 100th in the World Golf Ranking.

9. The top two players from any secondary foreign tours (e.g., Canadian, South Africa, or Asian)—which is different from Australasian, for those keeping score at home).

A total of 190 players were exempt into second stage. Some of those who were exempt to second stage but not to the finals were eye-popping. Larry Mize, who had won the 1987 Masters, would play second stage. So would past tour winners Steve Stricker (who had won the Match Play title in 2001 and had finished second to Vijay Singh in the 1998 PGA Championship), Bill Glasson (seven tour wins), Dan Forsman (five), Blaine McCallister, Mike Hulbert, Donnie Hammond, Guy Boros, Brian Henninger, Tom Byrum, Matt Gogel, Jim McGovern, Rick Fehr, Mike Springer, and Grant Waite. There were others who'd had significant success on the tour but were now back playing second stage, such as Tommy Tolles and Skip Kendall, who had finished second on four different occasions and had been in the top 50 on the money list (with a high of 32nd) from 1999 to 2001.

In all, 232 players were exempt from first stage. They would also save a little money on the entry fee: those exempt to the finals paid $3,500; those exempt to second stage paid $4,000; and everyone else, 973 players in all, paid $4,500 and headed for first stage, knowing that the chances that they would tee it up in golf nirvana, the 2006 PGA Tour, were slim. But they also knew that in 2004, nine players had started at first stage and ended up on the tour. In addition, 19 players had made it from first stage to the finals and had played on the Nationwide Tour. Each of them was convinced that he was going to be among the handful of players who would beat the odds.

Most of them would, of course, be wrong.

———

ONE OF THE FEW PLAYERS who wasn't thinking he was going to beat the odds was Casey Martin.

It hadn't been that long since Martin had been one of the best-known golfers in the world. At the 1998 U.S. Open, the only player in the field with a larger gallery was his onetime Stanford teammate Tiger Woods. Back then, everyone who followed golf—and many who didn't—knew who Martin was. He was the talented, bright, outgoing kid who had something called Klippel-Trenaunay-Weber syndrome, a degenerative disease in his right leg. He had been born with the disease, which caused him to walk with a noticeable limp and made walking golf courses for a living close to impossible, especially as he got older and his leg got worse.

In 1997 Martin petitioned the PGA Tour to allow him to use a golf cart. The tour's rules were clear: everyone walked. The only exception had been during Q School, when players were allowed to ride because it was a six-day tournament and frequently the only caddy a player could afford was his wife or girlfriend. Some players didn't use a caddy at all. But that loophole had been closed in 1996, and Martin was told that if he wanted to play in the Q School finals in 1997, he would have to walk.

That was the first time Martin took the tour to court, and he won. He got a court order saying that the tour had to let him use a cart based on the Americans with Disabilities Act (ADA). He used a cart during the Q School finals in 1997, and although he missed qualifying for the PGA Tour (by two shots), he did play well enough to gain full status on the Nike Tour. Still using a cart, he won his first Nike Tour tournament early in 1998. That was when the attention—and the controversy—started to build.

The tour decided to take a hard line against allowing Martin to use a cart. Commissioner Tim Finchem and many top players took the position that walking was part of the game and allowing someone to ride could give him a competitive advantage (since riding isn't as tiring as walking). Martin's position was twofold. Legally, he said, the ADA gave him the right to a cart the same way a disabled person who bought a ticket to a golf tournament was allowed to use a cart while a healthy person could not. Logically, he added, watch me walk from my cart onto the tees or the greens or into a bunker, and see if you think I'm not going to be tired at the end of a round.

Martin wasn't even on the PGA Tour when the controversy began making news. But after he qualified for the U.S. Open on a searingly hot day in Cincinnati, riding 36 holes while everyone else in the field walked, he arrived in San Francisco for the Open as the most talked about player in the tournament other than his old friend Tiger Woods. "I remember feeling incredible pressure both that week and that year because I was under the microscope all the time," Martin said. "The interesting thing is, I probably played my best golf during that period. I seemed to thrive on the attention and on the pressure."

"Cart-gate" divided the locker room. Some players were adamant that no one should be allowed to play from a cart. Veterans with their own physical problems, like Fred Couples and Scott Verplank, said that they would apply for carts, too, if Martin was granted one. Legends like Jack Nicklaus and Arnold Palmer said that the traditions of the game would be violated if players were allowed to play in carts. Others saw it differently. The late Payne Stewart argued that there was a clear difference between something that caused discomfort (such as Couples's sore back) and a degenerative disease that made one legally disabled. "We should give the kid the cart," Stewart said. "It makes us [the tour and the players] look bad to be fighting him on this. You take one look at him trying to walk, and there's no doubt he's hurting."

What's more, those who met Martin almost immediately jumped on board (or on cart) with him. He is bright and has a disarming, self-deprecating sense of humor. The players who knew him best, notably Woods and Notah Begay, another Stanford teammate, were adamantly in his corner. "If you had seen Casey try to walk 18 holes on a regular basis like we did at Stanford, you would feel differently," Woods told doubters. "Plus, he's a guy who would be great for golf."

No one doubted that. Martin's is the kind of story the tour would have latched onto and publicized if not for the cart issue. He grew up in Eugene, Oregon, and never thought he would be good enough or strong enough to play even college golf. But he blossomed as a high school player and was recruited by all the national golf powers. He chose Stanford and was part of a national championship team in 1995, when he was a senior. Although his leg hurt when he walked, he was able to handle it. But he knew the leg was getting worse. Doctors had told him there was a chance that, at some point in his life, he would face amputation.

Martin turned pro after graduating with a degree in economics and sailed through the first stage of Q School. But he missed making it through second stage by two shots and was devastated. "It meant I had no status at all for '96," he said. "I wasn't even focused on making the PGA Tour that year. I just wanted to get to the finals and get on the Nike Tour. I thought I was good enough to at least do that, and I didn't. It was definitely a setback."

He ended up playing most of his golf the next two years on the NGA/Hooters Tour, with some mini-tour events thrown in. The Hooters Tour (named for the restaurant chain famous for scantily clad waitresses and mediocre food) is at least a level down from the Nationwide (then Nike) Tour. For one thing, as on mini-tours, players have to pay fairly substantial entry fees each week. The purses are less than half of what they are on the Nike Tour, and the golf courses and locales are second-rate as well.

"It is not a fun way to live," Martin said. "After a while, you get sick of the towns and the hotels and the places you go to eat. It's a lonely life, and it certainly isn't a lucrative life, even if you play well. By the summer of my second year out there, I was sick and tired of the whole thing, and my leg was getting worse. I quit midway through the summer to rest my leg. I figured I'd take one more shot at Q School, and if I couldn't at least make the finals, I'd be done. I'd go get a job."

This time, he sailed through first stage and in second stage went into the last round at the Bayonet Course at Fort Ord, California (considered one of the toughest Q School courses) right on the cut line. "I knew I needed a good round to get through," Martin said. "I shot 69, one of the best rounds of my life under pressure. I was thrilled. After the round, I started talking to one of the tour officials about needing a cart to get through six rounds at the finals. The guy had just been telling me how happy he was for me, and when I brought up the cart, his face just turned to stone. 'There's no way,' he told me. 'Don't even bother applying.' It really took me aback."

As it turned out, the official was right. Martin's request for a cart was immediately rejected, despite the facts that players had been allowed to use carts in the finals for many years and carts had been allowed during the first two stages that year.

"When the court ruled in my favor and gave me the cart for the finals, that's when my life changed," Martin said with a laugh. "You know, all kidding aside, the PGA Tour made me. If not for them making such a big deal out of the cart, no one would ever have heard of me. I probably wouldn't have gotten the endorsements I got, the attention I got, and I *certainly* never would have seen the inside of the Supreme Court."

PGA Tour v. Martin ended up in the Supreme Court after one lower court ruled for Martin and another ruled for the tour. The Martin case became front-page news, one of those stories that the nonsports media latched onto. It had just about everything you could want in a story: a young athlete taking on what appeared to be a heartless bureaucracy; political implications; and superstar athletes divided over a kid whom they never would have known anything about if not for his bad leg and his golf cart.

The cart controversy not only changed Martin's life; it also changed his outlook on life. "I grew up a dyed-in-the-wool conservative Republican," he said. "Heck, if it had been someone else in my shoes and I was just an observer, I'd have probably been one of those guys saying, 'He can't have a cart. If he can't walk, get him out of there.' But I wasn't. I was the guy living it. That made me rethink a lot of things, like, just as an example, how I felt about welfare. I couldn't help but wonder if I was the one living *that* life, I might feel differently on that subject, too. I found myself looking at things through a different lens.

"To tell the truth, the Republicans really disappointed me. I'll be completely honest and tell you I was appalled by the positions taken by Justice [Antonin] Scalia and Justice [Clarence] Thomas. I just think they're completely heartless. Bob Dole was the exception, but his experience was like mine—he'd been through it, knew what it felt like to be handicapped. I remember going on Bill O'Reilly's show and walking away thinking, 'This guy is a complete schmuck.' It pains me to say it, but most of the people who showed compassion for me, who seemed to want to help out someone who was downtrodden, were Democrats. I came away from the experience with a lot of different feelings on a lot of different subjects."

The case was heard by the Supreme Court on January 17, 2001. Martin remembers most of that experience as being thrilling. "Not that many people get to have a case tried in the Supreme Court with their name on it and [that] doesn't involve life or death," he said. "That was an amazing, once-in-a-lifetime experience to sit there. I came away with so much respect for the lawyers on both sides. I mean, arguing before the Supreme Court is the Super Bowl or the Masters for them. They're getting grilled from all directions, and they better be right when they answer a question. Eight of those nine judges were intimidating and impressive, regardless of which side they came down on. Watching the whole thing just made my jaw drop."

The one justice who wasn't intimidating or impressive was Thomas. He never asked a question. In fact, throughout most of the arguments, he sat back in his chair with his eyes closed. "My lawyer had warned me about that before we went in," Martin said. "He told me, 'Don't be shocked if you see Judge Thomas napping. He does that.' Even so, it was shocking to see."

Martin had finished 29th on the Nike Tour money list in 1998, fading down the stretch when he'd had a chance to make the top 15 and earn a trip to the PGA Tour in 1999. (In those days, the top 15 made the tour.) A year later, while his case was still winding its way through the courts, he put together a more consistent year and finished 14th on the Nike money list. His ticket to the PGA Tour was punched for 2000. He was twenty-seven years old, and now he had his chance. He didn't play horribly on the tour. He had some good rounds and some tournaments where he went into Sunday with a chance for a big check. But it never quite came together for him. He made fourteen cuts in twenty-nine events with only one top-25 finish (tied for 17th in Tucson). That left him 179th on the money list, sending him back to Q School and then to what had now become the Buy.com Tour.

On May 29, 2001, four days before Martin's twenty-ninth birthday, the Supreme Court ruled 7–2 in his favor, his friends Scalia and Thomas dissenting. He no longer had to worry about losing his cart. In his dissent, Scalia accused the majority of looking at the ADA far too liberally, saying that the law was intended for "no such ridiculous thing" as Martin's case. By then, just about everyone in golf had accepted Martin and his cart as part of the scenery, and even players who had come out against him in the past congratulated him on his victory. In the movies, he would have won the U.S. Open shortly thereafter. In real life, his golf game went south.

"I wish I could figure out why, but the fact is, my golf has sucked since the Court ruled for me," he said. "I've thought about it a lot, and I honestly don't have any answers as to why. Has my leg gotten worse? Yes. There are times when I make a swing that I know is good and the teachers I'm working with say is good, and I feel pain. When I make a swing that's completely pain-free, it isn't a good golf swing. So most of the time when I swing a club I feel pain—mental or physical. But I don't think that's why I haven't played better. With me, [the problem] has always been my putter. When I was playing my best golf, my strength was my ball-striking. If I could make some putts, I played very well. The last couple of years, my ball-striking hasn't been as good as it was when I was younger, but it's still good enough—if I can make putts. I haven't made putts, and that has nothing to do with my leg."

He sighed. "Maybe I just couldn't live up to people's expectations. When I was uncertain about whether I was going to be able to keep the cart, I was just thankful to be playing golf. I know I felt pressure, but it was different. When the Court ruled for me, it felt like expectations just exploded. I remember people saying to me, 'Dude, you're going to tear it up now.' But I didn't. I kept grinding, kept trying, but I couldn't play the way I wanted to—or the way people expected me to. It's disappointing."

Martin became a Q School regular after the ruling, but he never made it back to the PGA Tour. "I've thought about Q School a lot," he said. "It's interesting how my attitude toward it changed through the years. At first it was exciting; it was an opportunity. As the years went by, I began to feel as if I was taking golf's version of the bar exam—except that [I] didn't just take it once; I took it over and over." He laughed. "It's almost as if you're working in a law firm, and if you don't bill enough hours, they make you go take the bar again. And if you don't pass, you spend the next year working in the law firm—as a janitor.

"It *is* like a final exam, because you can't rationalize or fool yourself or anyone else. If you aren't good enough, you can't say, 'But I'm getting better' or 'I'll do better next week or the week after.' You're either prepared and you come through or you don't.

"Before I played on the tour, it was like an adventure. But afterward, it was different. I felt like I had worked hard to get to the tour, very hard, and it became a part of my identity—one that I wanted. So when I ended up back at Q School, I felt like I was playing for my identity. Part of it was the perks and the money, but it was more than that; it was my identity. When I was young and first played Q School, I thought I felt pressure. But I didn't, certainly not compared to the pressure I felt when I had to go back. I've heard guys who have won on tour and had to go back talking about how tough that is, but at least they know they have *some* kind of status if they don't make it, as past champions. Guys like me have nothing if we don't play well.

"It's tough sometimes to explain what has happened to your life to people who aren't golf knowledgeable. They tend to think because they've seen you on TV that you're a big star, that you have it made forever. Of course, that isn't even close to being true. When you first come out of college, if you don't make it, you don't feel as if you've lost anything—because you've never had it. When you go back, though, there is a feeling of loss—something you once had is gone."

After the Court ruling, Martin never again finished in the top 100 on the Nationwide money list. He played less and less, partly because he didn't have full status, but more because he knew his game wasn't there. He could have applied for sponsor exemptions and probably gotten them because, especially on the Nationwide, his name would still sell some tickets. But he thought it pointless to take a spot in the field from someone else when he was likely to miss the cut.

In the summer of 2005, he made a decision: he would work hard at his golf game one more time to try to prepare for Q School. He would have to go back to first stage, but that was okay. "I figured if I wasn't good enough to get out of first stage, there was a message there," he said.

He had quietly been told by people at the University of Oregon that there would likely be a coaching change for the school's golf team in the spring of 2006, and if he was interested, he would be a prime candidate for the job. That was nice to know, but he wanted to take one more crack at Q School. Most golfers don't quit the first time they think about it. They go back and forth. On the one hand, they know they aren't playing well enough to compete. On the other hand, playing golf is all they know, and they still love the game. And, the last few times out, if a few more putts had fallen...

Martin had already played the back-and-forth game. "My approach going in was PGA Tour or bust," he said.

He signed up to play first stage and spent a lot of time on the range looking to find his swing. When he got to his first-stage site, he was struck by two things: "I felt kind of old being there at thirty-three," he said. "It was hard to believe it had been ten years since I'd been one of those kids just out of college so excited and eager to tee it up. The other thing was the overall quality of play. Even ten years ago, you would go to first stage, and probably half the field simply had no chance. You didn't really feel as if you had to beat seventy or eighty guys; you had to beat maybe forty. Now you go to first stage, and there are a lot of good players."

Martin had chosen San Juan Oaks Golf Club in Hollister,

California, for first stage. He wanted to play at San Juan Oaks in part because it wasn't that far from Eugene, but also because he believed it was a golf course where the scores wouldn't be that low. A player who is a good ball-striker but not that good a putter usually wants a golf course where hitting fairways and greens isn't that easy, because he doesn't want to find himself in a putting contest.

San Juan Oaks wasn't a pushover, but the scores were lower than Martin had anticipated. Two days in, having shot 72–71, he knew he was going to have to come up with a low round to make it into the top 20 and ties who would advance to second stage. "It wasn't all that different than the kind of golf I'd been playing for a while," he said. "I was hitting the ball well but not scoring well—sort of the story of my golf game the last five years."

Martin knew that, barring a radical change in weather conditions, the number was probably going to be somewhere in the vicinity of five under par. Starting the third round at one under, he was certainly in the hunt, but he knew that another round around even par would put him in a hole going into the last round. Needing to make a move, he did—backwards. "I just couldn't make a putt all day," he said, remembering the disastrous 75 he shot in the third round. "I think because I wasn't making putts, I tried to be too precise with my shotmaking, and I ended up hitting the ball worse. I found myself starting to think, 'I'm not going to spend my entire life being a struggling golfer.'"

He went to bed that night knowing he would have to go low—way low—to have any chance on the last day. The thought also occurred to him that he might be about to play the last meaningful round of his professional career. "I wasn't terribly emotional about it," he said. "It wasn't as if it crossed my mind for the first time then; it had been there for a while. But I did want to go out and give the round everything I had. I figured if I could shoot five or six under, maybe get to four under, I might have a shot."

Martin would have needed to shoot a seven-under-par 65 to get to the number, which turned out to be five under par. The last day was a lot like the many days before it: a lot of birdie chances, very few putts going in the hole. "With about four or five holes to play, I was even par for the day, and I realized it just wasn't going to happen," Martin said. "Even if I birdied in at that point, I knew it wasn't going to be enough. The conditions were perfect. I knew people were going to score; they weren't going to be coming back. Those last few holes, I just kind of took everything in. I wasn't so much emotional as I was numb."

He signed for a 72 — even par — which left him at two-over-par 290 for the week, tied for 46th place in the seventy-one-man field. That left him seven shots behind the four players who tied for 20th place. One of them was another ex–tour player, Joel Kribel. Mark Wurtz, another player who had once been on tour, didn't do much better than Martin, finishing in a tie for 33rd place. Martin knew it was time to go home and stay home.

"At that point, it wasn't that tough a decision to make," he said. "The farther I get from it, the more I think about some of the heartbreak and how close I came to really making it. But I also think how lucky I was to do the things I did, to be involved in the things I was involved in. Part of me wakes up in the morning and thinks 'comeback.' Fortunately, there's a bigger part of me that knows better."

The coaching job at Oregon became a reality in May 2006 — a big story in Eugene, a couple of paragraphs in most newspapers around the country. Most of the stories began something like this: "Casey Martin, the handicapped golfer who took the PGA Tour to the Supreme Court and won..."

Which is true. "I wish people would remember me for more

than just that," Martin said. "I would rather be remembered as a U.S. Open champion or something like that."

Perhaps. But there is no doubt golf people will remember Casey Martin not just as the guy who beat the tour inside the hallowed halls of the Supreme Court, but as someone who dealt with adversity — *real* adversity, not the kind that comes because of a wayward tee shot — with dignity and grace.

4

Nine Hundred and Seventy-three Dreamers

THERE WERE TWELVE first-stage Q School sites in 2005 after Steve Carman decided to make the two preliminary-stage sites into first-stage sites. A total of 973 players were required to play first stage. Since the weather in October is still relatively mild almost anywhere south of the Mason-Dixon Line, the tour spreads the sites out across the South. The farthest north it ventured was Kannapolis, North Carolina. There were three sites in Florida, three in Texas, two in California, and one each in Georgia, Arizona, and South Carolina. Most players chose their sites based on geographical convenience, although some were willing to travel a long distance to play a specific course they knew, liked, or had had luck on before. Some wanted to stay west to play on Bermuda grass greens; others wanted to stay east to play on bent grass greens.

Some of the courses are almost always part of the Q School rota. In recent years, Carman has made an effort to find new sites in an attempt to improve the quality of the courses. Also, the event has become old hat to the locals in some places that have hosted it for a long time, making it tougher to find volunteers to help out during the week.

"It isn't that easy to go to a club and ask them to give up their golf course and a lot of their facilities for a week," Carman said. "In all, we need nineteen sites [twelve for first stage, six for second stage, and one for finals], so it isn't as if we can pay them a ransom in rental. They make money, but the more high-end the club, the less likely that kind of money is going to make the members eager to have their course taken over—especially at a time of year when the weather is usually nice for playing. You go to new places where it's a novelty and say 'PGA Tour' and you're more likely to get a positive response."

One place that has become a traditional first-stage site was the TPC Tampa Bay, which has the advantage of being owned and operated by the tour. It is also one of only eight courses within the twenty-nine-course TPC system that isn't fully private. Technically, it is a public course, although the club sells memberships for $1,600 annually to people, which allows them to play unlimited golf and receive advantageous tee times. Still, TPC Tampa Bay is not a place where angry members are going to walk in and wonder what the heck all these guys are doing inside their locker room.

To say that the TPC Tampa Bay is located off the beaten path is something of an understatement. It is a twenty-minute drive north of Tampa, through numerous stoplights, to a turn that takes you another three miles down a two-lane road filled with nearly identical homes before the PGA Tour's logo comes into view. The clubhouse is unimposing—one story, with a small dining room and equally small locker rooms. It is anything but pretentious, although there are photos throughout the building of players like Arnold Palmer, Jack Nicklaus, Gary Player, and Hale Irwin. That's because the TPC Tampa Bay annually hosts a Champions Tour event, and those men have taken part in the past. Nicklaus won the tournament in 1996; Irwin was the champion in 2005.

The TPC Tampa Bay is also home to a very good golf course. It has become a popular first-stage site for just that reason. "It's very straightforward," said rules official Dillard Pruitt. "There are no tricks. It's all out in front of you, and it's fair. The players like that, especially under this kind of pressure. They don't like surprises."

Pruitt knows how players feel about Q School golf courses because he played in six Q Schools during his professional career, which lasted from 1984 to 1996 and included a victory in Chattanooga in 1991 and a tie for 13th in the Masters in 1992. He first made it to the tour in 1988 after playing in Europe for a couple of years. "I played horribly that year," he said. "I missed at Q School at the end of the year and took a job as an assistant pro and played some mini-tours. I qualified for the [U.S.] Open in '89, got my confidence back, and made it through Q School again in '89. After that I played well enough that I never had to go back."

Pruitt retired in 1996 because, at thirty-five, he didn't think he was ever going to putt the ball well enough to be a consistent winner on tour. "I bounced around a couple years, because when you quit young, no one really believes you're retired," he said. "They think you're going to go back. I was lucky the rules guys gave me a chance." In 1998 he became a rules official, and even though he now has enough seniority that he doesn't have to work Q School, he chose to work it in 2005 because he thought it was important. A lot of rules officials who are ex-players work Q School because they remember what it was like for them as players, and they want to make it as painless as possible for the current players. "There are a lot of guys playing here this week who have stories pretty similar to mine," Pruitt said, riding around in his cart on a muggy Tuesday morning. "I can relate to their struggle."

Most of the sixty-eight players arriving in Tampa for the week would be delighted to have their careers follow the same path as Pruitt's. To reach the PGA Tour at all would be a major victory. Two players in the field had accomplished that goal: Mike Grob, an easygoing forty-one-year-old from Billings, Montana, and Stephen Gangluff, a not-so-easygoing thirty-one-year-old who lived in Ponte Vedra Beach, Florida, headquarters of the PGA Tour. Even though he was an ex–tour player, he had no access to the TPC Sawgrass, the tour's home club, not even to practice.

"I guess if they let every guy who ever played the tour practice there, they'd be overrun," Gangluff said. "I understand."

Gangluff has loved golf since he was little. As a boy, he played a municipal golf course in Marysville, Ohio, with his father, an assistant prison warden, and his friends. He played as much as he could and watched the tour on TV all the time. Being from Ohio, he had to be a Jack Nicklaus fan, but he also admired Payne Stewart. "I liked his style, the way he dressed, the way he acted, but most of all the way he played," Gangluff said. "I remember saying to myself, 'Someday, maybe I'll be good enough to wear plus fours on the golf course.'"

He was a good enough player to get a scholarship to Ohio State, but left after three years to try mini-tours, thinking that playing golf full-time would better prepare him to make a run at the PGA Tour. The problem was, when he thought he was ready, he hadn't saved enough money to pay the entry fee, and he couldn't find any sponsors to step up and pay it for him. So he spent a year working as a cart boy at Wintergreen Resort in Virginia and saved enough money to play Q School at the end of 2001. Remarkably, he made it through all three stages and found himself on tour in 2002 — a long way from jockeying carts at Wintergreen a year earlier.

"Just to be out there was an amazing experience," he said. "What a life! I mean, the whole thing — the courtesy cars, the phones in the locker room, the food, and the golf courses. Once you've seen what that's like, you don't want to go back and play anyplace else. But you have to earn the right to stay out there."

Gangluff made a little more than $187,000 and finished 176th on the money list in 2002, went back to Q School, and missed getting back on the tour by two shots at the finals. That was disappointing, but he didn't think a year on the Nationwide Tour would necessarily hurt him. He was wrong. "Bomber's paradise," he said with a laugh. "They play a lot of short, outmoded courses, and a lot of the young guys can hit it nine miles. Even if they miss the fairway, they've got a wedge in their hands. I just couldn't make enough birdies out there." He finished 90th on the Nationwide list, then didn't make it back through second stage at the end of 2003.

"Now," he said, "I was in full reverse. I'd gone from the tour in 2002 to the Nationwide in 2003 to nowhere in 2004." He played mini-tours in 2004 and then decided, on the advice of some friends, to try the Canadian Tour in '05. "Better golf courses, decent money, and it feels like a real tour," he said. "The only problem was, I needed a place to practice during the winter, and I needed to make some money because I didn't have any."

He had moved to Ponte Vedra Beach at the end of 2003, thinking at the very least he would have access to places to play and practice. When the tour told him he couldn't play at Sawgrass, he made a deal with Ponte Vedra Golf and Country Club: he'd go back to jockeying carts but would have complete access to play and practice when he wasn't working. "I had to swallow my pride," he said. "Most of the members had no idea I'd been on the tour, but a few recognized the name. I had to deal with it because it was my best chance to get through the winter and get back to playing."

He had played reasonably well on the Canadian Tour, finishing ninth on their money list, making about $37,000. His standing on the Canadian money list had gotten him into the Nationwide event in Calgary, and he'd finished fifth, a boost to his confidence.

The top-ten finish there had gotten him into the following week's event in Utah, but he missed the cut.

"I need the Jason Gore effect," he said with a smile. "I need about three hot weeks to get on a real roll again."

Jason Gore had become the new poster boy for all struggling golfers in 2005. He had been one of those players good enough to compete on the Nationwide Tour, good enough to make it to the PGA Tour (twice), but never good enough to make a dent once he got there. He had played horribly the first half of 2005 but had managed to qualify for the U.S. Open at Pinehurst. There, for three days, he was blessed by the golfing gods and found himself playing in the final group on Sunday with two-time Open champion Retief Goosen. The wheels came completely off on the final day—he shot 84—but his easy smile, his paunch, and his sense of humor had made him an instant star. He returned to the Nationwide Tour and, as if the 84 had never happened, picked up where he had left off on Saturday at Pinehurst. He won three times in five weeks, actually winning three straight starts since he took off two weeks after the second win. Prior to that streak, he had won only three times on the Nationwide in eight years and not at all since 2002. The third victory earned him a "battlefield promotion" to the PGA Tour. (Any Nationwide player who wins three times in the same year is immediately promoted to the PGA Tour.) To prove that neither Pinehurst nor the three-tournament string on the Nationwide was a fluke, Gore won the 84 Lumber Classic playing with the big boys in September, earning a two-year tour exemption and a slew of sponsorships. In less than four months, he had gone from 668th in the World Golf Ranking to 89th. He had gone from being a struggling thirty-one-year-old journeyman trying to support his wife and infant son to being a folk hero—a suddenly very financially comfortable folk hero.

Every player going through the Q School experience wanted to become Jason Gore. Every one of them was convinced he was just one good round away from getting on that kind of roll. If it could happen to Jason Gore, why couldn't it happen to them?

"Of course you need a shot of confidence," Gangluff said. "My problem right now is, I'm playing scared. I'm letting the golf course intimidate me. I feel like I'm fighting all sorts of demons, and I know, even if they go away next week, it will be too late. I have to figure something out *now*."

Gangluff started the first round on Tuesday feeling as if he had the demons under control. He was two under par walking to the 17th tee and thinking he was on his way to putting himself in good position after 18 holes. But he missed the green at 17 and made a bogey. He could feel the demons encroaching. "I should have been thinking, 'Okay, let's just play 18 well and get inside, one under is just fine,'" he said. "But I wasn't thinking that. I was losing it again. I hit my drive about 500 yards to the right of where I needed to be."

From there he hit one ball in the water, and by the time he tapped in and limped off the green, he had made a quadruple-bogey eight. What should have been a comfortable one-under-par 70 — or, at worst, an even-par 71 — had become a 74 that put him well back in the pack. "This is what I've been doing for a while," he said, sitting in the clubhouse eating lunch. "I've got to find something to get my confidence back." He forced a smile. "And I've got about forty-eight hours, max, to find it."

He stood up to head back to the range to pound balls and continue his search. The midday temperature was about 90, and the humidity was thick enough to peel. Gangluff, like almost everyone else, didn't notice. He had too many other things to worry about at that moment.

GANGLUFF'S DAY HAD ENDED BADLY, but not nearly as badly as Chris Wisler's. Wisler was a twenty-five-year-old pro from

Dover, Delaware, who had teed off on the 10th hole in the fourth group of the day with Jon Turcotte and R. E. Winchester, a young player from Great Britain who was giving U.S. Q School a shot.

Dillard Pruitt was patrolling the front nine, checking on the pace of play among the early groups, when he got a call on his radio saying he was needed at the 16th hole. There was, he was told, "an issue." Pruitt shook his head. That was never good news. When he arrived at the 16th, Wisler explained to him that while playing the 14th hole, he had hit a ball into a lateral water hazard and had gone to his bag for another ball. He'd finished the hole with that ball, then teed off on the 15th. When he'd gone to mark his ball on the green, he'd noticed that the ball was a different brand than the one he had started the round with. Not wanting to hold up play, he had not asked for an official to come out to explain the rule to him. "He knew something was wrong, but he wasn't sure what," Pruitt said. Instead, he had gone to the 16th tee and teed off, still using the same ball.

When Wisler finished his story, Pruitt's heart sank. The tour's rules on ball branding are very strict. A player can't start a round playing Titleist, then switch to Nike, or vice versa. This is true at every level of the tour, right down to the first stage of Q School. In a sense, the rule is archaic, because it dates back to the days when golf balls were different than they are today. Years ago, most tour players used balls that were wound on the inside, made of balata. Others used balls with a hard center. The balata balls, which were far more likely to suffer cuts because of their soft centers, flew higher than the other balls. It was not uncommon for a player to change from one kind of ball to another depending on how much distance he wanted. On a long par-five, a player might play a hard-core ball, wanting a lower flight or more bounce. On a par-three, playing a short iron, he might switch to balata, wanting a high flight and a soft landing.

These days, all balls have hard-core centers, so that is no longer an issue. Now the issue is avoiding what tour officials call "a golf ball hitting demonstration." If Nike or Titleist or Callaway is unveiling a new ball that flies longer or lands softer or spins more — whatever the twist may be — it could ask a player who is under contract to the company to use the new ball on specific holes to demonstrate that quality. Thus the rule remains: once you begin a round with a certain brand of ball, you must finish the round with that brand of ball.

Wisler clearly wasn't trying to put on a golf ball demonstration. At the moment Pruitt arrived to talk to him, there was only one spectator who appeared to be watching the group: a man carrying a tackle box who had been fishing in a water hole nearby and had stopped when he saw Pruitt's cart pull up. That didn't change the rule. "When he noticed he was playing the wrong ball, he needed to take it out of play right away," Pruitt said. "The penalty would have been two strokes for the 14th and two strokes for the 15th. That would have hurt him, but he could have kept playing until the moment when he knowingly played a wrong ball. Once you do that, you have to be disqualified."

Pruitt had Wisler repeat the story so that he was absolutely certain of the facts. Wisler admitted that he had knowingly continued with the wrong ball, apparently because he thought that changing again might involve an even more serious penalty.

"If he was unsure and his fellow competitors weren't sure, he should have waited until I got there," Pruitt said. "We tell players that all the time: if you aren't 100 percent sure, ask. I felt awful. I mean, the guy spent $4,500 and no doubt spent weeks or months preparing to play four rounds. The penalties obviously would have hurt him, but it's a 72-hole event; a lot can happen. The guy handled it with amazing grace. He went and shook hands with the other two guys in his group and actually said, 'I'm sorry for causing this trouble.' I mean, my heart really sank when I heard that. Made me feel even worse."

Wisler was, in fact, a legitimate player, not someone just taking a crack at first stage. He had made it through first stage in 2002, 2003, and 2004, so he had every reason to believe that he would be among those advancing out of Tampa. Instead, he never got to finish his first round. On tour, where there are several rules officials patrolling each nine, it rarely takes more than a minute to get word from a marshal to a rules official that a ruling is needed. But with no marshals—or fans—at a first stage and with Pruitt the only PGA Tour official on-site (the rest of the officials at first stage are local PGA of America officials who volunteer to help out), the wait would have been much longer. That's why Wisler had decided to continue playing until Pruitt arrived. That proved to be his undoing.

Of course, stories like Wisler's aren't uncommon in golf. Greg Norman was once disqualified from a tournament because even though he was playing a golf ball that had been approved by the U.S. Golf Association (all golf balls must receive USGA approval before they can be played), it had not yet been officially placed on the approved ball list. But when these things happen at Q School, they are that much more poignant, because the disqualified player can't just go and tee it up someplace else the next week. He has to wait an entire year for another chance.

Mark Russell, a longtime tour rules official, remembers a second-stage qualifier in the late 1980s when a player came to him after the second round to tell him he believed one of his fellow competitors had signed for a wrong score that day. Russell asked him what he was talking about.

"He said this guy, his name was Ivan Smith, had hit a bad tee shot on a hole and, thinking it was out-of-bounds, grabbed another ball, teed it up, and hit again. When they got down the fairway, Smith found his ball was inbounds, so he played it. According to the guy who was playing with him, he had never said, 'I'm playing a provisional' before he hit his second tee shot. When he didn't say that, under the rules the second ball was in play, and he couldn't play his first ball. What really upset me was that the guy clearly knew Smith had forgotten to declare a provisional and never said anything to him then or before he signed his scorecard. If he had called it before he signed, it would have just been a two-stroke penalty. Instead, he comes to me after he's signed and tells me this. I was furious with the guy. I told him he was completely outside the spirit of the game and the rules. I don't think he cared.

"I had to go find Smith, who I knew because he had played some on the tour. He was in pretty good position, if I remember correctly. I asked him if he had declared a provisional on the tee when he'd hit the shot he thought was going out-of-bounds. He just stared at me for a second and said he didn't remember saying anything. I asked him to think again. I could see this look coming over his face. He started shaking his head and telling me that, no, he was angry, and he just grabbed a ball and hit again. I told him that once he did that, he had to play his second ball, that it was in play. He asked me what the penalty was.

"There was nothing I could do. The rules of golf don't let you let a guy off the hook because he didn't intend to do anything wrong. Intent doesn't matter. I said, 'Ivan, you signed for an incorrect score that was two shots lower than what you actually shot. I've got no choice but to disqualify you.'

"His face went completely white, and then he looked at me and said, 'Do you know that you're ruining my life? Do you know that? You're ruining my life!' I can still hear his voice clear as can be to this day."

Russell swears he can't remember the name of the whistle-blower, but he does remember checking to see how he did the rest of the tournament and being relieved when he didn't qualify. "I don't often root against a player," he said. "But I rooted against that guy. The day after this incident, he came to me and started asking me some other rules question. I said to him, 'What're you trying to do, get someone else disqualified today?'"

Most DQ's happen the way Wisler's did: an innocent mistake. Very few players want to see another player disqualified. Most are so worried about their own games that they don't pay that much attention to what their competitors are doing, although they're all aware of their obligation to "protect the field." The Ivan Smith incident is rare. Even rarer are accusations of outright cheating. In one case, however, Joe Ogilvie, who has played on the tour for six years now, refused to sign a fellow competitor's scorecard because he believed he had cheated.

SOME PLAYERS ACTUALLY WITHDRAW from Q School voluntarily. These are usually veterans who are coming to grips with the fact that they no longer have what it takes to compete. They get so far behind after a couple of rounds that they decide to pull out. Most players, however, slog on, believing that there is a 63 somewhere inside their bags.

Marc Turnesa was one of those players. He is from a golfing family on Long Island. His dad, Mike, was a longtime club pro at Rockville Links Country Club. His older brother, also Mike, is now the pro at the Apawamis Club. For as long as he could remember, Marc had played golf with his father, his brother, and his older sister, who was also a good player. He had spent two years at the University of South Florida before transferring to North Carolina State, where he graduated in 2000 with a degree in communications. But he had no desire to use that degree anytime soon. He'd had his heart set on being a golf pro—a playing pro—all his life.

"I had a good amateur career, not a great one," Turnesa said. "I won the Long Island Amateur, and I did well, but never overwhelmingly well, in college. I always wanted to take a shot at doing this. I guess the best thing I can say about myself right now is that I still feel as if my swing and my game are improving. Still, I need to make something good happen here pretty soon."

Turnesa had been living the mini-tour life for five years. "My results have been decidedly average," he said. "This past summer I paid $18,500 in entry fees, and I made about $35,000 in prize money. That's pretty much the way it's been since I got down here. If you want to be able to make a reasonable living, you need to make at least $80,000 in prize money. I can only go on doing this for so long."

His dad owned a house in Palm Beach, which helped since the rent was quite reasonable. He'd made a lot of friends, and each year he felt closer to having the kind of game he needed to make it to the tour. But he was still struggling to get out of first stage. "There comes a point where you have to start to question yourself," he said while cooling off in the clubhouse, literally and figuratively, after the second round. "Each year I've had what I thought were bad breaks. One year I shot nine under par, and it took ten under to get through. Another year I played a golf course that just wasn't very good for me—it was a bomber's course, and I'm not a bomber. Another year I got DQ'd because I forgot to get a signature on my scorecard and turned it in that way."

He forced a smile. "Today I could blame what happened on the rules guys, but in the end, it comes back to me. I was the one who couldn't get out of my own way."

Turnesa had shot a two-over-par 73 on the first day, which put him back in the pack, but with no reason to panic with 54 holes to play. But he had blown up on the back nine in the second round and added a 76 to the 73. That put him a long way back of the leader, Ted Potter Jr., who was at seven under par. More important, it put him nine shots outside the cut line with a whole lot of players to pass to get into contention. "I lost my cool," he said. "No one's fault but my own."

He lost his cool because his threesome had been put on the clock by the rules officials. They had fallen behind the group in front of them soon after making the turn and looked up to see themselves being warned and then watched. Rules officials always walk a fine line when it comes to pace of play, especially at Q School. On tour, a slow player is subject to fines but isn't penalized on his scorecard. At Q School, where there is no prize money until the finals and that money is essentially irrelevant, the only way to penalize a player is by penalty—in this case, two shots if you get a slow time while on the clock. Unless there is an exceptional situation—being behind a tree, being forced to change clubs, or, for example, needing a ruling—a player on the clock has forty seconds to put the ball in play once he pulls a club.

A rules official is highly unlikely to penalize a player if he's anywhere close to forty seconds. In fact, the player would probably have to go well over forty seconds on a consistent basis to be penalized, because no rules official wants to be the guy who costs a player a chance to advance by penalizing him.

The flip side, though, is not wanting the golf course to come to a complete halt because one group is slow—which can easily happen. It often happens at Q School because players slow down as the pressure builds. The last day at Q School can make the Last Supper look like a trip to a McDonald's drive-through. Players can be seen changing clubs two or three times, walking off yardages they know cold, and lining up six-inch putts.

Most of the time when a rules official puts a group on the clock, it is just to get their attention and get them moving faster. The official has no intention of penalizing any player unless he starts walking backwards or on his hands. "Usually [when] you put a group on the clock, you're doing them a favor," Dillard Pruitt said. "I would say 99 percent of golfers play better when they play fast. The slower they play, the more they overthink.

You'd be amazed how often when you make guys speed up, they play better."

Unfortunately, that wasn't the case for Turnesa. He let the thought of being timed get to him. "I'm over the ball, and instead of thinking about my shot, I'm thinking about time. Has it been thirty seconds? Thirty-five? Am I about to get nailed for two? I got pissed off for three holes and made bad swings that led to bogeys. I looked around, and the group behind us was way behind, so I got more pissed off." He sighed. "Next thing I know, I've shot 40 on the back nine, and I'm sitting in here stewing about it. I go to the range and stripe every shot. That doesn't do me a lot of good right now, though, does it?

"You know, I like to think of myself as a realist. If I didn't think I was good enough to compete, I'd go do something else." He paused. "Of course, I have no idea what that would be. All I've known my whole life is golf. I don't see myself as a club pro. And yet, when I think about what else I might do if I don't do this, I come up blank.

"There are still 36 holes to play. I don't see myself as being out of this by any means. I go out and shoot 67–67, and I'll definitely have a shot to advance. Is that easy? Obviously not. But is it impossible? No. My game has always been built on chipping and putting. I haven't made a putt for two days. I've got to make some putts. That's a familiar-sounding story, I know, but that's what it comes down to in the end for all of us.

"You know, the funny thing is, my buddies back home think it's really cool that I'm down here playing golf. To some degree, they're right, of course. It is cool, and I'm lucky to have this chance to follow my dream. But if people ask me about playing great golf courses, I tell them, 'Stay amateur.' The good amateur events are played on great golf courses. Mini-tours are played on terrible golf courses, often under lousy conditions. It's hardly a glamorous life. A gallery consists of friends and family—when you're lucky. I'm not complaining; I'm just saying that's the reality of it. It isn't glamorous. But you do it because you love the game and because you honestly believe that someday you're going to be good enough to go to that next level, and someday you'll go all the way to the tour."

He stood up. It was time to call his dad and give him a report. "He's always great in situations like this. He never lectures, never gets down. He's always encouraging. He always says, 'Okay, get back to work, and you'll get 'em tomorrow.' He's right, of course. The problem is, at some point you run out of tomorrows."

5

Nineteen and Ties

THE MAIN HANGOUT at a qualifier is almost never the club-house, although players will always stop there after a round to eat something and cool off a bit before heading back out into the heat to hit balls, chip, or putt. No one goes straight home. Home is almost always a cheap hotel room, and there's nothing to do there but think. Or wonder why you aren't out hitting balls like everyone else in the field.

The favorite hangout is the scoreboard. There is never more than one at a qualifier, and it is always a far cry from the computerized scoreboards that are prevalent on the PGA Tour. At the TPC Tampa Bay, Karen Widener, who worked at local golf tournaments throughout the year, was in charge of the scoreboard. Prior to the start of the event, she had carefully written down the names of all the players on long strips of cardboard, leaving room to fill in their scores for the four 18-hole rounds. (There are no cuts at any stage of Q School, the tour having decided several years ago that for the kind of money a player pays to participate, he should be allowed to play all the rounds, no matter how far behind he might be.) The players' names were arranged across the board in alphabetical order. Once the scorecards from a group were signed and attested, they were walked over to Widener, who filled in each score, hole by hole, and then the total. In the middle of the board, she kept a tally of all the scores for the day and, in parentheses, how many under par (or over par) that was.

That was the section of the scoreboard everyone paid the most attention to. As the scores came in, players, caddies, and friends and family would stand in front of the board and count to 19—that was the magic number, since the top 19 players and ties would advance to second stage—and see what number the 19th player was sitting on. At the end of the first day, exactly 19 players had shot 70 (one under) or better. What that told the players was that if the conditions stayed the same—warm and humid, with a breeze but no high winds—the number after four days was likely to be around four under par. If it rained and the course got wet, the number could go lower. If the wind came up, it could go higher.

At one time, the number of players who would advance from first stage to second stage or from second stage to the finals had been exact. Ties were broken by play-offs. In those days, most first stages advanced exactly twenty players. Now, most advance nineteen and ties, although occasionally if a site has more or fewer entrants, the number can go up or down by one. "In the end, we usually end up with about the same number of players advancing as in the play-off days," Steve Carman said. "Ideally, you want seventy-eight players at each of the six second-stage sites, but if you have to add a threesome at a couple of places, it isn't that big a deal. In the end, I'd rather give a few more guys an opportunity than a few less guys."

The TPC Tampa Bay is often used as a first-stage course, so a lot of the players were familiar with it. Jamie Neher, who lives only a few hours away in Hobe Sound, had reason to be confident playing the course: he had won the first-stage event there the past two years. Of course, a first-stage qualifier is one golf tournament where players would prefer *not* to defend a title.

Neher, who hadn't made it through second stage yet, was back at
Tampa Bay trying to advance for the third—and, he sincerely
hoped, last—time.

"There are a lot of players who have the first-stage thing down
pretty well," said Alex Rocha, standing in front of the scoreboard
as scores went up on Tuesday afternoon. "I'm not going to say
that's the easy part, but it is definitely a lot different at this level
than the next. Second stage, you routinely see guys who have
not only been on tour but have been successful on tour. You don't
see that too often at first stage. This isn't a whole lot different
than a mini-tour event. You see a lot of familiar faces."

Like a lot of players, Rocha knew the TPC Tampa Bay's
Q School history. "Usually the number here is about three or four
under," he said. "If the wind blows, of course everything changes.
Chances are, if you shoot four under, you're going to move on."

Rocha was born in Brazil but raised in Florida. He was
twenty-seven years old and, like a lot of players, had studied the
course's Q School history. He had shot 69 in the first round,
which put him in solid position. The low score of the day had
been a remarkable 62, shot by Vince Covello, which had included a 28 on the front nine. No one else had shot better than
66. A lot of players in the field were playing without caddies.
Most of those working as caddies were friends or relatives. A few
local caddies were working, but several players, including Rocha,
had opted to rent a pull cart. Mike Grob, one of the two ex–PGA
Tour players in the field, was carrying his own bag in the searing
heat. "Good exercise," he joked, sweating profusely after shooting 69 the first day.

The weather was a concern for everyone in the field and for
Dillard Pruitt. Not the heat—everyone knows that comes with
playing in Florida—but Hurricane Wilma, which was heading
toward the state. Six weeks after the devastation of Katrina, people were even more uptight about the approach of a hurricane

than usual. The qualifier was supposed to end on Friday afternoon. The hurricane wasn't likely to make landfall before Saturday, perhaps as late as Monday. Still, Pruitt was worried.

"A lot of these guys live in Florida, in places right in the path of the thing," he said. "Some of them have already been nailed this year, and a lot of them just want to get home, get their houses ready, and, in a lot of cases, get their families out. From what I'm seeing, we can get the thing finished by Friday evening without being affected, but I know the closer the hurricane gets, the more uptight players are going to be."

Pruitt didn't like the idea of asking the players to play more than 18 holes a day, but by the end of the second day, he was considering it. He was in communication with tour headquarters in Ponte Vedra Beach but had basically been told, "You're there; you make the call."

On Thursday, while the players were grinding through the third round, Pruitt made the call. The players had been re-paired after two rounds, just like at any PGA Tour event, with the leaders going out last. At Q School, they use a re-pairing format called "reverse horseshoe." Because there's no cut, the players continue to tee off on both the front and back nines for all four rounds. In a regular PGA Tour event, unless pressed for time because of weather delays or a West Coast TV finish, players go off only one tee after the field is cut. That makes it easy: the player with the highest score for two rounds tees off first, and everyone falls in line after that, with the leader going off last. When two tees are used, the field is divided in half. In this case, with sixty-six players still playing after DQs and withdrawals, eleven three-somes went off the first tee and eleven went off the 10th tee. The thirty-three players with the best scores went off the first tee under the normal tour weekend format: highest score first, lowest score last. On the back nine, the format was reversed: lowest score first, highest score last. The reason for this, especially at a qualifier, is to have the players in the middle of the field playing at the same time under the same conditions. "You want to make it as fair as possible, and the more guys with similar scores who are on the course together, the better it is," Pruitt said.

A breeze had kicked up on Wednesday and the scores were slightly higher than on the first day. Instead of nineteen players at one under or better, there were now just fifteen players who were under par after 36 holes. There were, however, eleven more players bunched up at even par. Amazingly, one of those twenty-six players who had shot 142 or better was *not* Vince Covello. Living proof of the vagaries of Q School, Covello had gone from 62 to 83 in a period of twenty-four hours. Even more amazing was the fact that the entire 21-stroke swing had come on the front nine, when he had gone from 28 to 49 — 49! — on the front nine, including a 10 on the fourth hole, which had started his spiral.

In a sense, Covello was living proof that players like Marc Turnesa who insisted they weren't out of it even when they were way behind, weren't just mouthing hopeful pabulum. If a player could go from 62 to 83, he could also go from 83 to 62, or, at the very least, from 73–76 to 66–66. That's what the players in the bottom half of the field were hoping for when the third round began — a low round that would bump them back into contention. If there is one good thing about a qualifier, it is that 19th place is just about as good as first place. The only advantage a high finisher has is that he is guaranteed being assigned to the second-stage site listed as his first choice on his application, although most players get their first choice anyway.

Just before the third round started, Pruitt made a decision: he would err on the side of caution. As the players were about to tee off, they were told to be prepared to play again in the afternoon. There wouldn't be time to re-pair them based on their third-round scores, so they would be given about an hour off to eat and relax, then would go out and play for as long as they could. It would get dark by about six thirty. Pruitt's goal was to get in enough golf that the final round could be completed by noon on Friday, to give everyone a chance to get home and prepare for the hurricane.

"I figure they've got enough to worry about without being uptight about getting out of here and getting home," he said. "The sooner they finish, the happier most of them are going to be."

For most players, the third round is critical. Those near the front know that a good round could give them a good deal of leeway for the last 18 holes. Those in the middle want to move up, to get inside whatever the number will be. Those behind know that they have to fire at flags to at least get within shouting distance.

One of those in the middle was a player whose last name is familiar to people who follow golf: Josh McCumber. His uncle is Mark McCumber, who won ten times on the PGA Tour, including victories in the Tour Championship and the Players Championship. He had also finished second in the British Open in 1996. Now he plays only part-time on the Champions Tour, in part because he's had surgery on his shoulder and legs and has never felt quite the same physically, but also because he and his older brother, Jim, spend a lot of time working on their golf course design company. Josh is Jim's son, but it was Mark who inspired him to want to play big-time golf.

"I still remember going to the Western Open in 1989 when I was thirteen and seeing Mark win," he said. "I thought it was cool. I thought the whole deal with tour life was cool. I had the chance to be exposed to a lot of good players and a lot of good golf courses as a kid. I feel as if I have a realistic sense of what it takes to play on the tour. Having said that, I know it's hard—really hard. The number of players I've played with in juniors, in college, [and] on mini-tours who could really hit the ball is staggering. When I play with Mark, it isn't so much that he hits the ball that much better than guys like that, but that he has this ability to always get the ball close to the hole. I'm not sure that's something you can teach. He just does it, one way or the other, and he does it all the time. That's what really good players do — they get up and down four or five times in a round when other guys won't. On a good day it's the difference between 66 and 71, and on a bad day [it's] the difference between 71 and 76. Add it up — that's a lot of shots."

Josh McCumber graduated from Florida and then turned pro after playing in the U.S. Amateur at Pebble Beach in 1999. He had gone to Q School twice and made it through the first stage but not second. By the end of 2001, he was feeling frustrated and a little burned-out. When Buddy Alexander, his college coach, offered him the chance to return to Florida as assistant coach, he took it. "I enjoyed coaching," he said. "I enjoyed the guys and working for Buddy. But two years into it, I had the itch to play again. I began to feel as if I hadn't really given myself a chance to make it. I remembered that Mark went to Q School six times before he got to the tour. In fact, he won the regionals [now second stage] twice and then didn't make it at the finals. I wanted to see what would happen if I really worked on my game for a while."

After he finished the '04–'05 season at Florida, he turned his attention to playing golf. He qualified for the U.S. Open at Pinehurst, a big confidence boost, and played mini-tours during the summer and fall to prepare. In September he took a break from his preparation to get married. His dad and his new wife, Kerry, were his cheering section in Tampa. He had chosen the TPC Tampa Bay as his first-stage site because Mark McCumber had played in the Champions Tour event there in February. "Mark and my dad both thought it would be a good course for me," he said. "I came out here and checked it out and agreed. So here I am."

For the first three days, Josh's game was almost agonizingly consistent: 70–71–71. That left him just inside the cut line after 54 holes, with the fourth round beginning shortly. Almost all the contenders knew they would play for a while Thursday afternoon, then come back to finish on Friday. In some ways, that would make things more difficult, since they would be walking to the clubhouse in mid-round, not really knowing where they stood. The only scores posted on Karen Widener's scoreboard would be for the first three rounds. Other than through gossip, they wouldn't know who was rallying or who had it in reverse up to that point in the fourth round.

"I'm trying as best as I can to play relaxed," Josh said. "If I make a mistake, make sure it's only a bogey. If I make a birdie, great, try to make another one at the next hole. Being on the clock [as part of Marc Turnesa's group] the first two days was a little bit distracting, but I thought I handled it well. I know Marc was fighting himself a little bit Wednesday. He apologized to us on the 15th tee. I told him not to worry about it. We're all grinding out here."

"Grinding" is the word golfers use for working hard — when every hole is pressure-packed, and there's no chance to ease up and relax. Players on tour talk about grinding to make a cut on Friday afternoon. Those on the Nationwide Tour talk about grinding to make the top 20 on the money list so that they can avoid Q School. In the Q School finals, everyone is grinding for a spot on the PGA Tour, or at least a full exemption on the Nationwide Tour. At second stage, everyone's grinding to make the finals and guarantee himself some kind of job playing golf the next year. But there may be no grind like first stage. One reason for that is that players who don't make it to second stage have absolutely no place to play the next year except the mini-tours that have cropped up around the country, where the first goal is to re-coup your entry fees. Beyond that is the cold recognition that if you can't get past first stage, you're a long way from where you want to be as a professional golfer.

"That's the hard part," Marc Turnesa said. "In my heart of hearts, I think I can be a good player, good enough to play on the PGA Tour. But my results don't say that right now. I'm still a long way from the tour, not a short way. The guys who make it to the finals and play on the Nationwide, they can honestly say, 'Hey, if I improve just a little, I can be out there.' The guys who are fall-ing short at second stage, at least they've shown they can get through first, and they're on the cusp of being able to make a de-cent living on the Nationwide. All of us struggling in first stage are about three big steps removed from where we want our games to be, and even though we can go home at night and tell ourselves, 'It's this close,' the numbers say it isn't as close as we think it might be or want it to be."

What keeps players like Turnesa out there is that the differ-ence between a first-stage failure and a tour player is not that great physically. Players like Turnesa can hit the ball far enough to compete on the PGA Tour. They can shoot low numbers on occasion, and when they go home and play with their buddies, they are clearly a cut above those guys. The gap between a good amateur player—the kind of guy who competes for his club championship or even in amateur events around his region—and a player good enough to play competitively at first stage is mam-moth. If you walk out onto the range at a first-stage qualifier, you won't see a lot of difference in the swing quality of most of the players—barring the occasional ringer who gets through the system and can't break 80—and the swing quality of those on the tour.

Two things separate the first-stage player from the tour player, and both are far more mental than physical: the ability to control his swing under pressure and the ability to make putts under pressure. In 2005 Tiger Woods did not miss one putt inside four feet on tour. That's an astonishing statistic. Most first-stage players miss at least one short putt per round when playing under pressure. Frequently, those four putts are the difference between advancing and not advancing. Or there might be one wayward drive or iron shot when the player can least afford it. Dealing with nerves—Stephen Gangluff's demons—is the hardest thing for any golfer, especially one who is trying to crack the elite levels of the sport.

Gangluff's demons were still chasing him throughout the third round. He started the morning at three over par, just three shots outside the number, but he couldn't get his swing under control. "I never gave myself any kind of real chance the whole round," he said after shooting 75. Like most players, Gangluff had ducked inside the clubhouse to cool off during the break between rounds. He sat in an armchair in the lobby staring into space, clearly baffled and upset, knowing that he now had no chance—barring a 59 the last 18 holes—to advance.

The third round is the one where a lot of dreams go up in smoke. If you shoot 75 and go from three shots outside the number to nine shots out, you know you're a dead man walking those last 18 holes. Vince Covello didn't even want to play the last round after shooting 75 in the third. He had gone from nine under par after his first round to seven over par, meaning that even another 62 probably wouldn't be good enough to advance. Like everyone else, he was hot, tired, and frustrated. He told Dillard Pruitt he wanted to withdraw and go home.

"Are you injured?" Pruitt asked.

"No."

"Are you sick, I mean physically sick, not sick about your golf?"

"No."

"Then I really think you owe it to yourself and to the event to finish. You signed up to play 72 holes. Unless there's a reason you can't, you should at least be able to say you finished. You might feel worse about it now, but when it's over, you'll be glad you posted a score, regardless of what it is."

Covello listened, nodded his head, and walked to the range to get ready to play the last round.

As the players headed back to the tees shortly after two o'clock, the tension was apparent. Steve Carman calls Q School "the quietest event in golf. Someone can make a hole in one, and you'll barely hear a whoop or a holler."

Having already played 18 holes in the heat and knowing they were going to play one of the most important rounds of their lives, the players weren't up for much chatter. One of the few with a smile on his face was Garrett Frank.

Frank was one of those second-stage perennials, someone who always seemed to survive first stage but not second. For two days, it had appeared that he might not survive first stage this time around. He had started horrendously. Through 33 holes, he was six over par and felt as if he was running in quicksand. "Just couldn't get anything going at all," he said. "I kept telling myself that I just needed a couple of good holes to get going."

Actually, he needed only one good hole — one shot, in fact — to get going. Playing the 16th hole in the second round, a relatively short par-five, Frank found himself 230 yards from the hole after a good drive down the left side. He took out a "rescue club," a wood (all woods are metal these days, of course, but most golfers still call them woods) that can be used in the rough, in the fairway, and for almost any kind of shot. "There was wind from the left, so I aimed for the left side of the green," Frank said. "When I hit it, I knew I'd hit a really good shot. My swing felt perfect. I saw the wind taking the ball right just as I thought it would. The ball hit and went over a knob on the green and disappeared. Joey Whitaker had walked up toward the green because he had laid up, and I saw his arms go up in the air in the touchdown signal. That's when I knew it had gone in."

It was the first double eagle Frank had ever made. "Heck, it was the first one I've ever witnessed," he said. A double eagle is the rarest shot in golf, far more unusual than a hole in one because it almost always involves a much longer shot than the tee shot on a par-three.

Buoyed by his sudden change of fortune, Frank parred his last two holes and then, filled with confidence, shot 66 in the third round to jump to two under for the tournament. That put him right on the number beginning the last round. "Now I'm confident," he said, relaxing in the locker room to get out of the heat. "For 33 holes, I had nothing going on. One shot turned me right around. Amazing game, isn't it?"

Most players weren't quite as buoyant. A few appeared to be in very strong positions. Alex Rocha was the leader at 11 under par, meaning if he could finish 18 holes standing, he was likely to make the top 19. A number of players were bunched between two under par and seven under par, with everyone else trying to catch up. Pruitt had told everyone that when they heard three blasts from his siren, that was it for the day. A player could finish the hole he was playing or stop right there and mark his ball, if he preferred.

The three sharp blasts came at 6:48 p.m. with dusk rapidly closing in. The player in the field who least wanted to stop was Marc Turnesa. He had played better in the third round, shooting 70, but that still had left him way outside the number at six over for three rounds. Knowing he had to go low — or, as the players say, "go deep" — on the last 18 holes, he was doing exactly that. "Third round I wasn't close to making a bogey," he said. "Honestly, 70 was the highest score I could have shot. I didn't make a putt longer than five feet."

Playing in one of the later groups off the back nine, Turnesa began dropping birdie putts from all over. He didn't miss a fairway, and the putts that hadn't dropped in the third round were now dropping. When the horn went off, he had finished 14 holes and was eight under par for the round, meaning he was now two under par for the tournament. "I didn't want to stop," he said. "I'd have kept playing in pitch dark at that point if they'd let me. I was in such a zone, the kind you only get into once in a while. I knew it was going to be very hard to keep that kind of momentum going in the morning, and I was guessing I still wasn't inside the number, that I needed to make at least one more birdie, maybe two, to make it."

That's what everyone was doing on Thursday night — guessing. The consensus was that the number was going to be three under, perhaps four. The weather report for the morning was hot without wind, the kind of weather that had led to the saying "the calm before the storm."

A handful of players finished their rounds on Thursday. One of them, Chang Hong, playing in the first group, had rallied after an opening 74 to shoot 70–68–70. But he had come to his last hole, the ninth, almost convinced that two under par wouldn't be good enough. His second shot had stopped just short of the green, and he'd had a 60-foot chip, which he almost holed. The ball curled to a stop about two inches from the hole. Hong's shoulders slumped.

"Last year I was nine under par with nine holes to play and shot six over the last nine to miss by one," he said. "I think I may have just missed by one again."

He wouldn't know until the next day. Some players took the suspense out of their last rounds early. Nicholas Thompson, who had graduated from Georgia Tech in the spring and had played on the U.S. Walker Cup team before turning pro in August, shot 65–63 the last two rounds to finish at twelve under par. That tied him with Rocha. Colby Beckstrom, a twenty-two-year-old who had left Texas Christian after his junior year, was one shot behind them. Mike Grob put his experience to work during the final round, shooting 66 to finish at nine under par, and went off to hire a caddy for second stage. Garrett Frank tagged a 67 onto his third-round 66 and was comfortably in at six under par.

It wasn't as easy for most of the others. Jamie Neher, the two-time TPC Tampa Bay king, had one hole left when play was stopped. He came out tight and nervous on Friday morning, hit a ball into the water on the 18th, and made double bogey, dropping him from a comfortable-feeling five under to a not nearly as comfortable three under. Since Neher's group was the first of the day to finish, he knew it would be a long wait before he would know whether he was in or out.

"I can't do this," he said to his caddy. "I can't just stand here and watch these scores go up. I'm heading home. Call me in the car."

Josh McCumber also had a nervous finish. He had played superbly in the afternoon round and was five under for 12 holes and six under for the tournament when play was called. "I felt like I was inside the number at that point," he said. "I think I came out playing too carefully in the morning. I wasn't trying to make birdies anymore."

He made no birdies in his last six holes but did make two bogeys. "The first one was just a bad break. I had mud on my ball off the tee at 14," he said. He smiled. "The second one was probably some nerves."

McCumber flew the green with his second shot at 18, then chipped carefully to 10 feet and missed the par putt. "I didn't want to do anything crazy at 18," he said. "I figured I would still be okay at four, and I wanted to make sure I didn't make worse than bogey."

He signed his card and walked to the scoreboard, where the crowd was growing as more and more groups finished. When he saw the number of players at five under or better, with several of the leaders still on the course, his heart skipped at least half a beat. "I hadn't expected to see that many guys ahead of me," he said. "But then I heard that some of the guys in the late groups were struggling, so it made me feel a little better."

It is one of the mysteries of Q School just how word gets out that a player is going deep or has it in reverse. Perhaps a relative walks on ahead and mentions to someone following another group that the player has just made three straight bogeys or hit a ball out-of-bounds. Somehow, word gets out.

Just as McCumber was carefully finishing at 18 with a bogey, Marc Turnesa was finishing at nine, also with a bogey, but for entirely different reasons. His concern about finding the magic that had been in his clubs on Thursday afternoon had been justified. He had parred the sixth, seventh, and eighth holes and came to nine, a 425-yard par-four, thinking he had to make one more birdie to have a legitimate chance to get to the number.

"All week we had talked about three under or four under making it," he said. "I'd heard it was four under last year, but this year the scores had been a little higher because it had been windy on Wednesday. I knew the conditions were calm but nerves would come into play. I'd have loved to get to four under, but I thought three under would have a chance. I figured at two under I was dead."

Standing in the middle of the ninth fairway after a perfect drive, his white shirt already soaking wet at nine thirty in the morning, Turnesa had 165 yards to the hole. He took a seven-iron and, as the ball left his club, thought he had hit it "absolutely perfect."

But there was just a hint of a breeze, and the ball wasn't flying in the direction of the pin, tucked over a knob in the green, the way Turnesa had thought it would. "Be right," he hissed with the ball in the air, a golfer's reference not to wanting the ball to go to the right but to the club selection being correct. When the ball landed just in front of the green and skidded to a halt instead of bounding toward the hole, Turnesa's heart sank. When he got to his ball, he still had 84 feet to the hole and knew he needed a miraculous shot.

"I went for the chip," he said. "I figured I had no choice."

He hit a good shot, right at the flag, but the ball slid by the hole and stopped six feet behind it. Disheartened, he missed the par putt, finishing with 64, which he knew was going to be too little, too late. He signed for a four-round score of 283—one under par—and dragged himself over to the scoreboard to join the others who were watching Karen Widener do her work. At that moment, he wasn't officially dead, but he knew there were too many players on the course for his score to hold up.

"I might as well stand here and watch," he said. "I like dying a slow, painful death."

It didn't take long for him to die. Before long, those at two under were gone, and those at three under—including Jamie Neher, somewhere in his car en route to Hobe Sound—were in serious jeopardy. Stephen Gangluff, who had finally shaken his demons to shoot a last-round 67, which still left him nowhere near the cut line, paused for a brief look before heading for the parking lot. "Back to the drawing board," he said quietly.

The word about players in reverse had proven to be true. While young Colby Beckstrom was cruising to a final-round 65, the two men playing with him, Ted Potter Jr. and George McNeill, were struggling. McNeill had lost much of his cushion with a third-round 74, but Potter had appeared more than comfortable starting the last 18 holes at six under par.

"I wanted to shout at him [Potter], 'Put your driver away, dude!'" Beckstrom said. "He kept hitting his driver and getting into more and more trouble. I really felt for the guy because you could see by the look on his face that he knew it was slipping away, but he didn't know how to stop the slide."

By the time he got to the 18th hole, Potter was six over par for his last round and had no chance. McNeill stood on the tee at three under, thinking he might need a birdie, but a par might be good enough. He was an experienced player, who had played his college golf at Florida State and had been to second stage several times. He had also qualified for the U.S. Open in the past, so he had been in pressure situations. But, after opening with a 66 in the first round, the rest of the week had been a struggle. Now he was just trying to hang on.

He couldn't. His second shot missed the green left, and he chipped to 12 feet. Knowing he almost certainly had to make the putt, he watched it die an inch—one inch—to the right. That was the difference between making it to second stage and not making it. He finished at two under par along with Chang Hong, whose prediction that he would miss by a shot had proven true. Marc Turnesa was another shot back, tied for 27th. His gut feeling that he needed one more birdie had been exactly right.

Jamie Neher was an hour down the road when he got the call telling him that he had finished tied for 19th along with Barry Roof and Bryan Clarke.

At Q School, everyone has a story to tell—one way or the other. George McNeill's one-inch tap-in for bogey at the 18th hole had been the last shot of the week. It had come at 10:31 a.m., giving people time to head home and prepare for the hurricane. A number of players went straight to their cars, flinging clubs into the trunk and changing shoes right there before heading down the highway. Others lingered by the scoreboard. Some knew it would be at least another year before they competed at this level again. Others knew it might be longer than that.

Chris Wall, who had finished four shots outside the number

at one over par, stood with his bag slung across his shoulder and shook his head. "I wish I could have played nine more holes," he said, echoing a familiar refrain.

Joey Whitaker, who had witnessed Garrett Frank's double eagle, had deferred graduate school for a year to take another shot at Q School. He had worked on a golf course maintenance crew on the early-morning shift so he could have the rest of the day to practice. As the scores went up on the board, his father, who had caddied for him, stood and watched sadly. His son had shot 306, 22 over par, and had finished second to last. "A week ago, he played in a tournament and shot 65–67 and won," Joe Whitaker Sr. said. "I don't know what happened to him this week. I've never seen him play like this. All the time and all the work, and this is how it ends."

The one player who had finished behind Whitaker was Toddy Brown, who had shot 311. He was delighted. "I just wanted to see what this would feel like," he said. "This was a chance to get my feet wet against players at this level."

Brown was a businessman from Greensboro, North Carolina. He played college golf at Wake Forest and decided at the age of forty-seven that he wanted to take a crack at the Champions Tour when he turned fifty. He had taken time off from his job to work on his golf, and this was the first time he had tested himself. Clearly, he had a long way to go, which was no surprise to him. "This golf course was just too long for my game," he said. "I knew that would be the case. My nerves held up, though, and that's a good sign."

Those who had survived lingered longer than most of those who hadn't. They talked about where they were going for second stage. There were two Florida sites, and most had signed up for one of them. Younger players like Nicholas Thompson and Colby Beckstrom were all smiles. For them, first stage had been a successful adventure. Most were just glad it was over.

"There's a little bit of a double-edged sword to this," Garrett Frank said, watching the last scores get posted, knowing he was safely inside the number. "If you want to play big-time golf, this is a week you have to deal with, have to survive. But when you walk away from it, you understand you still haven't done anything yet. This is the first hill. Second stage is the mountain."

And what are the finals? "I don't know," Frank said. "But I'd sure like to find out."

6

On to November

IN ALL, 294 PLAYERS had advanced from the fourteen first stages, an average of 21 players per site. That was slightly more than the ideal number of 20 per site that Steve Carman hoped for, but it wasn't anything that couldn't be handled. Second stage was scheduled for the second and third weeks of November, three sites each week. With cooler weather approaching, there would be two sites in California, two in Texas, and two in Florida.

A number of players with familiar names had taken part in first stage with varying success. Scott Ford, the grandson of 1957 Masters champion Doug Ford (he had caddied for his grandfather once at Augusta as a teenager), had made it through at the Florence, South Carolina, site on the number—which was eight over par, in large part because the weather was frigid the entire week. Codie Mudd, the son of Jodie Mudd, who won the Players Championship in 1990, wasn't nearly as fortunate in Florence, shooting 20 over par—12 shots outside the cut. Patrick Damron, the younger brother of tour player Robert Damron, cruised through in Lakeland, Florida, finishing tied for third. One brother team advanced: Ron Whittaker got through in Cypress, Texas; his brother John made it through at Tampa Bay. Warren Schutte, best known for beating Phil Mickelson to win the NCAA championship in 1991, finished tied for eighth at the Kannapolis, North Carolina, site. Ricky Barnes, the 2002 U.S. Amateur champion, who had gotten a lot of attention by outplaying Tiger Woods while paired with him at the 2003 Masters, finished tied for second at Rio Rico, Arizona. Jeff Curl, the son of Rod Curl, the only full-blooded Native American to have won on the PGA Tour (Colonial, 1974) finished tied for fourth in Spring, Texas, and reached second stage for a third straight year.

There were, as usual, some eye-catching scores. Isabelle (Izzy) Beisiegel, who in 2004 had become the first woman to enter Q School, was allowed to enter again even though she had shot 324 in '04. She had full playing status on the LPGA Tour in 2005 after finishing 81st on the money list in 2004, so her entry was accepted on that basis. She proceeded to shoot 339—51 over par—at La Quinta and missed advancing by 55 strokes. Her score wasn't even close to being the worst one posted. In Florence, Sergei Pidukov pieced together rounds of 94–100–99–89 (a strong finish) to shoot 382—102 over par and 108 shots behind medalist Scott Parel. He only missed the cut by 94 shots. Pidukov might have had some competition for high score if not for the fact that Greg Moak, playing the same site, was disqualified after shooting 85–97 the first two rounds.

Robert Floyd also played in Florence. He finished tied for 32nd, seven shots outside the cut. Floyd was the second son of four-time major championship winner Raymond Floyd. He and his older brother, Raymond Jr., had both been very good junior players and had received a good deal of attention as the sons of a Hall of Fame player. "I think it was a lot harder on my brother than on me, because he was older and he had my dad's name," Robert Floyd said. "For the most part, being dad's son was all good. We got exposed to teachers like Butch Harmon and David Leadbetter. We had dad there as an adviser—never a pushy one, just there for support. We played great golf courses, and there wasn't any new equipment we didn't get to try."

Ray Jr. went to Wake Forest, tried to play professionally briefly, and then decided Wall Street and amateur golf were the right combination for him. Robert had a better junior record and was recruited to play at Florida by longtime coach Buddy Alexander. He did very well in college and reached the semifinals and quarterfinals of the U.S. Amateur in 1996 and 1997. Had he won his semifinal match in 1996, he and his father, the 1976 Masters champion, would have been the first father and son to play in the Masters together.

"That would have been neat, no doubt," Robert said. "I wish it had happened, but it didn't. To be honest, at the time I thought it was just postponing something that was going to happen. I had a lot of confidence in my ability to get better and to make it on the PGA Tour. If I had thought then that would be my best chance, I'm sure I would have been more upset. Back then, I was just unhappy about losing the match."

He decided to leave Florida after his junior year and turn pro. "I was playing well, I'd done well in college golf and amateur golf, and I thought I was ready," he said. "When I was in college, I was pretty confident. I didn't think anyone was all *that* good."

Because he was his father's son, he had a quick opportunity to find out just how good the players on the PGA Tour were. "I got five sponsor exemptions right after I turned pro," he said. "I had some decent rounds, but I went zero-for-five making cuts."

Welcome to the tour. As the marketing slogan goes, "These guys are good."

He played a few mini-tour events to get ready for the 1997 Q School and then breezed through first stage. He still remembers the first hole of his first round at Bear Lakes Country Club in West Palm Beach, Florida. "It was soggy because it had been raining. One of the guys I was playing with hits a shot into the green, and it plugs. He thinks he has to play it plugged. I tell him he can lift, clean, and place on the green, but the guy says no, he's sure we can't. I'm about to argue with him or call a rules official when P. J. Cowan, the third guy in the group, says to me, 'Let him go ahead. I want to see this.' P. J. was a veteran. I shut up. The guy punched the ball out, and it went about six feet straight up into the air, bounced and rolled, and stopped eight feet short of the cup from 30 feet. I felt kind of guilty I didn't do more, but it *was* funny."

With Alexander, his old college coach, volunteering to caddy for him, he played second stage at Hombre Golf Club, a course in Panama City, Florida, often used as a Q School site. On the second day, the wind howled, rain fell in sheets, and Floyd shot 68. "I think I passed just about the entire field," he said. "Then I went to a restaurant with a bunch of guys, and they were all talking about how they were going to have to rain the round out and replay it. I'm thinking, 'Oh, God, please don't do that.'"

They didn't, and Floyd was comfortably inside the number until the last nine holes, when he began to feel the pressure. "I started hitting it all over," he said. "I was leaking oil all the way. I think I shot 40 the last nine holes and made it by a couple. The only person more nervous than me was Buddy. He told me afterward, 'I didn't want to be the one to call your dad and tell him you shot 42 the last nine holes and missed by one.'"

Floyd didn't miss, and there he was in the finals, still not twenty-two years old and brimming with confidence. "I think the first time you're in the finals, especially when you're that young, there's a tendency to be relaxed," he said. "You've already guaranteed yourself a place to play, and even though you *say* the only thing you want is the PGA Tour, you know you have a fallback position. I think for some guys, that can work well, because they aren't nervous. For me it was different. I need some kind of extra incentive, some kind of push, I think. I just never got going the whole week."

He landed on the Nike Tour in 1998, which was fine. He started the year playing well. He made seven straight cuts and was in contention several times. He heard his name mentioned on the Golf Channel as already being one of the best players on the tour. He was breezing.

Only it didn't last. "When I didn't win when I had those chances, I went backward instead of forward," he said. "I went from contending every week to missing cuts. Next thing I knew, the year was over, I was 82nd on the money list, and there I was back at first stage. To be honest, I was kind of shocked."

This is what golf can do to young players—even confident, talented, and, in Floyd's case, privileged young players. All of his father's contacts, all the equipment, all the lessons, and all the publicity could do nothing more than get him the occasional sponsor exemption. The rest he had to do on his own, even as it became increasingly difficult.

He again made it through first stage with ease in 1998 but missed second stage by two shots. All of a sudden, he found himself playing mini-tours. "Even that didn't bother me that much," he said. "I played some good golf and played with some good players. Briny Baird went from the Golden Bear Tour that year to the PGA Tour and has done well ever since. You can learn there, and I thought I was learning."

But even as he was improving, Q School was becoming a wall he couldn't get over. One year Rick Smith, now Phil Mickelson's teacher, came out and caddied for him. He had long talks with his father about what he needed to do. "Dad had never had to go because when he came on tour, they didn't have Q School yet. He tried very hard to relate to it, though. He said he tried to imagine how he felt on a Friday when he was grinding to make a cut and needed to make key four-footers just to play the weekend. When that happened, that meant you were struggling, and there's no struggle quite like Q School.

"That's the thing, though, it *is* different than missing a cut. You can go play next week. At Q School, if something's wrong that week or if you have a bad round or if you're in a bad mindset for whatever reason, that's it for the year."

Floyd continued to plug away at mini-tours for the next few years. He had some success and played the occasional Nationwide Tour event. But he never made it back to the finals. In 2003 he got married and started thinking it was time to find another way to make a living. He got a real estate license, even though he continued to play golf and continued to enter Q School every year. "The thought of not making it through first stage never occurred to me—until I missed first stage three years ago. It's amazing how quickly things change in golf. Now, when I go to first stage, I see kids with a look on their faces that's familiar. Then I think about it and realize it's the same look I had on my face seven, eight years ago—a look that says, 'I know I can beat *you*.' They look at me now and see an old guy who has been around and hasn't made it. They're not wrong. I'm about to turn thirty. That's a long way from twenty-one or twenty-two in any sport, especially when you're still trying to get to the big leagues."

Floyd skipped Q School in 2004, but the bug was still nipping at him in 2005. He tore some ligaments in his wrist midway through the year after playing well in mini-tour events. He was back and forth about whether to send in an entry. On the one hand, he'd played well and felt less pressure to succeed than he had in recent years. On the other hand, he wasn't sure if he would be 100 percent ready physically for the mid-October first stage. He finally sent in his entry just prior to the September 7 deadline. Because his was one of the last entries to arrive, and because the two Florida venues he had requested first were already full, he was sent to Florence.

"Didn't bother me at all," he said. "I figured it would be 70 degrees instead of 90, and maybe it would be good to try a new route. Then, a few days before I was supposed to go up there, someone gave me an unsolicited tip on the range, and I couldn't seem to get it out of my head." He laughed. "If you've got confidence in your swing and your game, something like that doesn't bother you. You don't even hear it. But I'm a long way from that. Then I got to Florence, and it was about 30 degrees and the wind was blowing like crazy. The scores were very high [Florence had by far the highest cut line number, eight over par], but I just couldn't play well enough.

"After all these years, I'm mentally fragile. It didn't used to be that way. I've learned, if nothing else, that being naive is king. You need to put yourself in a cage mentally so nothing bothers you."

The year 2006 would be a watershed year for Floyd: he was turning thirty and becoming a father. "My deadline for making it or going home has passed," he said, laughing. "But there's still a part of me that hasn't quite given it up yet. I did play some good golf last summer before I got hurt. This year, I'll try to get into some Nationwide events, and I'll play some mini-tour events once the real estate season quiets down in June. I'll go back to Q School. I think if you're a pro and you can only play one tournament every year, it should be Q School. You hear stories about guys finding it in their thirties. I know it doesn't happen often, but it does happen. I'd like to see what might happen if I can play some tournaments, go in there fresh and healthy mentally and physically.

"I know there are about a million guys out there saying the same thing. But golf is full of one-in-a-million stories."

He paused. "You know, I remember when I was a kid playing. I wasn't afraid of anything. There wasn't a shot I couldn't hit, a putt I couldn't make. I always thought that I'd always feel that way. Now I'd just like to feel that way again one more time."

Robert Floyd wasn't the only golfer who was searching for those feelings of supreme confidence again. In fact, it's probably fair to say that almost every player facing second stage was searching for that boyhood feeling that he could do anything. The number of well-known players dragging themselves to the six second stages around the country was staggering. The first name that jumped off the page was Larry Mize, the 1987 Masters champion, whose chip-in to beat Greg Norman is one of golf's most memorable shots.

In addition to Mize, there were no fewer than thirty-five players who had won at least once on the PGA Tour. Bill Glasson had won seven times. Steve Pate had won six times and had played on two Ryder Cup teams. Dan Forsman had won five times. Steve Stricker had three victories and had played on a Presidents Cup team. Duffy Waldorf, Rick Fehr, Donnie Hammond, Mike Hulbert, and Blaine McCallister had all won multiple times. Matt Kuchar was a U.S. Amateur champion who had been a phenom at the 1998 Masters and U.S. Open and had won on the tour in his second year. David Gossett had won as a rookie.

Brian Watts had never won on the PGA Tour, but he had lost a play-off to Mark O'Meara at the 1998 British Open and had dominated the Japan Tour for a number of years as an American playing overseas. T. C. Chen had been leading the U.S. Open in 1985 when he infamously hit the ball twice while trying to slash a wedge from the rough and ended up losing the tournament by one shot to Andy North. Bubba Dickerson had won the U.S. Amateur title in 2001 but still hadn't made it to the tour.

And Kelly Gibson liked to tell people he was responsible for Tiger Woods becoming Tiger Woods. "People forget I was leading the tournament at Las Vegas in '96 until I hit it in the water at 17 and then bogeyed 18," he said with a smile. "I par in and I win, and Tiger and Davis [Love] are a shot behind me. Instead, I finish one shot behind them, and Tiger beats Davis in the playoff. Since then, Tiger's won $50 million, and I've won $500,000. I launched him. It all started because of me."

It took Gibson six tries to get all the way through Q School to the PGA Tour. He was on the tour full-time from 1992 to 1998 and had bounced back and forth between the PGA Tour and the Nationwide since then. He had never won, although he'd had several near misses, including the one in Las Vegas that he liked to joke about. He was one of the best-liked players on tour because of his easygoing manner and sense of humor and because he enjoyed byplay with the fans. During a practice round for the U.S. Open in 2004, he had demanded that the starter introduce him as "the 2004 United States Open champion." When the starter simply introduced him as "from New Orleans, Louisiana, Kelly Gibson!" he enlisted the fans standing around the tee to demand that he be introduced as the soon-to-be U.S. Open champion. The starter finally gave in at that point.

When Gibson arrived for the qualifier at Lake Jovita Golf and Country Club—technically in Dade City, Florida, but actually somewhere between Tampa and Orlando on back roads that made the place almost unfindable—he was not in his normal jovial mood.

With good reason. "I've played 18 holes of golf since August—nine holes of practice yesterday and nine the day before," he said quietly on the opening day of the qualifier. "I haven't had the time or the desire to play any golf at all since August 29."

Most Americans might not remember that date as vividly as someone who had lived in New Orleans his entire life would. That was the day when Hurricane Katrina blew through the Gulf Coast and New Orleans, leaving unparalleled devastation in its wake. Gibson, who lives in downtown New Orleans, didn't lose his home, although it was looted after he and his wife, Elizabeth, evacuated. "We got off easy," he said. "The kinds of things I saw are the kinds of things you never forget, the kinds of things that change your perspective forever.

"It isn't that golf became unimportant, not at all. I love golf, I love to play. It's still what I do, and I still believe, even at forty-one, that there are things I can still get done in the game. That's one of the reasons I'm here. The last couple of days before I came down, I really didn't want to come. I just felt as if my heart wouldn't be in it. But people back home told me they wanted me to play, that I am the pro from New Orleans, and there are going to be people following how I do and enjoying it if I do well."

Still unsure, Gibson called David Toms, another native of Louisiana who he had worked with setting up a relief fund after Katrina. Toms, winner of the 2001 PGA Championship and eleven tour events, was in a very different place in his career. But he also encouraged Gibson to play—for himself and for others. "He told me I needed to start to move on with my own life and also let other people know it could be done," Gibson said. "He also said I might pull a Bruce Lietzke and just go out and play great."

Lietzke, a longtime tour player, is legendary among his peers for taking off months at a time and then coming back and playing well without ever seeming to practice. During the opening round, Gibson did a decent Lietzke imitation—getting to four under par for 11 holes. Having played the back nine first, he made his first bogey of the day on the third hole and then mis-clubbed himself on the fourth. "Having only played the hole once probably hurt me there," he said. "I had 210 to the pin into a stiff breeze. My caddy thought, with the wind, I couldn't fly the green with a three-iron, that I'd get it to the back where the pin was. Well, he was wrong. I flew it over the green onto a downslope and had no shot. Hey, it's on me—I made the decision, and I hit the shot.

But occasionally you depend on a caddy and he gets it wrong. Happens."

From an impossible lie behind the green, Gibson ended up making a triple-bogey six. In an instant, he had gone from four under to even par. He managed to right himself the last five holes and finished the day with a one-under-par 71, which left him in a tie for 34th place with lots of holes to play. Still, his mind wasn't really on his golf as he sat on a golf cart outside the clubhouse trying to convince himself to go hit some practice balls.

"I've never needed to hit that many balls," he said. "I've never been injured. That's why I still think I can play and play successfully. Regardless of where I play or how much I play the next couple of years, it'll be different.

"When we went back to our house, a SWAT team took us inside, because we weren't sure what we'd find or who we might find. I mean, guys carrying M4s. Later, they took me up in a helicopter so I could get a good look at what was going on. I saw people being rescued. I also saw people who weren't rescued. My wife and I worked feeding rescue teams. I didn't dive in after anyone, but I helped take care of the guys who were. There's part of me that thinks I should just take the next year off and work in New Orleans. There are a lot of things I can do. I've already talked to some people about helping to bring back some of the golf courses. That's an area where I have expertise. Plus, I'm good at networking. The last couple of months were good for me in terms of feeling like I can do things besides play golf. I got things done — that was a good feeling."

Being at Q School, playing 18 holes on a sun-drenched day on a gorgeous, scenic golf course, almost felt strange to Gibson after what he had seen the previous eleven weeks. "Part of it is Katrina, but part of it is just being old," he said, laughing. "I remember playing Q School back in the late '80s. It was entirely different than now. You would never be at a golf course this nice, especially at second stage. There weren't nearly as many good players then as now. I remember in '89 I played with a guy the first day who got sick on the golf course, *twice,* because his nerves were so bad. The young guys now, they've played so much tournament golf before they get to this level, I don't think they're as nervous. I don't think you see as much choking as you used to. And it felt more private back then. I liked it that way. You're a golfer. Part of you is a performer—but in certain settings.

"To be honest, I don't like the fact that the Golf Channel televises the finals. I understand it, but I don't like it. If you're in a tournament and you're inside the ropes and there are crowds and you're playing well and you see a TV camera, that's okay. You aren't on camera unless you're playing well, so you want to show off. But if you're at Q School, it's because on some level you're struggling. You want the quiet. You want to feel as if you're alone, and a lot of the time, you *can* feel that way. You get out on that golf course, most of the time it's you and the other two players and the caddies. Period.

"A couple years ago on the last day of the finals at La Quinta, I made a big run. I was way back, and all of a sudden I started making birdies. Next thing I know, I'm eight under par for the day, and I know I'm right around the number. I'm playing my last hole, thinking I need one more birdie. I'm in the middle of the fairway waiting to hit, and all of a sudden I see a guy with a camera running right at me down the fairway. It just kind of stopped me. I was in a zone at that moment, totally focused, just hitting good golf shots, and then I see the guy with the camera, and I think, 'Oh, my God, the whole world has noticed I'm making this run. I'm either right on the number or one off it.' In an instant, everything changed for me out there. The rhythm I'd had wasn't there anymore. I flinched just a little. I ended up hitting a lousy second shot, made a par, and, sure enough, missed by one. I just walked straight to my car, got in, and sat there and cried. I had been so wound up, and it all came out.

"I know the tour isn't going to tell the Golf Channel to go away. I just wish there was a way to make them understand when they're out there that this isn't the same as a regular tournament. You have to be inside a player's head to really understand how different it feels. You never feel more alone than when you're playing Q School. You succeed, you get all the credit. You fail, you get all the blame. That's golf. You don't have any teammates who can carry you through on an off day or in an off year. When you get it going right, you don't want anything to change that feeling. At Q School, you look up and see cameras and it *feels* wrong. I'll never forget the feeling in the pit of my stomach that day when all the work turned out to be for nothing. Every golfer has had that feeling at some point. But when you're one shot short with the next year of your life riding on the result, it makes you want to cry."

He smiled. "Which, on that day, is exactly what I did."

BECAUSE GIBSON HAD NEVER WON on the PGA Tour, he didn't have the luxury that the thirty-six players taking part in second stage who had won tournaments did: status on the tour.

Once you have won a PGA Tour event, you have lifetime status as a past champion. That means that each year you can get into a handful of tournaments because enough players ahead of you in the pecking order (the fully exempt 125, tournament winners from the previous two years, players with medical exemptions, the top 20 on the Nationwide list from the year before, those who make it through Q School, and those who finish between 126th and 150th on the money list) choose to skip them. The tournaments that players with past champion status get into are some of the tour's least glamorous events — midsummer tournaments like Milwaukee and Quad Cities, and fall tournaments that come after the major championship season is over and the stars have gone home to rest.

"That's not exactly what any of us are looking for," Donnie Hammond said, cooling off after a lengthy postround session on Lake Jovita's range. "I want to choose the tournaments I play in, not have them choose me because the guys who can choose have stayed home. I'm not that far from fifty. I'd like to go back and play Memorial again, play Riviera [Los Angeles] again, play Colonial again. Going through this is the only way I'm going to have that chance."

Hammond has the distinction of winning by the largest margin (14 shots) in Q School finals history. He accomplished that feat playing the TPC Sawgrass in 1982, the first year when getting through Q School got you into every tournament the following year without dealing with Monday qualifying — the dawn of the so-called all-exempt tour. Hammond had just turned twenty-five when he made it to the tour, and for the next fifteen years he pieced together a solid career that included victories at the Bob Hope Chrysler Classic in 1986 and the Texas Open in 1989. But he seemed to hit a wall when he turned forty and had struggled since then, never finishing higher than 165th on the money list after 1997. He had been fully exempt in 2003 after getting through Q School in 2002, but other than that year, he had lived in the netherworld of the "partly exempt" player, waiting for his number to come up as a past champion while spending some time on the Nationwide Tour.

"Not exactly the ideal life when you've got four kids," he said, shaking his head. "It's funny how your attitude toward the game seems to change when you're in your forties. I'm not sure if it's having kids or feeling different physically or just being at a different point in your life where it's harder to just keep your head down, play golf, and not worry about anything else. Nowadays, there are more guys playing well into their forties because of better conditioning, but with 97 percent of us, you do start to see the slippage as your forties move along."

Hammond had plenty of Q School experience. His first one had been in 1982, when everything had seemed so easy. During the last eight years of his career, he had been forced back on a regular basis. He had successfully negotiated his way through the finals on four different occasions. "Getting through in 2002 at PGA West was, without question, one of my top three days in golf," he said. "If I'd ended up missing, it would have been one of my worst. That's what makes this so tough. For most guys, the difference between success and failure is extremely narrow—a shot here or there, a made putt or two, catching one lucky break or not catching it. You really feel it at second stage because there's no gray area at all. If you don't make it, you can't walk away saying, 'Well, I've got the Nationwide.' You've got nothing—unless you're a past winner, in which case you might get ten or twelve starts the next year. How many guys in this field are past winners? Everyone else is playing for their lives."

He smiled and waved a hand around the driving range, where he was sitting on a hill, a few yards behind a line of players pounding balls in the late-afternoon heat. "Listen to how quiet this range is. At a regular tournament, the range in the afternoon is like a bar after work—guys talking, joking, standing around in groups. You don't see that at Q School. There's too much at stake. You do your work, and you go home. The pressure here is so intense, I think the birds and the squirrels hide out. All the Q Schools I've played, I don't remember ever feeling comfortable while I was awake—and I don't sleep very well either."

He sighed. "You know what this is like? A really big four-day funeral. In the end, there are nineteen survivors. The rest of the bodies just get carted away."

The seven men at Lake Jovita who were guaranteed past champion status were a decidedly mixed bag. At forty-eight, Hammond was the oldest in the group. "I feel like I'm ready to move on to the Champions Tour," he said. "I played with a kid named Matt Davidson today who was plenty young enough to be my son. I think I've figured it out: I'd rather try to compete against Charles Coody [the 1971 Masters champion, who was sixty-eight] than Charles Howell III [who was twenty-six and averaged just under 300 yards off the tee, according to official tour statistics]."

David Gossett, at twenty-six, was the youngest of the past champions. Mike Hulbert was forty-seven, Blaine McCallister was forty-six, Grant Waite and Guy Boros were forty-one, and Matt Kuchar was twenty-seven. Gossett and Kuchar had come to the tour in their early twenties labeled as can't-miss stars.

Kuchar had burst into the public's consciousness with spectacular performances at the 1998 Masters and U.S. Open. Still a Georgia Tech undergraduate, he won the 1997 U.S. Amateur, which gained him automatic entry to those two events and the British Open. Playing the first two rounds at Augusta with defending champion Tiger Woods, he made the cut and went on to finish in a tie for 21st place—which not only made him low amateur but also earned him a trip back in 1999, since he had finished in the top 24. He did even better at the Open, finishing in a tie for 14th, which got him a spot in the '99 Open (the top 15 automatically qualify for the next year).

Most people expected Kuchar to turn pro once he had played in the British Open. He was a hot commodity and would have made a lot of money in endorsements at that moment. He had an endearing smile, and the only criticism anyone had of him was his father's performance as his caddy in the majors. Not being a professional, Tom Kuchar was a bit overenthusiastic about his son's play, and he upset a number of players and caddies—notably, Justin Leonard, who was paired with Kuchar for the last round of the

Masters and the first two rounds of the Open. Everyone liked the kid; the father was the issue. Once he got on tour on his own, he would do fine.

Except Kuchar decided not to turn pro. He was the rare athlete who meant it when he said he wanted to finish college. He graduated in the spring of 2000 and, even more surprisingly, opted not to turn pro then either, deciding to go into finance. That notion lasted about six months, and he finally turned pro at the end of 2000. Playing on sponsor exemptions in 2001 — he was still a popular name among tournament directors, who remembered his hot play in 1998 — he earned more than $572,000, enough to make him exempt for 2002. When he won the Honda Classic early in 2002 and finished the year 49th on the money list with $1,237,000 in earnings, he seemed to be on his way to stardom.

But things don't always work out the way people expect. Kuchar struggled the next three years and lost his fully exempt status for 2005 after finishing 139th on the money list in 2004. He dropped to 159th in '05 and found himself back at second stage, trying to find the magic again.

Gossett's drop-off had been even more precipitous. Coming out of the University of Texas in the spring of 2000, he had been labeled one of the "young guns" (along with Kuchar, Howell, Luke Donald, and Adam Scott, all early twentysomethings who hit the ball a long way and appeared to be exceptionally mature) likely to challenge Tiger Woods over the next few years. Gossett was the son of a pilot — his dad had flown F-4 Air Force phantoms before retiring to fly for Fed Ex — and had grown up in Memphis after spending four years in Germany while his father was stationed there.

Gossett starred at Texas, being chosen a first-team all-American as both a freshman and a sophomore before deciding to turn pro after his second year of college. He breezed through the first two stages of Q School that fall and came to Palm

Springs for the finals as one of the players being closely watched. For three days, he played mediocre golf, failing to break 70 and falling back in the pack.

After the third round, his mother arrived in town, and they went and had an early dinner at Macaroni Grill. Gossett remembers telling her that he'd left a lot of shots on the golf course the first three days. "I know I need to relax," he said. "But that's easier said than done."

He started the next day on the 10th hole at the Jack Nicklaus Tournament Course at PGA West and promptly knocked his tee shot into a bunker. But he got a seven-iron to within 15 feet of the hole and made the putt for birdie. He can recite every shot and every thought he had for the rest of the round. He missed a birdie putt on the 18th hole (his ninth hole of the day) and walked off the green "hacked off" because he had shot 30 on his first nine holes and he'd never had a 29. He birdied the first hole, making a 15-foot putt, then knocked an eight-iron into the cup at the par-three second hole for a hole in one. All of a sudden, he was nine under par after 11 holes. "The amazing thing about that day is, I parred two par-fives," he said, "and still shot what I shot."

What he shot was 59—the first person in history to do it in competition on a par-72 course. He birdied the last four holes, hitting his second shot at number nine to five feet and making the putt to make history. It was the first time—and is still the only time—anyone had broken 60 at any stage of Q School. "I remember standing on the eighth tee with Mike Smith after I had birdied seven," Gossett said. "Rick Fehr was supposed to be the third guy in our group, but he'd withdrawn, and it was just the two of us. Mike said to me, 'Well, David, we're a combined 11 under par so far today.' He was even. That was when it first dawned on me that 59 was possible."

The 59 caused a sensation and made Gossett the center of

attention for the remaining two days of Q School. But he couldn't recapture the magic of that day, shooting 74–72 the last two days to finish in a tie for 68th place—three shots outside the number he needed to make the tour. Remarkably, he never shot a round in the 60s that week—he had five rounds in the 70s and a 59.

"I had a lot of mixed emotions when the week was over," he said. "On the one hand, I didn't meet my goal—making the tour—and that was very disappointing. On the other hand, I'd played one amazing round and had a piece of history to show for it. When I got away for a while and thought about it, I was able to focus on the positive side of it. I had to be a good player to shoot a round like that. I decided I needed to go out and build on what I had accomplished."

He did, finishing second in a tournament in Australia while waiting for the Buy.com Tour schedule to begin. He top-tenned in four straight Buy.com events. "What was disappointing about that was I had a chance to win each of those weeks but didn't," he said. "I had to tell myself to stay positive and good things would happen."

Gossett received a sponsor exemption for the John Deere Classic in July 2001. He was still considered a rising star, and the second-tier PGA Tour events were eager to have him. He took the lead after 36 holes and never lost it. He hung on to win by one, and just like that, he was a fully exempt player on the tour through 2004 (thanks to the two-year winner's exemption). He was the first player to win a tournament playing on a sponsor exemption since a twenty-year-old kid named Tiger Woods had won in Las Vegas in 1996. His young gun status was fully restored.

"Actually, I was the first of the group to win," he said. "Kooch [Kuchar] won the next year, and Luke and Charlie and Adam have all won since, but at that point, they hadn't won. I felt great. I had played well in the clutch, and I had done something I'd been building to for a while."

He had just turned twenty-two, and it looked as if he was on the road to stardom. Only it didn't happen.

"I had always wondered if expectations could be a burden," he said. "Looking back now, I'd have to say yes, they can be. You hear a lot of stories about guys changing things to try to get better and ending up getting worse. I'm one of those stories."

He changed teachers, going from Jonathan Yarwood (who also taught Michael Campbell) to David Leadbetter. For all the success Leadbetter has had helping good players become great (Nick Faldo and Nick Price come to mind), he is not for everyone. He is very exact and methodical in his teaching, something that some players find difficult. Gossett was one of those players who wasn't cut out to be a Leadbetter pupil. "I do *not* want anyone to think I blame David in any way for my last couple of years," he said. "He's a good man and a great teacher, and I have absolutely no issues with him. It just wasn't right for me, and I learned that the hard way. No sour grapes, though. Whatever went wrong, that's on me, not on David."

Gossett played decently in 2002 and 2003, finishing 100th and 84th on the money list, but he plummeted to 245th in 2004. He arrived at Lake Jovita with Yarwood in tow and a belief that he was headed back in the right direction.

"The proof is in the pudding," he said, his Texas cap firmly in place after an opening-round 70. "I hit 16 greens today and shot 70. I have to believe if I keep hitting the ball like this, there are lower numbers to be shot. I feel confident I can get this done." He smiled. "Three days from now, I'll know whether I'm right."

7

Lake Jovita Blues

LAKE JOVITA WAS AN EXAMPLE of the kind of golf course Steve Carman was looking to add to the second-stage rota. It was a relatively new club, having opened in 1998, and it had two golf courses, which made it easier to convince the membership to give up one course for a week to the tour. It was also located off the beaten path, on back roads between Tampa and Orlando. Tim Petrovic, who had won his first PGA Tour event in 2005 (New Orleans), lived at Lake Jovita. So did Garrett Willis, who had won his first event as a rookie on tour at Tucson in 2001 but had since fallen back to the Nationwide Tour. Willis was exempt to the finals based on having finished 33rd on the Nationwide money list in 2005 and had volunteered to caddy for Mike Hulbert at Lake Jovita.

Willis had not been the most popular guy on tour after his victory at Tucson. Some found him cocky; others found him immature. One of the locker room stories told about him dated to the first year of the Wachovia Championship in Charlotte 2003. The people running the tournament had made a deal with one of their sponsors, Mercedes, to supply each player with a courtesy car during the week. Willis arrived to pick up his car at the same time as Nick Price. When he was handed the keys to his Mercedes—a smaller model than the one being given to Price, a former world number one player who had won three majors in his career—he demanded, "Why does he get a bigger car than I get?" To which the Mercedes rep replied, "Because he's Nick Price, and you're not."

Perhaps being forced back to the Nationwide Tour had humbled Willis a bit. Or perhaps, being on the verge of his thirty-second birthday, he had matured. But more likely, as some players speculated, there just wasn't anyone in the world who didn't like Mike Hulbert.

Hulbert—"Hubby" to almost everyone in golf—had been a consistent and successful player on the tour from the mid-1980s until the end of the 1990s, finishing in the top 100 on the money list for thirteen straight years while winning three tournaments. He had finished as high as 18th on the money list (1989) and had finished in the top 25 on three occasions. Like a lot of the over-forty players Donnie Hammond talked about, it had gotten harder for Hulbert after he turned forty, and he was now a part-time player, spending more time doing TV commentary than playing golf. He had made two cuts on tour in the past three years, both at the B.C. Open, his local tournament, since he had grown up in nearby Elmira, New York.

Hulbert looks and sounds more like a schoolteacher or a bank teller than a professional athlete, with his thick glasses and squeaky voice. Always in shape, he still has the same wiry build that he had when he was a big moneymaker on tour. The warm smile hasn't changed either. The major difference was the confidence level.

Hulbert was one of three players who had come out of upstate New York at about the same time and found success on tour. Jeff Sluman, the 1988 PGA champion; Joey Sindelar, a seven-time tour winner; and Hulbert were born within nineteen months of one another between 1957 and 1959 and grew up within a few miles of one another. "We were always together as kids," Hulbert said. "We'd play golf all summer, and when the weather got cold, we'd put the clubs up for the winter and bowl."

Sluman, as he still likes to point out, was the best bowler in the group. They all made it to the tour at about the same time. Sluman made it through Q School in 1982, although he had to go back in 1984. At second stage in 1984, Sluman brought Billy Harmon to the TPC Sawgrass as his caddy. Sluman's teacher then, as now, was Harmon's brother Craig, one of the four golf pro sons of Claude Harmon, the 1948 Masters champion. (Butch Harmon is the most famous of the four because of the work he did with Greg Norman and, later, Tiger Woods.) Billy Harmon had done a lot of caddying and volunteered to help his brother's young pupil try to get his playing privileges back.

"I thought it was a great idea to have Billy on the bag," Sluman said. "I knew it would relax me to have him with me, and it had to help to have someone with me who knew what he was doing. First day, I walk to the first tee and go over to Billy to get my driver. There's one problem: he picked up the wrong bag on the putting green. We've got someone else's bag. He sprints back to the putting green, finds my bag, and sprints back with my driver just in time. There's still one problem: my putter is in the other guy's bag. So he has to sprint back again and get my putter while I'm walking down the first fairway."

Sluman survived those travails to make it back to the tour and has been a human ATM machine for most of the past twenty years. He has six tour victories, including the win at the PGA, and has won more than $1 million in prize money in seven of the eight years since he turned forty. Sindelar got through Q School in 1983 and was 12th on the money list in 1985, his second year on tour, after winning twice. He won again as recently as 2003. Hulbert first made it to the tour in 1984, went back to Q School the next year, and was a consistent money winner after that.

Although Sluman and Sindelar have continued to play well on the tour, it hasn't been as easy for their buddy Hubby. "I keep thinking that I'm close to getting back to where I want to be," Hulbert said. "You know, every great golfer has to have a little bit of, well, turd in him. I mean, you have to be selfish, you have to be mean, you have to be able to worry only about yourself, and you have to believe completely in yourself. I had that for a lot of years, and somewhere along the line I lost it. Being around the top guys all the time because of doing TV makes me want to get it back. I see those guys up close, and a lot of time I find myself thinking, 'I can still do that.' That's why I'm here. I know I've done it before. I think I can do it again."

It is difficult to picture Hulbert being selfish and mean. Greg Norman and Tiger Woods, neither of whom is noted for having an especially wide circle of friends, consider him one. He is the guy on the practice tee who is always willing to offer help. He is the guy who plays in everybody's charity tournament. "I'm flattered that a lot of guys—really good players—will come to me and say, 'Hey, check me out, will you?'" he said. "A few weeks ago, Davis [Love III] is having trouble on the range, and he asks me to look at him. I do, and it takes me about five minutes to get him fixed. *Him,* I can fix in five minutes. *Me,* it's not so easy.

"It's always been the turd factor for me. I swear to God that's it. I remember in '85 I had to go back to second stage after I lost my card. We're playing in Boca, a hundred guys for twelve spots. The first two rounds I shoot something like 72–73, and I'm in the middle of the pack. After the second round, one of the guys I'm playing with, a lifer on the mini-tours, starts lighting me up—really getting in my face. He says to me, 'What the hell is wrong with you? You've got more talent than any of us, and you don't look like you care or you want it. You want to come and spend your life on the mini-tours with me? That's where you're heading right now unless you kick yourself in the butt and start playing like you care.'

"I went back to the Days Inn where I was staying and lay there staring at the ceiling for a good long while. I finally decided the guy was right. I was just out there playing, not competing. I needed to compete. I shot 65–68 the last two days and finished second. After that, I rolled pretty good for a long time."

He wasn't rolling now, though, and it bothered him. He didn't need to play financially, and the TV work kept him around the game and around his friends. But he wanted to play; he wanted to compete. He wanted to be a turd again.

On the first day, a warm day with just a hint of a breeze, he shot 74, two over par, which left him way back in the pack, tied for 61st place in a field of seventy-four players. The leader, Brad Klapprott, shot a seven-under-par 65. Eighteen players shot four under par or better, and ten more were at three under. Hulbert had a lot of work to do to get back into contention. "It's there," he insisted. "I just have to stop leaving shots out on the golf course like I did today."

He smiled. "I'm going to go home and get pissed off."

THERE ARE NO BAD PLAYERS at second stage. The people who shoot 100 over par or can't break 80 are long gone from the competition. Everyone in the field has some kind of golf résumé, even if it's just having gotten through first stage. That in itself is no small achievement.

Second stage is a mixture of players frequently going in opposite directions. On the one side are the Hulberts and Hammonds, the Boroses, Waites, and Gibsons—players who have had success in golf but don't think they're done yet. On the other side are the kids, youngsters for whom Q School is still an adventure—albeit a scary one. They know the names and faces of the older, more accomplished players, but they are long past being intimidated by them.

There were a number of examples of that kind of youth and confidence at Lake Jovita. No one had more of both than Colby Beckstrom, a rangy twenty-two-year-old who had dropped out of Texas Christian University (TCU) after his junior year to turn pro—a move that had surprised friends and family if only because few had expected him to stay in college even that long.

"I can remember sitting on my bed talking to my mom one night when I was in tenth or eleventh grade," Beckstrom said. "I was starting to get letters from college golf coaches, and I said to her, 'Mom, I don't want to go to college.' I was never a good student; school was always a struggle for me. I knew then—just *knew*—that I wanted to play golf. My mom was great. She said to me, 'Colby, college isn't for everybody. Let's see what happens.'"

What happened was TCU coach Bill Montigel. Having grown up in Michigan, where the golf season is relatively short (he was a hockey goalie until age fourteen), Beckstrom wanted to play golf someplace where the weather is warm most of the year. TCU fit that bill. "I just really liked Coach Montigel," Beckstrom said. "He let me know who he was and what he would expect of me if I came. He convinced me, without a hard sell, that a couple of years of college would benefit my golf. My high school coach told him straight-out, 'Colby won't stay four years. If you get him for two years, you'll be lucky.' He was okay with that."

Beckstrom stayed three years because of his relationship with Montigel and his teammates, and because he could see steady improvement in his golf. He even made it to class enough to be on schedule to graduate in four years had he stayed. "It turned out to be a great decision to go," he said. "But after three years, I was ready—really ready. I knew in November I was ready to go. I finished my junior year so that I'd be there for the team in the spring. But I was done in terms of college. I couldn't wait any longer."

He waited until after the Michigan Amateur to turn pro and then, as a hometown kid, got a sponsor exemption into the Buick Open in Flint in early August. "It was the most unforgettable week of my life," he said. "I made the cut and played about as well as I could have hoped." He smiled. "I know Tiger, Vijay, and [John] Daly had their crowds, but I had a pretty good crowd of my own rooting me on. God, was it fun."

The only hitch in the entire week came on Sunday, when he hit his second shot into a bunker at 16. Even though he was in the bunker, he was closer to the hole than J. J. Henry, whom he was paired with that day. "J. J. walked into the bunker where my ball was to line up his putt. He was nowhere close to where my ball was. When he finished, as a courtesy, my caddy raked where he had walked. I played out, and [when] we finished, J. J. said to me as we walked into the scoring trailer, 'Don't sign your card yet.' He went and talked to a rules official, and then they came back and said I had to add two to my score at 16 because my caddy had raked the bunker before I played my shot. J. J. hadn't seen him rake, but someone did and told him about it. He was sick about it. He kept telling the rules guy how unfair it was, but I was saying, 'Hey, that's the rule. I understand.' It dropped me from a tie for 30th to a tie for 50th, but I'm telling you *nothing* could wipe the smile off my face that week."

Beckstrom had been in a pretty good mood throughout first stage. He had chosen the TPC Tampa Bay as his first-stage site strictly based on logistics. He had moved to Naples, Florida, in part for the weather but also because his mother, stepfather, and eight-year-old brother lived there, as did his older brother, J. J., who had just turned pro that summer. After an opening-round 71, Colby shot 65 the second day and cruised from there, finishing third. "I remember on the back nine the last morning feeling so in control of my game," he said. "I wanted to win because I thought that would have been good for my confidence, but it didn't matter that much. I just felt terrible for the guy I was playing with [Ted Potter Jr.], who shot 43 the last nine holes. I couldn't imagine what that felt like. He really handled it well at the end, though. That impressed me. A lot of guys would have just lost it."

Brimming with confidence, Beckstrom arrived at Lake Jovita feeling about as comfortable as a player can feel at Q School. "I know the golf course," he said. "We played our conference championships here twice, and I played well. That's why I asked for it for second stage."

Beckstrom had about as big a cheering section as anyone at Lake Jovita: his mom, stepdad, and younger brother, as well as his father, a friend from back home, and J. J., who had joined him playing mini-tour events. "His first tournament as a pro, he made the cut and I won," Colby said. "It was pretty close to perfect."

This week looked perfect, too. Playing in the first group of the day, on opening day, Beckstrom shot 66, holing out twice from bunkers, including on 18. During first stage, it had been just Colby and J. J. in Tampa, and they had gotten into a routine of going to the same Outback Steakhouse near their hotel and eating the same meal every night: a couple of gin and tonics followed by Monterrey chicken and mashed potatoes. Since they were staying in the same hotel (about forty minutes from the golf course) as in October, they went back to their old routine. Only now the table was for seven instead of two. "I can honestly say we were having the time of our lives," Beckstrom said. "I'm playing well, I've got all this support, and I feel about as confident as you can feel."

The opening-round 66 put him in second place, one shot behind Klapprott and in a tie with Bubba Dickerson, another young gun, and Hiroshi Matsuo, a perennial mini-tour player who was trying to break out of that life and jump-start his career at the age of thirty-six. Matsuo was a first-generation American. Born in Queens, he learned the game from his father, who was an assistant pro at Westchester Country Club. Matsuo played college golf at Auburn. Not long after graduating and turning pro, he decided that tour life or club pro life wasn't for him, and he went to work for his father, who had moved to Jupiter, Florida, and owned two restaurants there. "It took me a few years to figure out I wasn't ready for that sort of work," he said. "I decided to try golf again."

In a sense, his timing had been perfect. During the 1990s, the sport's popularity had created a boomlet in mini-tours. Prior to that time, there hadn't been very many mini-tours, and breaking even financially was about all a player could hope for once he got through paying his entry fees and travel expenses—even though travel was generally limited to cars and the cheapest motel that could be found. By the time Matsuo started playing mini-tours, however, the money for the top players on a number of the tours had become respectable. In 2001 and 2002, he was the leading money winner on the Golden Bear Tour, finishing 2002 by winning the season-ending tournament and a check for $60,000.

"It was a living, a decent one," Matsuo said. "But I'd had one year [2000] on the Nationwide and flamed out. I really felt I was a better player than that, and I've wanted to prove to myself that I can be better than I have been." He smiled. "It needs to start happening here pretty soon."

Matsuo is tall—6 feet 3—and very outgoing. By his own admission, he has also enjoyed himself in the past, at times to the detriment of his golf game. "I've always had a fallback position—my dad's business," he said. "I worked in the restaurants long enough that I know my way around, and I can go back there and do well if I want to. But now, as I've gotten older, I realize I'll be disappointed if I don't give myself a chance to live up to my full potential. I'm at the age where my wife and I want to start a family. So I can't say 'Wait till next year' too many more times. I need to at least get out of second stage this year."

If Matsuo didn't make the finals, his only option if he wanted to stay in golf was another year on the mini-tours. Klapprott, at thirty-six, was in the same boat. At the other end of the spectrum was Ty Tryon, a player who had seemed ticketed for stardom just a few years earlier. In fact, he had appeared, along with Charles Howell III, David Gossett, Adam Scott, and Matt Kuchar, in a PGA Tour public service announcement touting the sport's young guns. Scott was now ranked in the top 15 in the world, and Howell was an established tour player. Kuchar and Gossett were both at Lake Jovita, but each had won once on tour before falling back.

Tryon hadn't won on tour, but he had probably received more attention than the other four players combined during his one year as an exempt player. That was in 2002, when Tryon was seventeen and still in high school. In the fall of 2001, he had done what had been considered impossible: make it through all three stages of Q School before the age of eighteen. PGA Tour rules prevent anyone from being an official tour member before his eighteenth birthday (June 1, 2002, for Tryon), but after he played well in a number of tournaments for which he received sponsor exemptions, Tryon and his parents decided that he was ready to turn pro. Their decision was, to say the least, controversial.

Tiger Woods had waited until he was almost twenty-one and had been in college for two years before turning pro. History shows that those who have tried to make it on tour before age twenty-one — most of them prodigies like Tryon — have flamed out fairly quickly. The fact that Tryon had been able to stand up to the crucible of Q School, even with his every move and every shot being chronicled by the media, seemed to indicate that he could deal with all the pressures of life on tour.

But life on tour is about much more than what goes on between the ropes. In many ways, especially for a player as young as Tryon, that's the easiest part of his day. Dealing with media and sponsors, being ten to twenty years younger than most of your peers, living out of a suitcase—regardless of how fancy the suitcase or the hotel rooms may be—and knowing that you are now playing golf for a living rather than for fun are all far more difficult than standing up on a tee and hitting a golf ball.

It didn't help that Tryon struggled with health issues—another problem among young athletes who are pushed too hard, too early. (See women's tennis.) He had a bout with mononucleosis early in the year, which caused him to lose about fifteen pounds from an already thin 5-foot-10-inch, 160-pound frame. He couldn't play full-time until he turned eighteen on June 1, and he believes that the momentum he had coming out of Q School, hopped up and full of confidence, was lost during the six months when he was sick and played very little golf.

"Six months is a long time," he said. "Then when I started playing again, there was all the attention—which I thought I was prepared for, because it hadn't really bothered me at Q School. I've thought about it a lot since then, and here's what I think I've figured out: When you're playing well, attention doesn't bother you—nothing bothers you. When you're on the golf course, you don't hear anything; you're oblivious. But when you aren't playing well, everything bothers you; everything seems harder. You hear everything people say. You start to worry about not living up to expectations. For the first time in my life, I actually felt pressure to play good golf. That had never happened to me before. Golf had always been easy for me. It was what I did. When I was younger, I changed my school schedule so I could get out two periods early [missing a nonrequired music class and a physical education class] so that I could spend time with a personal trainer and have more time to play.

"A lot of people were critical of the decision my parents and I made, but college wasn't for me. I knew that, and, most important, I *was* good enough. If I hadn't been, I wouldn't have made it through Q School. Golf was what I wanted to do; it was what I always loved doing."

It was also quite lucrative at the outset of his pro career, because corporations love youth and they are all looking for the next Tiger Woods—or at least the next Phil Mickelson. Tryon seemed to have that kind of potential. He was the most Gen-X of the young guns, clearly still a kid with a love for video games and a tendency to call almost everyone he met "dude" (though always in a polite way). He signed a five-year contract with Callaway and shorter contracts with Target, EA Sports ("I was on a video game," he said proudly), and Red Bull.

"The good news is, I took the money from those contracts and invested wisely," he said. "I've got a nice house, and I'm in good shape financially, which means I can work my way through what's going on with my golf game without worrying about how I'm going to make a living." He smiled. "The only thing I have to do now is find my golf game again. It's been missing in action."

At twenty-one, Tryon looked a lot different than the seventeen-year-old who had blown through Q School four years earlier. His dark hair was long and curly, and he had a full beard that made him look more like a young biker than a young golfer. He was baffled by his golf game but still felt he was going in the right direction with his life. As he sat talking in the house right off the 18th green that he and Patrick Damron were sharing for the week, some of his laments—"I three-putted twice today for par on the par-fives; that's killing me"—were familiar to anyone who has ever talked to a frustrated golfer. But he made no excuses for his struggles and blamed no one for his fall from PGA tour phenom to mini-tour player.

"I try to remember that I'm still very young and golf is a

lifetime game," he said. "Sometimes I forget, and I feel like I have to get my act together *now*. But then I calm down and realize I'm still a work in progress. I've had some injuries, and I've had some growing up to do. But I don't have any regrets about the decision I made or about where I am."

He had broken off from his parents, most notably his father, for a while when things started to go awry. "We bickered," he said. "Some of it was natural teenage stuff. But some of it was probably the pressure we both felt when things didn't go the way we'd thought they would when I turned pro."

Now, though, he said, his relationship with his father was very good, and his dad had learned to let him do his own thing. "I travel with my girlfriend now, and that's about it," he said. "My parents live ten minutes away, and I talk to them all the time. But I'm making my own decisions, and they're fine with that." He smiled. "I've got one real issue in my life: I'm not making enough putts."

He had finished first stage tied for 10th and arrived at Lake Jovita feeling more confident, he said, than at any time since his run in 2001. He had come down to Lake Jovita a few weeks prior to the tournament and played a couple of practice rounds with Garrett Willis. "Shot eight under par one day," he said. "This is a good golf course with fast greens. You make putts, you can score."

The first day of second stage had been frustrating but okay—an even-par 72. "I'm leaving shots out there," he said, standing on the putting green not long before dark. "I can't afford to miss makeable putts. I'm hitting the ball great, but you can't score if you don't make putts."

He wore the look of a golfer who believes he's close—but knows close isn't good enough. "Q School is Q School," he said. "You can talk all you want about what-ifs when it's over. In the end, they don't matter. What matters is what is, not what if. And what is right now is that I've got to start making putts."

8

Moving Day

THE FIRST TWO ROUNDS of most golf tournaments carry a certain amount of trepidation for most players because of the 36-hole cut. Everyone knows that half the field will be sent home after two rounds, and except for those at the top of the leader board, players are concerned about what the cut number will be.

That's not the case at Q School, where there are no cuts. Everyone gets to play 72 holes — except at the finals, where everyone gets to play 108. What that does for most players is to keep either panic or calm from creeping in, regardless of where one stands at the end of two days.

At Lake Jovita, after two days of near perfect weather, twenty-two players were at five under par or better, led by Bubba Dickerson, who had shot 66–65 to take a two-stroke lead. Even though Dickerson was only twenty-four and was considered a future star, nothing had come easily to him as a professional.

He had decided to turn pro in the spring of 2002, which meant that he gave up the automatic exemptions he had earned for the U.S. Open and British Open as U.S. Amateur champion in 2001. (He had to remain amateur to use them.) He attempted to qualify for the U.S. Open but missed by two shots. Being just twenty-one and having a cool nickname — his full name is Benjamin Gordon Dickerson, but his older brother, Robert, had started calling him his "little bubba" when he was a baby—he was a sponsor exemption magnet during the rest of that year. He hoped to make enough money in the seven tournaments he was allowed to play under the tour's rules to enable him to skip Q School, as Tiger Woods and Justin Leonard had. But he came up considerably short. Then he flunked the second stage of Q School. In 2003 he again failed to get through second stage, and he ended up spending two years bouncing between the NGA/Hooters Tour and the European Futures Tour (the European version of the Nationwide Tour).

He made it to the finals in 2004, earning a spot on the Nationwide Tour for 2005. He played solidly there, finishing 38th on the money list, which meant that he was two spots away from getting to skip second stage.

"The good news is, I know I can play the Nationwide and make a living there next year if that's what I have to do," he said. "But it isn't what I want to be doing. I'll admit this has been tougher than I thought it would be when I left college. But what I've learned from all this is, you have to be patient to be successful. I've learned it; now I've got to actually do it."

Dickerson had left the University of Florida after two years. He was easy to spot on the golf course with his shock of red hair and, like most young players, his ability to hit the ball celestial distances. After he won the U.S. Amateur in his sophomore year, there wasn't much left for him to do. Add to that the lure of the sponsorship money that comes to a U.S. Amateur champion turning pro, as well as the belief that he was ready for the tour, and the decision was easy for him. Three and a half years later, he had few regrets, but he had learned some lessons.

"I made mistakes on and off the course," he said. "I signed with a management group that got me into some contracts where the guarantees were never met. I was younger than most of the guys I was playing with and didn't know people. Plus, I didn't really understand how much work I needed to do on my game to get where I want to go." He smiled. "Hey, I'm not exactly the Lone Ranger when it comes to dealing with some adversity out here. Everyone's got a story of some kind.

"I just believe I'm ready now. I watch the tour and I see some guy, and I think to myself, 'I can play better than that.' Maybe I'm wrong. I was wrong coming out of college about how easy it was going to be, that's for sure. But now I think I'm a little more mature and a little more realistic."

Dickerson had another reason for wanting to spend 2006 on the PGA Tour: he and his wife, Mindy (his high school sweetheart), were expecting their second child in March. "If it's time, then it's time," he said. "I'm trying to take the approach that this is just another tournament that I'm trying to win." He shook his head. "Of course I know that's not even close to being true."

THE CAST OF CHARACTERS at Lake Jovita was both fascinating and diverse, ranging from tour veterans like Donnie Hammond, Mike Hulbert, and Guy Boros to youngsters like Dickerson, Chad Wilfong, Steve Wheatcroft, and Colby Beckstrom. Wilfong had made the finals in 2004, eighteen months after graduating from Wake Forest. Wheatcroft and Beckstrom were trying to make the finals for the first time. One young player who almost certainly would have been a factor was a no-show. Alex Rocha, who had tied for first place in the first stage at Tampa Bay, had made it to the finals of the European Tour's Q School. He had planned to finish playing in Europe on Sunday and then fly in to Lake Jovita to tee it up on Tuesday. But weather delays in Europe had forced him to choose: wait out the finish of the European finals or fly home to take a shot at second stage.

Rocha, who was Brazilian by birth but lived in Florida, decided to go with the bird that was almost in hand and stay in Europe. He ended up tied for ninth in the European school, which gave him full status on that tour in 2006.

Beckstrom had finished third in Tampa and was still riding high when he opened with a 66. A second-round 72 left him in a strong position and still feeling confident. Most of the field was bunched close behind the twenty-two players who were at five under par or better after two rounds. Almost no one, even Dickerson, who was eight shots inside the cut line, and Grant Waite, who was two shots behind Dickerson, could rest easily. Those who trailed felt there was plenty of time to catch up.

"You don't have to do anything spectacular unless you're way back," said Blaine McCallister, the longtime tour veteran who was right on the number at five under. "It's a fair golf course, and if you don't make any big numbers, you can get a couple under every day and do just fine. Of course, you have to understand that. You can't go out there a few shots back with 36 holes to play and try to play the front nine in eight under. It's not going to happen."

Two players who were a few shots outside the number but still close enough not to panic were David Gossett and Jeff Curl, who had finished 36 holes at 142 — two under par. The two men were paired together along with Jimmy Green, another former tour player trying to get his card back, for the third round. They teed off on the back nine. Curl, who had missed at second stage the past two years, was trying to get to where Gossett and Green had already been: the PGA Tour. He was also trying to follow in the footsteps of his father, Rod Curl.

Anyone who followed golf in the 1970s was familiar with Rod Curl. He was only 5 feet 5, but he could really play golf. A solid money winner for many years, he beat Jack Nicklaus by one shot at Colonial in 1974. He was known as a fierce competitor during his playing days, and as he followed his son around the golf course now, it was apparent he hadn't changed.

"This is tough to watch," he said after Jeff's opening-round 71. "I watch him, and I'm reminded of how dumb I was at that age, the mistakes I made back then, because he makes the same ones. If I could have put my mind into his body today, the highest he can shoot is 69. Maybe better than that."

"Last year he played great golf at first and second stage and still didn't make it. This is like taking finals three times in a row. You pass the first time, they say, 'Okay, we're going to make the questions tougher, and you have to take it again.' If you pass the second time, they make you do it all over again, except it's for six rounds, not four.

"But if you're in the finals, you have a job. That's why this stage is *everything*."

It was quiet when Gossett, Green, and Curl teed off in front of a gallery that consisted of Rod Curl and Gossett's teacher, Jonathan Yarwood. He and Gossett had worked together during Gossett's formative years, before Gossett had gone to work briefly with David Leadbetter. Yarwood, whose profile had widened considerably when another of his pupils, Michael Campbell, held off Tiger Woods to win the U.S. Open in June 2005, was a dead ringer for Hall of Fame pitcher Dennis Eckersley: long, straight, black hair and a suave mustache.

Yarwood had flown in the day before to check Gossett's swing and provide moral support for him on the golf course. The day began routinely enough with all three players making par on the 10th hole. They hit their drives at number 11 and started walking off the tee. At that moment, Yarwood's cell phone rang.

Most people aren't allowed to bring cell phones to golf tournaments. Those who are (players, caddies, media, officials) know the phones have to be turned off when they are anywhere near the golf course. At the Masters, the rules are so strict that if anyone is caught carrying a cell phone on the course — even if it is turned off — it is confiscated, and the person may be asked to leave.

There aren't any rules like that at Q School, but it is so quiet on the golf course that a ringing cell phone sounds a bit like a cannon being shot off. As soon as he heard the phone, Yarwood knew he'd made a mistake. He reached into his pocket, took the phone out, and, without looking at the number of the incoming call, shut the phone off.

Before he could apologize, Rod Curl was in his face. "What's the matter with you?" he yelled. "You can't have a cell phone on out here. Don't you understand what's at stake?"

Yarwood apologized. "You're right," he said. "I forgot to turn it off. My fault."

"Apology not accepted," Curl said, heading off to find a rules official. He found Peter Dachisen, a longtime official from the Florida State Golf Association who had worked numerous Q Schools. When Dachisen asked Yarwood about the incident, Yarwood said that he had forgotten to turn the phone off and showed Dachisen that it was now off. That was good enough for Dachisen.

"I'm going to tell you this one time," Curl said. "That thing goes off in any way while my son is swinging, I'll kick your butt right here, right now."

"He was pretty hot," Dachisen said later. "I guess there was so much at stake for Jeff, and even though it was an innocent mistake, nothing seems innocent during the third round of second stage."

Yarwood was about half a foot taller than Curl, but seeing how angry the ex–tour player was, he felt intimidated. Yarwood asked Dachisen for his cell phone number. "I think he felt threatened," Dachisen said. "I felt pretty confident that nothing more was going to happen, but I think Rod made him nervous."

Neither Gossett nor Jeff Curl was close enough to the heated discussion to be aware of what was going on. Curl went on to shoot even par that day, but Gossett blew up, shooting 78, which put him 10 shots outside the cut line with 18 holes to play. "You look at that score, and you think I chopped it all day," he said. "I really didn't. I'd hit 16 greens each of the first two days, and I was only two under par. I probably pressed a little bit, and I made three bad swings that blew up my round. No excuses, I just didn't get the job done."

Jeff Curl was still in contention, still at two under par. Unlike his father he had kept his cool throughout the day. "Harder to watch than to play," Rod Curl said. "Especially here."

As evidenced by the Curl-Yarwood incident, tensions begin to rise on the third day of second stage. On the PGA Tour, the third round of a tournament is known as "moving day," because if you're behind and expect to contend, you have to make a move during the third round to give yourself a chance the last 18 holes.

Of course, on tour that's a reference to players trying to win the tournament. At second stage, a tie for 19th place is just as good as finishing first because there's no money at stake and everyone who finishes 19th or better is going to the finals and starting over again at even par.

No one dealt with the third-day pressure better than Tommy Tolles, who shot an eight-under-par 64. That gave him a four-shot cushion over Dickerson, who was in second place at 13 under after an even-par 72. Tolles had a seven-shot lead on everyone else in the field.

"The only good thing about being older [thirty-nine] is that I've learned to appreciate days like this more," Tolles said, relaxing on the range while one player after another congratulated him on the round. "It's taken me a while to figure a lot of things out about the game, but one of them is, there are very few players with 'the gift.' The rest of us are just out here scrapping it around. Guys like Tiger, Ernie, Phil, Vijay—what they do is like throwing a marble into a Coke can. Most of us can't do that. They've all got something special, whether it's Tiger's toughness or Ernie's hands or Vijay's diligence or Phil's creativeness. I don't have any of that. I spend my life trying to keep my club face from opening up and losing the ball right. I smile when I hit a duck hook. That's my game."

Tolles tends to be tough on himself, and he certainly hadn't had a free ride in the game. Growing up in Fort Myers, Florida, he was one of those kids who played everything. His father and one of his uncles were half of a foursome that started a concrete-pouring business as young men and sold it at a considerable profit in their thirties. Tolles tried football: "Got speared in the stomach. That was it." He tried baseball: "Got hit in the helmet by a pitch. That was enough for me." Golf was noncontact, and he was good at it.

"Good, not great," he said. "I walked on the team at Georgia and never starred there. Golf was what I wanted to do, though. In fact, it was all I did. That may be why I flunked out."

He turned pro, flunked Q School, and ended up playing in South Africa for two years after buying a plane ticket from Nolan Henke. Henke had been planning to play there but then made it through Q School and didn't need the ticket. Tolles finally made it through Q School in 1994—his seventh attempt—and looked to be well on his way to stardom when he finished second at the Players Championship in 1996 and ended up 16th on the money list at the end of that year. A year later, he was 27th on the money list, and he and his wife, Ilse, bought a five-acre farm in the tiny town of Flat Rock, North Carolina.

"I'm the story you've heard a million times," he said. "Guy

who is playing well and tries to change his swing to play better, only he plays worse. I worked with a great teacher when I was a kid—Jeff Heilman in Bonita Bay [near where he grew up in Florida]. I don't think he's ever told me anything wrong, but I've gone off and seen other instructors behind his back. It might take less time to list the guys I *haven't* seen than to list the guys I have seen: Jim McLean, Marty Fleckman, David Leadbetter. I've worked with [psychologist] Bob Rotella. I guess it's fair to say I tend to overthink about my swing.

"It isn't so much that you can learn too much, but you can *try* too much. I've listened to all these people through the years, but the thing is, when you're out on a golf course playing in a tournament, you're on an island all alone. It's almost as if I've gone to all these different guys so that someone else can swing the club for me. Problem is, it doesn't work that way.

"My swing, when I was playing my best in the mid-'90s, was never pretty. But it was effective. I was always a hooker, but I decided I'd be a better player if I could hit cuts like [Jeff] Sluman and [Tim] Herron. So I tried hitting cuts. It took me a while, but I finally figured out I can't hit cuts. I've got to hook the ball. Like with anything, I had to learn it the hard way."

Tolles also switched equipment, as so many players do when offered a lot of money while they're hot. In this case, the company was Tommy Armour, and the contract was for four years. "I'd been playing Ping for ten straight years. Look, in the end it's never the clubs; it's the player. But the Armour clubs *were* different, and I changed my swing to try to accommodate the clubs, and I just wasn't as good. My game fell apart. Was it mental? Physical? Both? Who knows? All I know is, I wasn't the same player."

Tolles went from 27th on the money list in 1997 to 115th a year later. He improved a little in 1999, finishing 85th, but hadn't been in the top 125 since. He went to the Nationwide Tour and played steadily there, actually getting his tour card back at the end of 2003 after finishing 20th on the Nationwide money list. But he languished on after his tour in 2004, making just eight cuts, and ended up 201st.

Tolles is one of those players others look at and wonder what has gone wrong. He has the personality to become a star, because he's just a little goofy. His hair color often changes from week to week, and he is disarmingly honest, with an occasionally off-the-wall sense of humor—most of it directed at himself. He is one of the few players who willingly admits that he likes chess.

"I've figured some things out about myself because of my failures," he said. "When I was young and starting out, I really thought there was nothing I wouldn't do to get to the top. I remember telling my wife when we got married, 'There is nothing and no one who is going to stop me from being the best, including you.'

"Well, that turned out not to be true. I found I could shoot 80 and come home and my kids still loved me, and I could live with the 80. I think [with] the guys that really burn inside, that isn't the case. I want to win, but I don't think I'm willing to push someone up against a wall to beat them.

"All that time I spent listening to all those teachers, trying to be Tiger or Ernie or Vijay, was wasted time. I'm not them, and I can't be them. I have to try to be the best Tommy Tolles I can be—whatever that is. I'd like to get back on tour now and see how I can do, because my perspective is different now. I've seen it from both sides."

Tolles sold the farm in Flat Rock—"between my golf and the end of the Internet boom, we had to downsize"—and he and his family were living in a smaller house in a bigger town (Hendersonville, population 25,000, as opposed to the 3,000 who live in Flat Rock), but still in North Carolina.

"It's very easy to get spoiled on the PGA Tour," Tolles said.

"Everything is spoon-fed to you. Whatever you want, you've got it. Going from there to the Nationwide is a little bit like going from a five-star restaurant to Kentucky Fried Chicken. Of course, that's not all bad. You have to think for yourself more, and you learn again how to do things for yourself.

"Still, I'd like to be out there on the big tour again. When I first got there in '95, I was just playing golf and letting the cards fall wherever they fell. After a while, I was protecting what I had. I think if I went back, I'd be able to get my '95 attitude back.

"Of course, I'm still a long way from getting there. [CBS analyst and swing guru] Peter Kostis once said there are two kinds of players. At one end is Nick Faldo, who plays with a wall around him. At the other end is Bruce Lietzke, who is always playing and thinking outside the box. Sometimes I think I'm both."

He smiled. "Which may explain a lot."

A LOT OF DREAMS DIE DURING THE THIRD ROUND. A player who is way back after 36 holes knows there is still time to get into contention. Not so if one is still way back after 54. Mike Hulbert, who had started the third round near the back of the pack, shot 67 to move into a tie for 21st—one shot away from the cut line, which was now at five under par. Steve Wheatcroft, a twenty-seven-year-old mini-tour player who had walked onto the golf team at Indiana after no one had recruited him out of high school, shot 69 to get to six under par, putting himself in position to make the finals for the first time. Tripp Isenhour, a Nationwide Tour veteran who had once been on the PGA Tour, also shot 69 to get to the cut line.

Twenty players were tied at five under par or better with 18 holes to play. Twelve more players were one shot back, and four more were two shots back. "In theory, anyone who is at even par or better has a shot tomorrow," said Grant Waite, who had stumbled to 74 but still appeared to be very comfortable at nine under par. "Someone who is way back will go low, and a couple of guys who are well inside the number right now will go backward." He smiled, his eyes fixed on the scoreboard. "I just hope I'm not one of them."

A lot of players were scoreboard-watching at the end of the day—many of them hoping they might somehow change the numbers by staring at them. Garrett Frank had started the day knowing he had to go low since he was at two over par. He spent the round running in place, shooting 72, meaning he made up no ground and was now seven shots outside the cut and behind so many players it would take a miracle round to keep his hopes alive.

"I need to shoot 64–65—at least," he said with a deep sigh. "Today I hit the ball about as well as I can hit it, and I just couldn't make a putt. Honestly, I don't think I had a birdie putt longer than 10 feet, and I couldn't make a thing."

Frank's shoulders sagged as he talked his round through with some friends. He winced at the thought of what might have been or, more accurately, what needed to be. "Last year when this happened, I said, 'That's it, I'm going home; time's up,'" he said. "I got through the holidays and all the questions about why I wasn't on tour. Then it got to be January, and, of course, the weather in Ohio was terrible, and I started thinking about the boys back in Florida teeing it up. I missed it—right away. So I went back. I honestly don't know what I'll do this time around."

For the moment, Frank headed to the putting green, hoping to find something in his putter for the next day.

Ty Tryon had been on that same green until dark the day before, also searching. He had started the day in the exact same spot as Frank and had gone backward, shooting 74, which, realistically, ended his hopes of getting back to where he had been four years earlier.

"The way I have to look at it is that golf's a game you play your whole life," he said. "I'm still only twenty-one. If I hadn't done what I had done at seventeen, this wouldn't be so discouraging—that's the irony of it. I try to keep telling myself I'm still learning and growing, and I know I *am*. But days like today are very hard to swallow. I know I've got the game, but knowing it doesn't mean a thing. Numbers don't lie."

The numbers on the board told other sad stories. Josh Mc-Cumber, who had started the day at three under par, shot 76, putting him virtually out of contention. Brad Elder, who had been labeled a can't-miss star coming out of the University of Texas in 1998, had been on the tour from 2000 to 2003. But he had dropped from 68th on the money list in 2000 to 217th in 2003 after having shoulder problems. He was now trying to make a comeback at the age of thirty. He had started the day in good position at five under par but could do no better than 74, which dropped him from a tie for 16th place into a tie for 36th place. David Gossett's 78 all but ended his chances, and Chad Wilfong, who had made the finals a year earlier and had started the day at one under par, had gone into full reverse, shooting 77.

Wilfong hadn't started playing golf until the age of thirteen and had improved steadily right through his college career at Wake Forest. "When I was a kid, I hated golf," he said, smiling. "I played some with my dad, but I figured it was a sport for old people. I played tennis and baseball and basketball. I liked to run, not walk.

"But there was a group of kids in my neighborhood who played all the time. One of them was the son of the pro at the club where we played—Thomas O'Brian. I just couldn't beat him. I started beating balls for hours just so I could beat him. Next thing I knew, I was a decent player."

Wilfong was recruited to go to Wake Forest by Jerry Haas, brother of Jay Haas and a former tour player himself. He ended up becoming a teammate of Jay's son, Bill. "Bill is the most talented golfer I've ever been around," he said. "Most of us on the Wake golf team would hit balls for hours. Bill would hit forty balls and go watch a football game. We used to joke that he never met a range that he liked. I'm not like that. I need to keep working at my game to improve."

Wilfong started 2005 with conditional status on the Nationwide Tour and finished 97th on the money list, even though he got into only sixteen events. "I'd like to believe if I had played a full schedule, I would have at least been in the top 50," he said, a notion backed up by the fact that he finished 40th in scoring average. "The key for me, I think, is getting a job playing out here for the next fifteen years. That's my goal."

Twenty-five, with a mop of light brown hair and a 6-foot-3-inch, 170-pound two-iron of a body, Wilfong looked as if he could still be in college. He had come to Lake Jovita fighting his swing but had managed to hang in contention for two rounds. "You have to do that this week," he said. "My game just isn't where I want it right now, but it doesn't matter. I have to go out and fight my way around and try to get through here.

"The biggest difference between the best players and the rest of us is that they *know* they're better than everyone else. It's not something that comes to most of us that easily. Bill's got it—you can see it; you can feel it when you talk to him. Toward the end of the year, he skipped an event even though he was trying to make the top 20 on the Nationwide list. I asked him why, and he said he'd played seven in a row, and he figured if he played well the last couple weeks, he'd make it. If he didn't, he wouldn't. Of course, he didn't figure on Miami getting canceled because of a hurricane. The point, though, is this: Bill *knows* he's going to be on tour; it's just a matter of when. Realistically, right now, if I had full Nationwide playing status next year, I'd be thrilled. I'm still trying to get good enough to feel as if I belong out on tour. Bill already knows he's good enough."

Wilfong lost the battle with his swing during the third round, meaning he would spend another year with conditional status (based on his money list finish) on the Nationwide. Like most of the players who had either failed to make a move or had gone backward in the third round, he walked off the course with a blank look on his face, knowing he would have to wait another year for another chance.

Those who had played well weren't celebrating by any means. For the trailers, 18 more holes wouldn't be nearly enough. For the leaders, 18 holes would feel like an eternity.

ONE OF THE TRAILERS decided to become a spectator for the last round. Guy Boros had one of the most famous last names in golf. He was the son of Julius Boros, who had won two U.S. Opens and a PGA Championship during his Hall of Fame career. His son, if you listen to those who have played with him, might have as much talent—which is saying a lot.

"When I was a kid, people would ask me all the time if I thought I could be as good a player someday as my dad," Guy said. He was sitting on a golf cart after the third round, watching other players pounding balls in the late-afternoon heat. "I would laugh and say, 'Oh, no, someday I'm going to be *better* than my dad. Of course, I had absolutely no idea at the time just how good—how *great*—my dad was. It wasn't until I really started chasing the game a little that I understood what kind of a player he had been. I still remember when I was ten, watching him at Westchester. He was fifty-five, and he ended up losing in a playoff to Gene Littler. It never occurred to me how amazing that was, or how amazing it was that he won the PGA [Championship] when he was forty-eight. Now, looking back, I realize I would have to be a hell of a player to be *half* as good as my dad was."

Guy Boros was a good player, blessed with the same kind of easy, natural rhythm for the golf swing that his father had. He looks almost exactly like his father: the same soft, broad features and stocky build, with an easy, laid-back manner. He was a three-time all-American at the University of Iowa and spent a number of years working his way up the golfing ladder, going from the Canadian Tour to the Nike Tour and finally to the PGA Tour. He often took time off from playing to caddy for his father on the Senior Tour.

"I loved doing that," he said. "When I first started playing golf, people always told me what a good man my father was, and I sort of nodded and said, 'Yeah, sure, I know.' But as I've gotten older and had kids of my own, and realized how he managed to spend time with all seven of his kids and got to see him with people, I realized he was a *very* good man.

"The problem for me has always been simple: I never loved the game the way my father did. He loved being on a golf course — anywhere, anytime. He loved hitting balls; he could do it all day. I was never that way. I always had talent, and I could always play, but I was never really passionate about it. You can't make yourself passionate about something. You either are or you aren't."

He smiled. "Growing up, what I really wanted to be was a policeman. I even majored in criminal justice in college. Now there's part of me that wants to go off and be a fishing captain. That's what my brother does, and I've got my license."

He sighed. "But golf is what I do. It's what I've always done. For a long time, it came so easy to me, other guys on tour called me 'the faucet,' because I could just turn it on when I needed to. Well, the faucet's rusted and not working these days. It's frustrating as hell, too, because I really have tried to figure out how to get it back, and so far it isn't happening."

Julius Boros died in 1994, while his son, then a rookie on the tour, was playing the Colonial, a tournament his father won in 1960 and again in 1963. Two years later, Guy Boros won in Vancouver and became part of golf history by becoming just the fourth son of a past PGA Tour winner also to win. But the faucet began to run dry a couple of years later, and he lost his exemption in 1999. After that, he played most of his golf on the Nationwide Tour, winning three times. In 2003, he finished 14th on the money list to get back to the PGA Tour in 2004. But that year he finished 208th on the money list and spent 2005 back on the Nationwide. He had just turned forty-one, and his curly hair was starting to show streaks of gray.

"No one ever thinks of themselves as being old, but when I play with some of the young guys and see how far they hit it, I feel old," he said. "I just can't find that kind of distance. Still, I see signs that it's still there. I played six PGA Tour events this year and made three cuts, so it isn't like I was just taking up space there. I still believe I can have a week where the stars align and I can win again."

He lit a cigarette. "Of course, there's been absolutely no evidence of that here this week."

Boros had arrived at Lake Jovita feeling confident. He knew the course well, since he often made the drive up from his home in Fort Lauderdale to play with Tim Petrovic and Garrett Willis, the two pros in residence there, and the Damron brothers, Robert and Patrick, who live nearby. He thought he would be able to draw on his experience down the stretch if he could play his way into contention.

Unfortunately, he never came close to contending. After he shot 74 the first day, he headed to the range, hoping to find something that would straighten out his swing. "To be honest, this sucks," he said. "I feel helpless right now. Part of me says I should walk away; part of me says I can still find it."

He was on the range again the next day after a 76 left him in second-to-last place. "I have to hope there's a low round out there for me," he said. "I have to keep trying. This," he gestured around the range at other players hammering balls, "is what I know."

A day later, he shot 76 again, leaving him 15 shots outside the cut line with one round to go. This time he skipped the range. "My head hurts," he said, "from the brick wall it's been beaten into all week."

9

The Unkindest Cuts of All

IT WAS WINDIER ON THE MORNING of the last day at Lake Jovita, meaning that low scoring was even less likely than it would normally be on the last day of second stage.

Colby Beckstrom woke up feeling completely calm, no nerves at all in his stomach—which surprised him. "To be honest, I love nerves," he said. "They make me feel as if I'm ready to play."

Beckstrom and his family had eaten their usual meal at their usual spot the night before, and it had felt like a pregraduation gathering. He had shot 69 on the third day, leaving him at nine under par for the tournament. That put him in a tie for sixth place and in the second-to-last group on the final day.

"Dinner on Friday night felt almost like a celebration," he said. "It wasn't as if I was cocky or overconfident. I wasn't. We were planning the real celebration for the next night. But we were all feeling good about things."

There was no reason not to feel good. His day had perhaps been summed up by the ninth hole, where he had hit his third shot up against a tree behind the green, leaving himself with two options: take an unplayable or try to chip the ball onto the green left-handed. Before he could go over and consider his options, Beckstrom was distracted by Akio Sadakata, who had hit his second shot into the water hazard fronting the green.

There was some question about where the ball had entered the hazard and where Sadakata should drop. Sadakata believed he was entitled to drop in a spot far more advantageous than the one Beckstrom and Joe Alfieri, the third player in the group, thought he was entitled to. After a couple of minutes of discussion, Beckstrom walked away.

"I'm up against a tree lying three," he said. "If that's what he thought, that's what he thought. I wasn't going to spend all day arguing about where his ball entered the hazard. In the end, he has to make the call."

Beckstrom decided to play his fourth shot left-handed, hoping to get the ball close enough to the hole to save par. He failed. The ball rolled straight into the cup for a miraculous left-handed birdie. He was on cruise control the rest of the day.

Now he figured he would find his nerves warming up on the range. If there is anything quieter than a golf course at Q School, it is a range at Q School—especially before the last round. Everyone is lost in his own thoughts, each trying to get himself into exactly the right mind-set for the day. Everyone knows it will be a long day. The pace of play is never fast at Q School, but on the last day, when players will frequently mark 1-foot putts, it slows almost to a halt.

"On the one hand, you don't want to see play get ridiculously slow," said Steve Rintoul, the former tour player who was running the qualifier. "On the other hand, I've been where those guys are, and I'm not going to put someone on the clock unless it's really getting bad out there."

For many players—Beckstrom among them—the stakes for the next 18 holes were the highest they had ever faced. For players who had no status on either the PGA Tour or the Nationwide Tour—Beckstrom, Jeff Curl, Joe Alfieri, Brad Klapprott, Patrick Damron, Hiroshi Matsuo, Garrett Frank, and Steve Wheatcroft among them—this was their chance to get off the mini-tour merry-go-round and secure a spot on the Nationwide, with a chance in three weeks to play themselves into golf nirvana—the PGA Tour.

For those who did have some kind of status—ex-winners like Donnie Hammond, Mike Hulbert, Blaine McCallister, Matt Kuchar, Grant Waite, and David Gossett—this was a step toward getting back to where they all thought they belonged. For players who had been on the Nationwide recently—Bubba Dickerson, Chad Wilfong, Tripp Isenhour, Tommy Tolles, and Kelly Gibson—this was what they needed to have the opportunity to take that next step.

Tolles might have been the only player with reason not to be that nervous. He stepped on the first tee that morning knowing he could shoot 80 and still qualify. "Of course, the last thing you want to do is start out thinking 'Let's break 80,'" he said. "You try to flush your mind and play a good round of golf."

That's what they were all doing in one form or another. In some ways, the lack of scoreboards at Q School is helpful. Sure, they all have an idea what the number will be, but because they aren't certain, they have to keep grinding regardless of where they think they stand.

"You might think you're safe and then find out you miscalculated," Bob Heintz said. "Or you might think you're a dead man walking and then find out you have life. That's why you keep playing no matter what."

Heintz was one of the twelve players who began the last day one shot outside the number. He had put himself in a hole with an opening-round 74, but back-to-back 69s had jumped him back into contention. "I'll take 69 and take my chances right now," he said early Saturday morning. "Just give me the card and I'll sign it."

Heintz was another player who didn't fit comfortably into the PGA Tour hunt/fish/vote Republican stereotype. (Of course,

Brad Faxon, the longtime tour player who listed his special interests in the media guide as "all sports *except* hunting and fishing," as a goof on his fellow pros, was not only a Republican but a close friend of the Bush family.) Heintz lists "collecting chess sets" as one of his hobbies, and you could bet serious money that those three words did not appear anywhere else in either the PGA Tour or Nationwide Tour media guides. He was actually a fan of the first President Bush but it may have had something to do with the fact that both were graduates of Yale.

He had ended up at Yale in part because Duke, his first choice, chose not to offer him a golf scholarship. Bob and his brother Chris had grown up in Syosset, New York (on Long Island), believing they were destined to be professional athletes. Their father was a high school basketball coach, and for a long time, Bob thought he would go to college on a basketball scholarship. By the time he was a senior, he was big for golf (6 feet, 200 pounds) but small for basketball. When Yale, which technically doesn't offer athletic scholarships, offered him financial aid to come and play golf, he took the university up on it. He got his degree in economics and was an academic all-American as a senior, but he wanted to take a shot at golf before deciding whether to use his degree or pursue an MBA. After struggling on mini-tours for three and a half years, he decided it was time to look for a job. In 1996 he was hired as a financial analyst by Raymond James.

"That was a good experience for me because it motivated me to work harder at my golf," he said, smiling. "If you have a degree from Yale, you can always get a job. But if you want a really good job in finance, you need an MBA. At one point, Nancy [his wife] asked me if I wanted to go back and get my MBA. I said, 'Hell no.' She said, 'Well, then, play hard.'"

His work began to pay off in the late '90s. He first made the Nationwide Tour in 1999 and then became one of those ping-

JAY AND BILL HAAS: The week was probably tougher on the father than on the son.　© STEVE GRAYSON/WIREIMAGE.COM

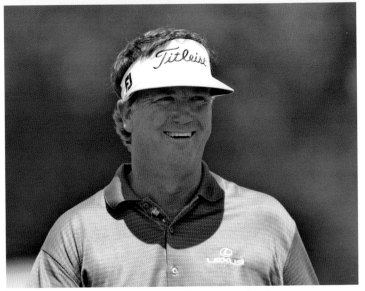

PETER JACOBSEN: Undoubtedly the only Q-Schooler ever threatened by a gun. © HUNTER MARTIN/WIREIMAGE.COM

LARRY MIZE: "The worst part is being called Mr. Mize."

© STAN BADZ/ WIREIMAGE.COM

BRIAN HENNINGER: Still grinding, still hoping.

STEVE STRICKER: One of the great comeback stories of 2006.

Ron Whittaker: A little Ambien and Pepto-Bismol and he was ready to play.   © STAN BADZ/PGA TOUR/WIREIMAGE.COM

DAN FORSMAN: A "Field of Dreams" that wasn't heaven.

NICHOLAS THOMPSON:
Full of confidence;
learning as he goes.

BRAD KLAPPROTT:
Injured at the worst
possible time.

B. J. Staten:
Hanging on for
dear life at the
finish.

© MICHAEL COHEN/
WIREIMAGE.COM

Peter Tomasulo:
A nightmare on the
107th hole.

© SAM GREENWOOD/
WIREIMAGE.COM

Tommy Tolles: One shot continues to haunt him.

pong balls bouncing back and forth between the Nationwide and the PGA Tour. His game was consistently good enough to play well on the Nationwide, but not good enough to keep him on the PGA. Three times he made it through Q School, and three times he failed to crack the top 150 on the money list, including in 2005. Now, at thirty-five, with three children and a degree from Yale, he conceded that thoughts of finding a new way of life crossed his mind.

"I'm not doing this because I don't have anything else I can do," he said. "If I wasn't supporting my family, I would stop. But I am. This year I was 171st on the money list, which technically makes me a failure because I'm back here. But I made $355,000 in prize money. I had a fifth [San Antonio] and an 11th [Vancouver]. I still believe I haven't lived up to my potential yet. I think I owe it to myself to keep at it a while longer and see if I can't put together one of those Jason Gore years. I believe I have that in me."

Heintz isn't nearly as rotund as Gore, but he does have a round face and a quick smile. He also has what would have to be considered a cerebral view of Q School. "The dichotomy is easy to understand, if you think about it," he said. "We're all trying desperately to do something in which the harder you try, the worse you'll do. You have to fight the idea that the consequences of failure are as bad as you make them out to be."

He smiled. "I keep telling myself that if I'm back on the Nationwide next year, my family really enjoys spending time at the Peek'n Peak Resort" (the site of a Nationwide event in Findley Lake, New York). "Of course, if I ever really got my game together, we could afford to go there on a vacation anytime we wanted."

Nancy Heintz is a graduate of Villanova who teaches preschool when she isn't taking care of their kids, ranging in age from four to ten. "The biggest problem for a tour wife is finding a sense of purpose and worth," she said. "People think all the wives just want to be 'Mrs. So-and-so' and hang out at the spa or shop. That might be true for some, but it isn't true for a lot of us."

Having spent time on both tours, her husband had found a simple way to describe the differences between them. "It's all in the walk from the clubhouse to the range," he said. "On the PGA Tour, [when] you make that walk, you have to deal with media, with fans, with club equipment reps, with agents. It's a traveling circus. You're talking thirty to sixty minutes a day to deal with all the chaos outside the ropes.

"The Nationwide is a lot more peaceful."

He stood up to make the quiet walk to the range. "I kinda like the chaos," he said, his spikes clicking in the silence against the paved cart path as he walked.

HEINTZ MADE A HABIT of not studying the leader board closely until after the third round. "At that point," he said, "you want to have a sense of what you're up against going into the last day."

His mission, like that of a lot of other players, was to try to shoot in the 60s the last day. With the wind up, there probably weren't going to be too many rounds in the 60s, and it seemed likely that anyone in contention who could shoot in the 60s would be in very good shape.

Colby Beckstrom didn't need to shoot in the 60s. He could probably afford to shoot a couple of shots over par and still qualify with ease. But that wasn't what he was thinking as he and his brother walked to the first tee at a few minutes before 10 a.m. to join Scott Parel and Deane Pappas in the second-to-last group of the day. "I just wanted to go out and keep doing what I'd done in Tampa and what I'd done for three rounds," he said. "Just play good golf and not worry about my score or anyone else's. It had worked for seven rounds. There was no reason why it shouldn't work for one more.

"The funny thing is, if someone had come up to me before the round and said, 'Hey, Colby, shoot 75 and you're in the finals,' I'd have laughed at them. The thought of shooting a score anywhere close to that high never crossed my mind."

Months later, looking back at the day, Beckstrom realized there were warning signals: the lack of nerves, the case of the giggles he had on the driving range. "It wasn't like I was laughing out loud at anything," he said. "I was just kind of giggly out there with J. J. That's really not me before an important round of golf. On the tee, I felt so relaxed. Again, that's not me. It was as if I couldn't get the adrenaline rush you need in that kind of situation."

He missed the green to the right on the first hole, chipped poorly, and made a bogey. A shaky start, but hardly a big deal. The second hole at Lake Jovita is a reachable par-five, but Beckstrom drove it into the right rough. Rather than take any chances, he decided to lay up. "I think I got a little too greedy with the shot," he said. "I left it in the thick rough on the right." His third shot was a chopped seven-iron from the gunk, and he was still well short of the green. He then hit a mediocre pitch that was still short of the green. He chipped to 10 feet and missed the putt for bogey. Two holes played, three shots given up.

"At that point, I was just a little bit baffled," he said. "I certainly wasn't panicked. I was telling myself, 'Calm down and let's go.' But I *was* calm. So telling myself to calm down really wasn't the answer."

He finally hit a good drive at number three and had 100 yards to the flag. He hit an easy gap wedge, knowing that with a full swing, the farthest he could hit the ball was 110. "I took what I thought was my 100-yard swing," he said. "The ball went five yards over the green."

It was at that moment that it first occurred to Beckstrom that he didn't have complete control of his body; that what he had thought was calm was something a lot closer to terror. He made another bogey from over the green, took a deep breath, and finally hit a green in regulation at number four, making a routine two-putt par that, at that moment, felt like a hole in one. "Okay," he thought, "the miserable start is behind me. I'm still in good shape if I just play good golf from here to the clubhouse."

But it wasn't behind him just yet. At number five, a hole he had played well all week by hitting a draw off the tee, he played the same draw. "I knew I'd hit it well," he said. "I looked up, expecting to see it going from right to left, and the ball was *slicing*. By now, I was in some kind of state of shock."

The ball landed in a bunker against the lip. By the time he hacked it out and got it on the green, he was looking at another long bogey putt—which he missed. He walked off the green in a state of panic and anger. His face was red, and he stood off to the side of the tee trying to collect his thoughts. Parel was sympathetic, saying softly, "Hang in there, Colby." Pappas said nothing. In fact, Beckstrom was convinced that he looked annoyed, which only served to make him angrier.

"At the time I thought he was being a jerk," he said later. "But when I thought about it, I realized it was a big day in his life, too. He's trying to grind through this thing, and he's playing with this guy who is hacking it all over the place."

The hacking continued on number six, a relatively easy par-four—if you hit the fairway. Beckstrom didn't. Completely unsure which direction the ball was going, he hit it deep into the left rough and had to pitch out. From there he knocked his third shot on and made a routine bogey, leaving him seven over par for six holes. On Friday, he had played the first nine holes in 34 shots. He had now taken 31 shots to play six holes. More important— most important—he had gone from nine under for the tournament to two under, which he knew was well outside the number he was going to need to advance.

Walking to the seventh tee, he heard J. J. talking to him for the first time all morning. He had kept quiet, not wanting to pick his brother up with false encouragement, but also not wanting to sound panicked by talking too much. Now he said, "Hey, Colby, let's play golf."

It was the quick slap in the face Beckstrom needed. "I knew I had to make birdies at that point," he said. "I went from the protecting mind-set back to the attacking mind-set. I started hitting the ball the way I had the first three days."

But he couldn't make enough birdies. The chances were there, but the putts, which now *had* to drop, weren't dropping. He played the next 11 holes at one under par — very solid golf, but not good enough because of the disastrous start.

"I hadn't thought about a number until the seventh hole," he said. "Then I began thinking I needed to try to get to five [under] to make it, and there was some chance I might make it at four. But my goal was five."

Standing on the 18th tee, he knew the only way to get to five was to hole out from the fairway. He hit a huge drive and had only 132 yards to the hole, which was tucked behind a bunker on the water side of the green. A classic last-day, last-hole sucker pin — as in, one had to be a sucker to fire at it, given how close it was to serious danger. At that moment, Beckstrom never thought about the bunker or the water. The only thing in his mind was holing the shot.

"Believe it or not, when the ball was in the air, I thought it had a chance," he said. "I hit it just about perfect."

But there was wind, and the ball came up just short of the green. As if to remind Beckstrom that it wasn't his day, it stopped dead rather than bounce up onto the putting surface. Even then he wasn't ready to give up. He had chipped in from behind the green on the second day and holed out from a bunker on the third. Maybe he could hole out one more time, and the number would somehow slip to four.

He came close, but the ball slid to the left of the flag at the last possible instant. He tapped it in for par and 78. Only two players among the seventy-one who teed it up that day carded a higher number. As Beckstrom shook hands with Pappas and Parel, he knew that his dream of going straight from college in the spring to the PGA Tour the following winter was gone. Pappas, who had started one shot ahead of him, hadn't played a whole lot better, but his 76 was good enough to get him in at six under par, safely inside the number. Parel had shot 74 to finish eight under.

As Beckstrom walked off the green, the first person he saw was David Schultz, a teammate from TCU who had also made it through first stage. Schultz had never been in serious contention at second stage and had finished 70th. He had just finished a few minutes earlier on the front nine and had a big grin on his face as he shook Beckstrom's hand.

"Congratulations," he said. "I couldn't be happier for you."

Beckstrom's family hadn't been able to warn Schultz about what had happened before he saw Beckstrom. "I felt terrible, because I knew how terrible he was going to feel when I told him," Beckstrom said. "I just looked at him and said, 'David, I didn't make it. I shot six over.'"

Beckstrom saw terror and shock in Schultz's eyes. "He didn't know what to say. I didn't know what to say," he said. "At that point, I was completely out of it. I kept thinking there had to be more to do, more golf to play, that it couldn't really be over. But it was."

He signed his card and accepted consolation hugs from his family. He didn't want to run out on everybody, didn't want to pout, so he hung around, accepting condolences from other players who saw his score and came by to tell him they were sorry. Beckstrom's face was blank as he spoke to them, the kind of look often seen at an accident or a fire. Or on the last day of Q School.

After a while, he and his girlfriend walked to the parking lot so Colby could change his shoes for the ride home. He put his clubs in the trunk and took a deep breath. They had been standing there talking for a few minutes when J. J. walked up. He had lingered by the scoreboard, watching the numbers go up, listening to people talk about who was in and who was out.

"I know you probably don't want to hear this right now, but I'm going to tell you anyway," he said. "The other players, the guys who have seen you play, are all saying the same thing over there: 'No way Colby Beckstrom shot 78. He's too good. He'll definitely be back.'"

J. J. paused for a moment, then threw his arms around his little brother. "I'm damn proud of you," he said softly.

Beckstrom felt a little better. "I loved him for saying what he said," he remembered later. "But it occurred to me that I had just missed the absolute worst cut you can miss in golf, and I'd missed it very painfully. I wasn't on the bubble starting the day. I was way inside the bubble. There were a lot of other guys with more reason to be nervous than me who played well. That was the part that was tough to take."

One other thought unnerved him a little, then and later. "They say it can happen to anyone," he said. "Of course they're right. But here's the worst part: there's absolutely no guarantee for any of us that it won't happen again."

BECKSTROM WASN'T THE ONLY ONE fighting final-day nerves. Grant Waite, seasoned veteran that he was, played the first 11 holes almost as badly as Beckstrom played the first five and found himself six over par for the day—and back to three under for the week. Just when he was becoming convinced he had blown it, he found his game, and, unlike Beckstrom, he made three birdie putts coming down the stretch to salvage a 75 and finish at six under.

Steve Wheatcroft, like Beckstrom trying to make the finals for the first time, managed to keep his golf ball under control the entire day, steadily making pars. At 18 he was even par for the day and still six under for the week. He was convinced that six under was a lock to make it but five under was not. He managed to get his second shot onto the green, about 30 feet behind the flag, then, with his hands starting to shake, putted to within three feet. He practically ran after the ball as it rolled toward the hole.

"I said to the guys I was playing with [veterans Kevin Johnson and Tripp Isenhour], 'I hope you don't mind if I finish right now, because if I have to wait a couple minutes, I don't know if I'll be able to grip the club, much less draw it back," he said. "They were great about it. I walked up and tried not to even think about what was at stake on the putt, and just managed to shove it into the hole."

Wheatcroft was one of a handful of players working with no caddy during the week, dragging his clubs around on a pull cart. As soon as his name went up on the scoreboard as a qualifier, a number of caddies who had shown up for the last day began searching for him.

"All of a sudden, I had these new friends," he said. "I just took their phone numbers and told them if I needed them, I'd be in touch."

Wheatcroft spent a lot of time at the scoreboard after he finished, just enjoying the moment. "I've dreamed of this my whole life," he said. "There's a part of me that can't believe it's true. I just keep staring at my name to make sure it's really me that finished six under."

Bob Heintz also headed straight for the scoreboard as soon as he signed his scorecard, but it wasn't to celebrate. He had shot 71, which put him at five under, and he knew that five under was very much on the bubble. "I hate to stand here and root against anyone," he said. "But I need some guys to go backward."

Some players can't bear to stand and watch scores go up when they know they're going to be a shot in or a shot out. Heintz couldn't bring himself to leave. "It makes no sense at all," he said. "But I feel like I'll miss something."

Others had no need to hang around. Matt Kuchar, the 1997 U.S. Amateur champion who had become such a hero with his play at the Masters and the U.S. Open the following year, could do no better than 73, leaving him at four under for the week. Mike Hulbert had a similar experience, also shooting 73. He came to the 18th hole at three under for the tournament, thinking that if he could make a birdie and get to four under, he might still have a chance. He hit a nine-iron to 12 feet, but missed the putt and walked off the green shaking his head.

"I still think I learned something this week," he said. "I've still got a little turd left in me. I'm not ready to give it up yet."

Donnie Hammond and Kelly Gibson ended up playing all four rounds with each other. They were both two under par after the first two rounds, and they were still at two under after third-round 72s. Hammond won their mini-tournament by one shot, shooting 71 the last day, but it left him tied with Hulbert at three under. Jeff Curl managed to shoot 70 — one of the better rounds on a day when only seven players broke 70 — but he still came up short at four under. Josh McCumber couldn't recover from his third-round 76. Shooting 72 the last day, he finished four shots outside the number. "Next year," his father said. "He's still got work to do, but he understands that."

Garrett Frank's 71 left him two shots farther back and wondering if there would be a next year. David Gossett (72) and Ty

Tryon (73) walked away shaking their heads, wondering how what had once been so easy had become so difficult.

The saddest ending of the afternoon belonged to thirty-six-year-old Ken Duke, who could aptly be described as a golf journeyman. He had played one year on the PGA Tour (2004), had played the Nationwide on and off dating back to 1995, had played mini-tours in the United States, and had played on the South American and Australasia tours. He had finished 47th on the Nationwide list in 2005, so his only Q School goal was to get back to the PGA Tour.

He stood in the middle of the 18th fairway at six under par, having hit a perfect drive. But he pulled his nine-iron into deep rough behind the green, chunked his first chip, chipped to 10 feet and missed the bogey putt. The double bogey dropped him to four under and punched his ticket back to the Nationwide for 2006.

There were also some success stories. Joe Alfieri II, who had been born on the July day in 1969 when Neil Armstrong and Buzz Aldrin first walked on the moon, shot 68 to go from just outside the number at four under to well inside it at eight under. His father, who had introduced him to the game as a child, caddied for him, using a pull cart in the midday heat. While Joe II went to sign his scorecard, Joe I collapsed in the arms of a friend and wept — partly from joy, partly from exhaustion, but mostly from relief.

As the late players came in, it began to look as if there might be eighteen players at six under par. The tour had sent word earlier in the week that only eighteen and ties would advance from Lake Jovita because there had been some withdrawals and because of larger fields at some other sites.

Bob Heintz was staring the scoreboard down when word began to circulate that someone in the late groups had gone backward. It was one of those rumors that had started someplace on the back nine and made it into the clubhouse as the later players began finishing.

The last group wasn't in any trouble. Tommy Tolles shot 71 to finish at 18-under-par 270. Bubba Dickerson shot 69 to finish two shots back. And Hiroshi Matsuo, fighting a case of need-to-make-it-through-second-stage nerves, produced a 72, which left him comfortably 10 under par at 278.

It was only when the second-to-last group — Parel, Pappas, and Beckstrom — arrived at 18 that people knew it was Beckstrom who had gone in reverse. The looks on the faces of his family were a dead giveaway. When Beckstrom's score went up, Heintz tried not to smile behind the sunglasses he was wearing, but he knew he had survived. When Tolles's, Dickerson's, and Matsuo's scores were added, there would be seventeen players at six under or better. That meant that Heintz, Tripp Isenhour, and Ryan Howison, who had finished at five under, were in.

Heintz let out a sigh of relief. "I feel sorry for the kid," he said. "But this is what happens at Q School. There's always someone with a sad story to tell. I hope for his sake there comes a time when he can look back on this day and tell people how this disappointment gave him inspiration to become a great player."

Someday, Beckstrom might do that. On that windy Saturday afternoon at Lake Jovita, he wasn't thinking about what might come someday, only about what could have come that day. Heintz, Howison, and Isenhour would play fifty miles up the road in Orlando in three more weeks. It would be two months before Colby Beckstrom could walk onto a golf course without feeling sick to his stomach.

10

What Is, Is

IN FIVE OTHER LOCATIONS around the country during the second and third weeks of November, several hundred golfers were fighting their way through second stage. The names that most golf fans would know were spread out around the country: Larry Mize was in Panama City, Florida, dealing with the fact that there were players in the field who had not been born when he first made it through Q School in 1981. Ken Green, a five-time tour winner who was best known for his frequent criticisms of tour policy, also was there. Bill Glasson, Steve Stricker, and Dan Forsman, all big money earners in the past, were in Kingwood, Texas, just outside Houston. Matt Gogel, perhaps best known for being the victim of an amazing Tiger Woods comeback at Pebble Beach in 2001 (Woods had come from seven shots down the last day to beat him) but better remembered by his fellow pros for bouncing back from that disappointment to win at Pebble Beach the next year, was in Beaumont, California, along with Steve Pate, Rick Fehr, Dennis Paulson, and Duffy Waldorf, all multiple winners on tour. Beaumont was also where T. C. Chen showed up.

One player in Panama City had a special place in golf lore — albeit one that no one would wish on his worst enemy. Jaxon Brigman had been knocking around between the Nationwide

Tour and mini-tours since his graduation from Oklahoma State in 1994. Playing at OSU had been a dream come true for Brigman. He had grown up in Abilene, Texas, the son of a CPA who bought a house right on a golf course. Brigman never took any formal golf lessons, but his parents had a golf cart to get around the golf club, and he and his friends would go out on the golf course after school and play. "By the time I was eleven, I was starting to get pretty good," he said. "That's when I started playing in tournaments a little bit."

Soon after that, Brigman and his friends went to watch an amateur tournament called the LaJet Classic. The best group of players in the event came from Oklahoma State, led then by Scott Verplank and Willie Wood, both future PGA Tour winners. "All I remember is they all had these orange golf bags, and they were the first team to have the stand-up bags, which I thought were really cool. Mike Holder was the coach, and he was kind of an icon even back then. My goal from that moment on was to somehow get good enough to go play there."

Brigman got good enough, winning a number of prestigious junior tournaments, which led to the phone call from Holder offering him a scholarship to OSU. "I'd been recruited by some other schools," he said. "But once Coach Holder called, that was pretty much it."

If Brigman had any doubts about wanting to play for Holder and OSU, they disappeared after Holder's first question to him: "Do you want to play on the PGA Tour?"

Brigman had started to dream that dream as a high school freshman. "Absolutely," he answered.

"Good," Holder said. "Because the only guys I want in my program are players who want to play on the tour."

"I was absolutely sold when I heard that," Brigman said.

He was on good teams at OSU, playing with future PGA

Tour players Bob May, Chris Tidland, Kevin Wentworth, Kris Cox, and Bo Van Pelt. But the experience wasn't what he had hoped for. "To be honest, I was intimidated by Coach Holder," Brigman said. "He's kind of an in-your-face guy, and I don't think I responded well to that. If he told me I was terrible, I believed I was terrible. My confidence got shaken. Finally, my junior year, I went in and told Coach that I didn't think I was doing a very good job responding to what he was telling me; that it wasn't his fault at all, but that I'd lost my confidence. He kind of eased up on me after that, and I had a great year and a great summer. Going into my senior year, I remember we had a team meeting. We had finished thirteenth in the national championships the previous spring, and Coach wasn't happy about that at all. He said, 'The only guy on this team who has a guaranteed spot is Jaxon Brigman.' That made me feel good."

It didn't last long. By the time Holder selected the team that would go to the Big Eight and NCAA championships, Brigman was first alternate. "I didn't even get to play in the big tournaments as a senior," he said. "It was definitely time for me to move on and try to start over."

His pro career began well. He made it to Q School finals and earned a Nationwide card in three of his first four years, although he never really got close to making the PGA Tour. "The good news was that I was good enough to make the finals, but I couldn't really get anything going on the Nationwide. The years I didn't make the finals and played mini-tours I think helped me, because I did well and it helped my confidence."

He made it back to the finals in '99 after a year on the mini-tours. "I actually missed at first stage in '98," he said. "That was the first time that had happened. But I managed to make a little money playing mini-tours in '99, so I actually felt a little better about myself going into Q School."

That was Steve Carman's first year running Q School and the

year the finals were played at Doral — not the famous Blue Course, but the Gold and Silver courses. "It was a logistical nightmare," Carman remembered. "We had to shuttle guys forever to get them out to the 10th tee or back in from the ninth green when they finished. There was construction in Miami right nearby, and the noise was deafening sometimes. Plus, there was all sorts of other play at other courses at the resort, so the whole thing had the feel of a giant outing. It was really tough on the guys, especially given what was at stake for all of them."

Brigman had sailed through the first two stages that year. He had arrived at Doral feeling as confident as he had ever felt going into the finals. "A lot of guys — and I'm one of them — the first couple of times they make the finals, they feel like their job is done just by getting there. Even if you finish dead last, you've got some kind of status on the Nationwide — you can make some kind of living out there if you play decent — so there's a feeling that you have a safety net.

"After a couple times, though, you don't feel that way anymore. For me especially, since I never played that well on the Nationwide and never made all that much money. The funny thing is, some people have said my game is better suited for the PGA Tour because I'm not a bomber, so I'm not that likely to make six, seven, eight birdies on a given day, and you almost have to do that to cash a big check on the Nationwide. On the PGA Tour, length sure helps, but getting it up and down matters a lot more — or so it would seem."

After five days at Doral, Brigman found himself several shots outside the number, but still with a chance to make the tour if he could go low in the last round. He played the back nine first at the Gold Course and was quite relieved when he parred the 18th hole — an island green par-four that required a nerve-wracking second shot. Several players, desperately needing either a birdie or par to have a shot at getting their cards, would find water there late in the day. With the 18th behind him, Brigman got on a roll. He wasn't even sure where he was or exactly what the number was going to be — "I'd never been that close before, so I didn't have a strong sense of what it was" — but he knew coming to his last hole that he was seven under par for the day. His parents and his girlfriend, Amy (now his wife), were walking with him, and he glanced over while walking down the eighth fairway and saw his father talking to a rules official.

"I figured he was trying to find out what the number was," he said. "I knew I was right around it."

He hit a good second shot to about six feet at the ninth, then got nervous for the first time all day. When he missed the putt, he looked over at his parents and Amy to see their reactions. "I figured if I was in good shape, they'd give me a thumbs-up or something. If I wasn't, I thought they'd look down or shake their heads. But I couldn't read them. It was nerve-wracking. When I went in to sign my card, I was kind of a wreck."

Because he had finished at the ninth hole, the scorer's tent was miles from the scoreboard, and the scorer — a volunteer — said he had no idea what the number was going to be, especially since there were a number of groups still on the course. Brigman went through his card, noting the seven circles that Jay Hobby, another Nationwide player, had made to indicate each of his birdies. He knew he hadn't made any bogeys, so the seven circles added up to a seven-under-par 65.

"I was completely whacked-out in there," he said. "I was confused, I was nervous, and I was having trouble focusing. I remember saying to the guy, 'Would you give me a check?' before I signed the card. He said, 'Yup, 65.' What I *should* have done was make the walking scorer check me, because she had been marking it down hole by hole and wasn't just reading my scorecard. The only thing I can figure is that the guy taking the scores just counted the circles, too. I signed my card, and then we had about a ten-minute van ride back to where the scoreboard was. My parents and Amy didn't know if I'd made it or not either, which was why they hadn't signaled me before I went into the scoring tent."

When they arrived at the scoreboard, his score still hadn't been posted, and it was tough to tell what the number was going to be. A few minutes later, though, his 65 went up, and a nearby television showing the Golf Channel feed had the number at 15 under par—which was exactly where the 65 had put him. He saw his name go up on the screen among those who had made it on the number. Soon after, people were telling him it was official: he was on the PGA Tour.

"I remember all sorts of crazy thoughts running through my head," Brigman said. "For a minute or two, I was kind of scared. I was thinking, 'Oh, my God, I have to go out on *that* tour and play with *those* guys?' That was kind of spooky. Then I started thinking, 'Man alive, I made the PGA Tour. How about that?' I remember a guy from Callaway came by and congratulated me and said, 'We'll be in touch. We'll work out a deal with you.' By now, it was starting to become a celebration. I was getting all sorts of congratulations from my friends, from strangers—it was just a great feeling."

It went on for about twenty minutes. By then, he and his parents and Amy were sitting on a golf cart making plans to celebrate. A golf cart marked "Rules," driven by Steve Carman, pulled up. Brigman recognized Jim Duncan, a Nationwide Tour official, sitting in the cart with Carman. He didn't know Carman by name, but he knew he was in charge of the tournament. "Jaxon, have you got a minute?" Carman said.

"I knew right away it was trouble of some kind," Brigman said. "He wasn't pulling up like that to congratulate me. I couldn't imagine what it was."

Carman was holding a scorecard. "I need you to take a look at your card for me," Carman said. "Do you remember what you made on 13?"

"Of course I do," Brigman said. "I made a three."

Carman handed the card to him. When Brigman looked at it, he began to shake. Hobby had circled his score for the 13th hole to indicate he had made a birdie, but he had written down the number 4.

The most famous moment in golf history involving a player signing for a higher score than what he actually shot came in the final round of the 1968 Masters, when Tommy Aaron (a future Masters champion) wrote down a 4 for Roberto De Vicenzo on the 17th hole when De Vicenzo actually made a birdie 3. Because he signed for the 4, De Vicenzo ended up losing by one stroke to Bob Goalby rather than being in a play-off with him. De Vicenzo, an Argentine, was quoted as saying, "What a stupid I am," perhaps the most famous self-put-down in golf history (until Phil Mickelson's "I'm an idiot" comment after his brain-lock double bogey at Winged Foot cost him the 2006 U.S. Open).

To this day, if a golfer accidentally gives another player a score higher than he made on a hole, it is called "pulling an Aaron" or "Tommy Aaroning him." None of the three men involved in the incident — De Vicenzo, Aaron, or Goalby (who had to deal with people saying he wasn't a "real" Masters champion) — ever completely got over it.

Brigman wasn't being watched by millions on TV when he looked at the scorecard Carman handed him, and there was no Masters at stake — just his livelihood and his future. Before he could find his voice, he heard his dad, looking at the card over his shoulder, say, "That's a 3. It looks like a 3 to me."

Years later, Brigman was able to laugh about his father's save attempt. "It was a nice try," he said. "But if anything, you would have had a better chance selling that it was a 5. There was no way it was a 3."

Brigman felt sick to his stomach. His first thought was that he would be disqualified for signing an incorrect scorecard. "The funny thing is, my initial reaction was, 'You just blew $25,000,'" he said, referring to the prize money the players who qualify for the tour received then at Q School. "My biggest check to that moment was $16,000. When the guy [Carman] told me I wasn't DQ'd, I just had to take the score I signed for—which meant I missed the tour by one shot—that's when I kind of came to my senses and realized, 'You idiot, forget the money. You just knocked yourself off the PGA Tour!'"

Everyone involved remembers feeling sick at that moment. Carman still shakes his head when retelling his side of the story. The person who might have felt worse than anyone was Hobby, who sought Brigman out to tell him repeatedly how sorry he was for the mistake. "I know he felt awful," Brigman said. "But it was my card and, in the end, my responsibility."

Brigman became the poster boy for how cruel the rules of golf can be. During 2000, playing on the Nationwide Tour, he became everyone's "early in the week" story at every stop on the tour. He somehow managed not to snap at anyone when he was asked to repeat the story over and over. "It wasn't their fault it happened," he said. "It was mine. And I could understand why people wanted to write about it."

He played better on the Nationwide that year, finishing 58th on the money list. In keeping with his luck, that was the last year only the top 55 on the tour were exempt from first stage. The next year, the number went to 60. He made it back through first stage and found himself tied for the last spot at second stage. Back then, ties for the last spot played off.

"It was three of us for two spots," Brigman said. "It was cold and rainy. I swear it wasn't more than 40 degrees. The two guys I was playing against were bombers. They're hitting mid-irons to the green on the play-off hole; I had my utility wood out. I make bogey from there; and I'm out. Then I find out that, unlike in the past, you no longer had conditional status on the Nationwide if you lost a play-off at second stage. They had changed that rule too. So in less than twelve months, I went from being on the PGA Tour for about twenty minutes to no status anywhere at all. It was discouraging."

One person who witnessed that play-off was Carman. "It just occurred to me then that it was unfair to ask guys to play one hole with their entire year hanging in the balance. You can get unlucky, or the conditions might favor one guy over another. If it's over four days or even 18 holes, okay. But one hole to decide an entire year of your life doesn't seem right."

So, in what might be called "the Brigman rule," all Q School play-offs were done away with beginning in 2001. Instead of a hard 20 as the number moving forward from first and second stage, it became either 18 and ties, 19 and ties, or 20 and ties, depending on the size of the field.

Since the play-off loss, Brigman has wandered through the pro golf netherworld, although his high moments have been remarkably high. In 2003 he made it through a Monday qualifier for the Texas Open and finished tied for 11th. In 2005 he did the same thing at the Byron Nelson and finished tied for 10th. "That one was a very big deal," he said. "Amy was pregnant with our first child, and I was having all sorts of doubts about my ability to make enough money to support a family. Talk about prayers being answered."

Brigman made $148,800 at the Byron Nelson, and by virtue of being in the top ten as a non–PGA Tour member, he earned a spot in Memphis two weeks later. He couldn't keep the roll going, though, missing the cut. He spent the rest of the summer trying to get ready for Q School, hoping the confidence boost he had received by playing so well against the world's best players would benefit him in the fall. Ultimately, he had an inconsistent year, playing only well enough to finish 103rd on the Nationwide money list. So it was back to first stage for the twelfth straight year. He made it through again and headed to Panama City, hoping he would make it back to the finals one more time.

"I'm thirty-five years old," he said. "I'm at the point where I know to make the kind of living I want to make to support my family by playing golf, I need to be on the PGA Tour. You can only scrape by for so long. The Nelson windfall gave me a little cushion for a while, but not forever."

Did he believe he had ever completely gotten over what happened at Doral?

He paused for a long moment. "I've thought about that a lot," he finally said. "To be honest, I think it hurts more now than it did then. Back then, I was almost nonchalant about it. I figured if I was good enough to do it once, I'd do it again. Back then, I told myself, 'Good things will come out of this.' Well, it's six years later, and I still haven't done it or even come close again, and I can't really see what good came out of it, at least not for me and my family. I'm not sure I'll be over it until the day comes when I make it to the tour. Then I'll be over it."

He shot 72–72 the first two days at Hombre Golf Club in Panama City, putting him right on the number with 36 holes to play. One good round and one okay round would clinch a spot in the finals. Of course, he had been a lot closer than that in the past, and, as everyone knew, regardless of where they were playing, a lot was bound to happen over the last two days.

IN KINGWOOD, TEXAS, there were no fewer than nine former winners on the PGA Tour playing, not to mention Brian Watts, the near British Open champion. One player who wasn't in awe of the competition was Ron Whittaker. He had too much on his mind to be awed.

Like Jaxon Brigman, Whittaker had gone to a great golf school: Wake Forest. In fact, Whittaker appeared to have been born to play at Wake and on the tour. Born in Raleigh, North Carolina, he was the nephew of Lanny Wadkins, a Wake Forest alum who went on to win twenty-one times on tour. His first golf lesson, at the age of two courtesy of Uncle Lanny, was from another Wake alum: Arnold Palmer. Whittaker grew up with golf and Wake Forest, and it only seemed natural when he was recruited by the school and enrolled in the fall of 1990. His game continued to improve in college, and by the time he graduated (unlike a lot of Wake's stars, including Palmer, Wadkins, and Curtis Strange, he *did* graduate), he had played well enough to be convinced he could be a pro. He spent 1995 playing mini-tour golf. At the end of the year, he finished tied for 37th at Q School, having made it through all three stages to land on the tour at the age of twenty-four. Life seemed pretty easy at that point. "Piece of cake," Whittaker said, smiling. "To me, it seemed a natural progression: play college golf, go through Q School, and then play on the PGA Tour for the next twenty years before you retire to your mansion and your yacht."

Things turned out not to be quite that easy. Whittaker made a measly $29,656 as a tour rookie, which put him 224th on the money list. By the end of 1996, he understood that the tour was a lot tougher than he had imagined, but he felt that he had learned a great deal and had improved as a player. "I wasn't all that upset about it," he said. "I was learning my trade: golf courses, how to compete, how to travel. I figured it was all part of the process."

He wasn't even that upset when he made it to the finals at Q School but didn't get his card back and ended up on the Nike Tour. He played reasonably well in 1997, finishing 46th on the money list, but again failed to get through finals. "That was prob-ably the first real disappointment," he said. "I'd made it once, I was now two years older, and I really thought I was good enough to get back on tour at that point. By then, though, I knew there were a lot of good players who had been up and down [between] the two tours, so I kept telling myself it wasn't a big deal."

It became a bigger deal at the end of 1998, his third full sea-son as a pro. Instead of improving his position on the Nike money list, Whittaker dropped and had to go back to the first stage of Q School. He survived that pretty easily but failed to get through second stage. That was, as the police like to say, when the trouble began.

"The first year, it was a shock to my system, but I just thought it was a fluke," he said. "I figured I'd get my confidence back for a year on mini-tours and then work my way back to where I wanted to be. I was still pretty young and single, so I wasn't panicked."

Seven years later, he wasn't as young and he wasn't single, and he and his wife, Gerritt, were trying to get pregnant. "We talked a lot this summer," he said. "Second stage had become such a wall for me that I just couldn't get through. I had played well on mini-tours, won tournaments, [and] made okay money, but if we were going to start a family, the time was probably past when I could be playing mini-tour golf for a living."

Although Gerritt never pressured him to make any sort of now-or-never decision, Whittaker had made one anyway: if he didn't at least get through second stage and back to the Nation-wide Tour, it was time to look for another job. Even if he made the Nationwide but not the PGA Tour, he might have to give some thought to quitting. But second stage was going to be the key. "I think the first couple of times you go to Q School, your nerves are kind of numb," he said. "I remember in '95, one of the guys I played with at second stage got sick on the golf course. I thought, 'Jeez, isn't that a bit of an overreaction to playing in a golf tournament—even an important one like this?" He laughed. "I can tell you now, my eleventh time through this, I understand just how the guy felt."

Whittaker knew what he was up against in Kingwood, but he wasn't daunted by the number of name players in the field. "This isn't like any other golf tournament you play," he said. "You aren't really trying to win. If you do, fine, but 19th place is just as good as first. What you're tracking during the week is where you stand in terms of the cut number, not where you stand in terms of first place."

For three days, Whittaker played steady golf at the Deerwood Course, avoiding major mistakes while understanding that the number probably wasn't going to be all that low because the weather was windy and the golf course was playing fast. If nothing else, having gone to Q School so many times had allowed him to figure out a routine he was comfortable with. "Sleeping is easy for me during Q School," he said with a smile. "Some Pepto-Bismol for my stomach after I eat and an Ambien before I go to bed, and I'm fine. Tricks of the trade, I guess."

On the last day at Kingwood, the wind blew harder than it had the first three days. Warming up on the range, Whittaker knew scores wouldn't be low. He was three under par, which at that moment put him one shot inside the number. He figured that if he could shoot even par, he would be a lock. He also knew shooting even par would be easier said than done. "The whole day was a battle," he said. "I had some birdie chances but didn't convert them." He scrambled for pars coming down the stretch but never threw in any of the big numbers that had caused him to miss at second stage in the past. "You know, you don't want to go around the last day thinking about what the number might be," he said. "I'd missed by one shot four times, and I didn't want to think in those terms. In the back of my mind, though, I was thinking it might be two under, could slip to one under."

By the time he played the 18th hole, he was three over par for the day and even for the tournament. In his heart of hearts, he felt he had played a decent round of golf. "The kind of round where you shoot 75 and you can't explain to people who weren't there that it was really a good round," he said. "I knew no one was going low, and I knew I'd hung in there. But I didn't know if it was enough. I suspected it might not be, but I didn't want to think in those terms."

When he signed his scorecard and walked over to the score-board, his heart sank. As he had suspected, no one had gone low. In fact, a lot of people had slid backward, as he had. But not enough — or so it seemed. There were still players on the course, but most of them had been far enough ahead of Whittaker that they would have to shoot very high numbers to finish at even par or worse. "I stood there adding up the numbers again and again," he said. "It was pretty clear it wasn't going to change. The number was going to be one under. I had missed by one — again."

He decided not to wait around until it was official. The sight of players who had made it through, or even the condolences of those who could understand his disappointment, was more than he could bear. He put his golf clubs in the car and drove back to the hotel where he had been staying. He called Gerritt and gave her the news. "I missed it," he said. "Probably by one shot."

He told her he was going to relax for a little while before starting the eight-hour drive back to their home in Little Rock, Arkansas. He was dreading the drive, but beyond that he was dreading what was coming at the end of the drive. A decision would have to be made. It was time to move on with his life. Part of him didn't want to. He'd been so close. He had played a good round of golf under very difficult conditions and huge pressure.

He hadn't choked. He could still play. And yet he was thirty-four, and if he and Gerritt did manage to get pregnant anytime soon, he needed a job with a steady income.

It was all rolling around in his head when the phone rang. It was Gerritt, and she sounded slightly breathless. Her brother Garrett had just called, she told him. "He was looking online at the final results," she said. "He says you made it."

Whittaker stared at the phone for an instant, then shook his head. "That's impossible," he said. "I checked the board over and over before I left."

"I know, but he says he just looked, and you're in — tied for 19th."

Whittaker didn't want to get his hopes up. He didn't have a computer with him, so he went downstairs to the hotel lobby and explained to the manager that it was urgent that he get online for just a minute. The manager found him a computer, and he went to PGATour.com, where all the Q School results were posted. His heart in his throat, he scrolled down until he found his name: T–19 at even par. Playing in the last group, Franklin Langham had shot 77 and Jason Enloe had shot 78. Both ended up at even par. Instead of 20 players finishing at one under or better, 18 had finished at one under or better. That left the six players who had finished at even par in a tie for 19th. They were all going to the finals.

Whittaker didn't know whether to laugh, cry, or yell. He called Gerritt back, screaming, "You were right! You were right! I'm in! I made it!"

Retelling the story, he shook his head and said, "Up until that minute, that might have been the happiest moment of my life."

Until about thirty seconds later. "I'm thrilled," Gerritt said. "I was going to wait until you got home to tell you this, but this is probably as good a time as any: I'm pregnant."

That was when T–19 at second stage became the *second* happiest moment of Ron Whittaker's life.

LANGHAM AND ENLOE had also let Dan Forsman, who had played one of the best rounds of the day (69), into the finals. Several of the veteran past tour winners had advanced to the finals easily, including Bill Glasson, Steve Stricker, Tom Byrum, and Brian Henninger. Several others hadn't been as lucky: Jim Gallagher Jr., the former Ryder Cup player, had missed by one shot. Glen Day, Mike Heinen, and Joel Edwards also had failed to make it, as had Brian Watts, who finished way back in a tie for 58th.

One of the late players Whittaker had thought to be out of his reach was B. J. Staten, who had reached second stage for the sixth consecutive year. "I've always played well at first stage but found a way some way, somehow to miss at second," Staten said. "I've missed by one twice and by two twice. If you don't think that will get you thinking, I don't know what will."

Staten is about as upbeat a person as you are likely to encounter. His father, Bobby Lee Staten Sr., played backup guitar for the group "Up with People" in his youth and first taught B. J. (Bobby Lee Staten Jr.) to play golf. To make it easier to demonstrate a golf swing his son could copy, the elder Staten had B. J. stand directly in front of him so B. J. could mirror the moves he made. Of course, that meant the right-handed B. J. learned to play golf left-handed. "At least," he said, "it gives me something in common with Phil Mickelson," who also learned to play lefty by mirroring his father and did everything except play golf right-handed.

B. J. also learned to play guitar growing up and had an older sister who had already recorded several successful country music songs. But golf was what he did best and enjoyed most. After paying official visits to five major golf schools, he decided to go to the University of Houston, which was close to home and to his teacher, Randy Smith, who he had started working with as a teenager. Having worked for years with Justin Leonard, Smith had a pretty good eye for talent and saw Staten as someone with tour potential. "The talent has always been there physically," he said. "The question with B. J. has always been getting him to believe in B. J."

Staten's path was like that of a lot of good, but not great, players. He had a solid college career and turned pro as soon as he graduated. In that sense he was different from a lot of college golfers, many of whom leave without degrees, especially those who aspire to turn pro. Backed financially by his father's company, he had labored on the mini-tours for five years. For many young players, getting some form of financial backing is critical because it gives them time to work on their games and try to get to the point where they can make it at least to the Nationwide Tour. Most mini-tour players are fortunate to make enough money to cover expenses. They're fortunate if they have a sponsor, but any sponsor who backs a player with the idea that he is going to get rich is probably making a mistake. Most sponsors do it because they have a connection to the player—family, friend, business partner—and want to help get him started. Frequently, though, they run out of patience.

Like Staten, Jaxon Brigman had started his postcollege career with sponsors from his hometown. "I think because they've seen you play and you're better than anyone else around, there's an assumption that it's just a matter of time until you get to the tour," Brigman said. "Of course, it isn't nearly that simple. Every town in America has someone who is pretty good—good enough to at least try to get on tour. The sponsor usually figures he'll get his investment back and maybe more in a year or two. After three or four years, it's like any investment—they start to wonder where the payback is."

Staten was lucky because his father was executive vice president of the company and because he and his family were well liked by those putting up the money. "Actually, at this point, after five years, I'm the one getting a little impatient," he said. "This past year is by far the best I've had on the mini-tours, but I need to finish the year off by getting something done at Q School."

Getting something done meant getting through second stage. After three days in Kingwood, Staten appeared to have finally accomplished that goal. He was tied for sixth place and in the second-to-last group along with longtime tour players Brian Henninger and John Engler. Players often refer to having a "good pairing" (or a bad one). By that they mean they're paired with a friend, someone they're comfortable playing with, or someone who makes a point of trying to make them feel relaxed—if that's possible at Q School.

Some players prefer to be with someone friendly and talkative. Others prefer someone who is quiet so they aren't distracted while they're working. Henninger, in particular, was a good pairing for Staten. He was friendly and, at forty-three, had reached a point in his career where he enjoyed mentoring younger players. Unlike a lot of veterans, he remembered what it was like to be young and struggling, and he also remembered older players—notably his fellow Oregonian Peter Jacobsen—who had reached out to help him in his early days on tour.

"I knew what a big day it was in his life because I remembered days like that in my life," Henninger said. "Actually, it was a big day for me, too. I wanted to get to the finals and try to improve my status [as a past champion, Henninger had a partial tour exemption already] and be full-time on tour. But I'd been through it before. I knew I could do it because I'd done it in the past. For B. J., it was different."

For 16 holes, Staten handled the pressure almost perfectly. He kept his mind off where he was trying to get by the end of the day and on the task at hand. Walking to the 17th tee, he was six under par for the tournament, which was well inside where everyone figured the cut line would be: two under par, with the outside possibility it might go up or down a shot. "I was thinking it was almost certainly going to be two," Staten said. "That left me with a huge cushion."

Which is why the decision he made on the 17th tee was completely baffling. The 17th at Deerwood is a tough par-three with water in front of the green and on the left. It was playing 217 yards that day, with a swirling wind that would blow the ball in the direction of the water on the left.

"What I needed to do was simple," Staten said. "Aim the ball to the right and play a cut. If the ball ended up right of the green, fine. Worst-case scenario, I chip it up and make bogey. Even if I three-putt somehow for double bogey, I'm still in great shape with one hole to play."

But Staten wasn't in protective mode. He was playing well, hitting the ball well, and without giving too much thought to potential consequences, he instinctively played the hole as if he had to make par. "I aimed it right of the flag and tried to cut it in," he said. "Only it cut too much, and then the wind got it."

The ball started left and then drifted left—and left. Staten watched in horror as it flew into the water. Now he had to re-tee, hitting three. "Even then, there was no reason to panic," he said. "Hit it in the middle of the green, take five if I had to, and get out of there. Six would be bad, but it wouldn't kill me. I'd still be playing 18 needing par to be 100 percent in, bogey to almost certainly be in."

Now, though, nerves were taking over. This time his swing was shaky, and the ball was headed left almost immediately. When it splashed into the water, Henninger looked at Staten.

His face was ashen. "I couldn't even look when he hit his third shot," Henninger said later. "I felt sick for him. I mean, we've all had moments where we've lost our composure, but this was stunning, because he'd been playing so well. Then all of a sudden, two bad swings, and now he's standing on the cliff—or maybe he's already over it."

Staten's legs were shaking as he teed up his third ball. "I'm not even sure how I got the club back at that point," he said. "In a way, I made one of the great pars of my life with that third ball." He just missed the green with the third tee shot, chipped it to four feet, and made the putt—for quadruple-bogey seven. At best, he figured, walking to the 18th tee, he had used up all his cushion and now needed a par. At worst, he might need a birdie.

Henninger thought about saying something encouraging but decided against it. "At a moment like that, you don't want to hear someone telling you to keep your head up," he said. "You're mad at the world, and you want to be as alone as you possibly can be."

The three players were alone as they teed off at 18, but, as is always the case on the last day, there were people waiting for them behind the green. Staten's parents had driven over from Dallas, expecting to take him out to dinner to celebrate his breakthrough. Nervous and still stunned by what had happened on 17, Staten missed the green at 18, chipped to 15 feet, and missed the par putt. He had played the last two holes in five over par after playing 70 holes in six under. His parents, who had arrived only a few minutes earlier and been told that B. J. had been six under when he'd made the turn a couple of hours earlier, went up to congratulate him after he had holed out.

"I missed," he told them, tears in his eyes. "I finished quad-bogey, and I missed."

There was nothing his parents could say. Staten walked slowly to the scoring area with Henninger and sat down to try to add up the numbers on his scorecard. "I remember my hands were shaking," he said. "I wasn't sure I was going to be able to sign my card."

Henninger, who was safely in by several shots, knew what Staten was thinking. "Do you have any idea what the number is?" Henninger asked the scorer.

"Looks like one under or even," the scorer replied casually.

Henninger looked the man right in the eye and asked him to repeat what he had just said. When he did, wanting to be sure, he asked, "So you're saying the one unders are in for sure?"

"One unders are in," the man said. "The guys at even are the ones that are shaky."

Staten was now staring at Henninger in disbelief. "It really hadn't occurred to me that the number might go back to one," he said. "I'd thought it might be three, two at worst."

"Did you hear that?" Henninger said, shouting, because he was excited for the kid. "One under is *in*. *You* are in!"

He held up his hands so Staten could high-five him—which he did—but then Staten hugged him, too, sobbing.

"I just lost it right there," Staten said. "I was completely convinced it was over, that I'd blown it, and then Brian was telling me I'd done it—finally done it. Talk about a roller coaster. I just lost my composure completely."

Henninger, an emotional type himself, had tears in his eyes as he hugged Staten. "You deserve it," he said. "You played great golf except for one hole."

Frequently at Q School, those last four words, "except for one hole," are a lament. In the case of B. J. Staten, they became a story he could tell with a relieved smile for years and years to come.

11

Endings

By the time dusk had fallen across the country on the third Saturday in November, the field for the 2005 Q School finals was set. In all, 165 players had qualified—42 through exemptions and 123 through second stage—for six rounds of golf to be played at the Orange County National Golf Center and Lodge in Winter Garden, Florida, beginning on November 30. That was the Wednesday after Thanksgiving. Many players would leave their homes the day after the holiday so they could have three or four solid days of practice on the two golf courses before the tournament began. A few would bring their families with them; most would not.

"You really have to look at it as a nine- or ten-day grind," said David Sutherland, who would turn forty in February and would be playing the finals for the seventh time. "I'll miss my kids [boys 4 and 3] every day, but this isn't something you can do as part of a family trip. You need to have your mind in shutdown mode—you shut out everything except the golf course and your golf game."

This from someone who wasn't even 100 percent sure he still wanted to be playing golf. Sutherland, whose older brother, Kevin, had become a successful and consistent player on the PGA Tour, had missed most of 2005 because of wrist surgery. David had been a solid player on tour until injuries began to take a toll on his career: shoulder surgery in 2001, a broken wrist in 2002, and then the wrist surgery in 2005.

"There's a part of me that thinks it's time to go get a job as a history teacher," he said. "Or maybe coaching and teaching, I know I'd enjoy either or both. But at second stage, when I was really in the crucible, especially on the last day, the feeling of competing again, of trying to grind my way through something that was *hard,* was intoxicating. I realized I had really missed that aspect of golf."

Sutherland, who had actually beaten his brother to the PGA Tour when he made it through the finals in 1990, had to rally on the last day of second stage in Seaside, California, to qualify. He had already decided that if he didn't make it, he would either look for a teaching job or enroll in a master's program at home in Sacramento, California. When he survived, he decided there was no point in going to the finals unless he put everything he had into trying to make it back to the tour.

"I've done the Nationwide Tour, and it's okay," he said. "But right now, I'm looking at this as PGA Tour or bust. I'm going to be forty. I've always told myself and other people I can walk away and do other things. If I don't make it, the time has probably come to call my own bluff."

Other veterans who had not made it through second stage were dealing with thoughts similar to Sutherland's. Rick Fehr had already quit the tour once and had gone back. After he missed the cut by five shots at his second stage in Beaumont, California, he was emphatically convinced he was done.

"I went out the last day knowing I needed to shoot 65 or 66 to make it," Fehr said. "That was doable if I got things rolling in the right direction. But as the holes slipped away and the putts didn't drop, I got to a point where I realized that, mathematically, I just didn't have a chance anymore. The last hour, I just wanted to get the round over and get out of there. I got in the car to drive home [five hours, to Phoenix] and waited for the tears to come. Nothing. By the time I was halfway home, I was on the phone talking to people about what I might do next and starting to feel excited about it. It was as if a burden had been lifted. If I needed any reinforcement that my time had come, I got it right there."

Fehr had been a reluctant traveler almost from the moment his first child was born in 1993. He talked often in those days about balancing his travel schedule with making time for his family. "Your kids only grow up once," he said soon after his third child was born. "I know a lot of guys out here go through this. On the one hand, you're doing something you love and making a good living. On the other hand, you're missing a lot."

Because golfers often don't begin to succeed and make serious money until their late twenties or early thirties, and because they can play longer than athletes in other sports, they frequently find themselves dealing with family issues that other athletes don't encounter. Athletes in team sports have lengthy off-seasons and play half their schedules at home. The only sport that mirrors golf in terms of length of season (endless) is tennis, and most tennis players are retired by the time they turn thirty. Tom Kite, whose three children were born during his peak years as a player, summed up the dilemma better than anyone: "When you're home, you feel as if you're missing something not being on tour," he once said. "When you're on tour, you *know* you're missing something not being at home."

Fehr was thirty-one when his first child was born, and he was just starting to make serious money. He won twice on tour during the '90s, which provided a good living for his family. In 2001 he injured his right thumb and struggled with his game. "I couldn't even practice," he said. "It just hurt too much."

When he finished out of the top 125 at the end of that year, he decided it was a sign. He had toyed with the idea of becoming a teacher, so when he was offered the chance to become the director of golf at a brand-new facility in Redmond, Washington—right near his home—he decided to take it. "It seemed ideal," he said. "I was the boss, it was a new venture, but the most important thing was that I would be home with my family. It seemed like a no-lose deal."

What he hadn't counted on was that his new bosses wanted the golf course up and running by the fall of 2002, and there was an extraordinary amount of work to be done. There were no phones in the clubhouse or the pro shop, so calls to the 800 number the club had set up for inquiries (about memberships, when the course would open, and where building materials needed to be delivered) were all routed to Fehr's cell phone.

"I was working until three o'clock in the morning most days," he said. "I was actually spending *less* time with my family than I had when I was on tour. I thought maybe when we opened it would let up, but it didn't. I remember one night I did make it home for dinner, and I fell asleep at the dinner table. I knew I had to rethink. This wasn't what I'd had in mind."

He had surgery on the thumb at the end of 2002. In the spring of 2003, he went out to hit some balls and found himself pain-free. He decided to give golf one more shot. He stayed at the club until the end of 2003 but spent a lot more time practicing than answering his cell phone. He went to Q School that year and didn't make it through second stage, but he had some status on the Nationwide Tour as a past PGA Tour winner. The world he entered in 2004 was a shock to his system.

"I honestly believe I would have been more competitive if I'd been on the PGA Tour," he said. "My game has always been about hitting fairways. On the Nationwide, you really don't have to hit fairways. The guys hit it so far and the rough most places is so forgiving, you can just go out and bomb the ball and play for birdies. That was never what I did.

"There were times I felt embarrassed because I'd be playing with some twenty-five-year-old kid, and he would consistently be 50 yards past me off the tee. I'm not exaggerating—50 yards. I'm a professional golfer, a guy who has had some success, and I could tell some of these kids were looking at me and thinking, 'What's he doing here?'"

Fehr decided to give himself two years to get back to the tour. After failing at Q School again in 2004, he started 2005 determined to have a more positive attitude and not to worry about how far anyone else was hitting the ball. His goal was simple: make the top 20 on the money list and get back to the big tour.

He never came close. Occasionally, he would make a cut, but he never finished high enough to cash any checks that he considered worthwhile or that would put him where he needed to be on the money list. By the end of the summer, he was heartily sick of everything about the Nationwide Tour.

"Maybe if you're playing well, you don't notice things as much," he said. "But week after week, you're staying in honky-tonk towns in crummy motels playing second-rate golf courses, and you can make the cut and beat two-thirds of the field and still lose money for the week.

"I think when you're young, it's part of the growing process. When you're forty-three, you're done growing. You don't need it, or you don't want it. Believe me, there is nothing romantic about going out week after week and beating your head against a wall—and losing money while you're doing it."

By summer's end, he had a clear plan about what he wanted to do next: take one last shot at Q School, and if he didn't make it all the way back to the tour, he would retire—this time for good. He had already been approached by equipment companies about being a tour rep—someone who works with the players at tournaments to make sure they have the right equipment. More appealing was the idea of working in player representation. "Not so much to make deals—there are a lot of guys who can do that," he said. "I'm more interested in the idea of mentoring players. I've been a top-30 player; I've been a struggling player. I think I've seen all sides of it. I feel like I have something to offer."

There would still be travel involved, but not the kind of grinding travel that comes with playing—especially on the Nationwide Tour. "You're out a couple, three days a week maybe, and you can pick your spots a little more," Fehr said. "Plus, I'll never slam a trunk [miss a cut] on Friday again."

The more he thought about it, the more he was convinced that this was the right plan. But he had already sent in his entry form and fee for Q School. So he decided to give himself one more week to play as hard as he possibly could and see what the results were.

He didn't play poorly, but he also never got anything going. The five-shot margin, he realized, was a pretty accurate reflection of where his golf game had been the past two years: not awful, but not nearly good enough to get him back on the PGA Tour. Two months after his Q School experience, he was ready to take a job as a player rep—"I've already got my agent uniform [a coat and tie] all picked out," he joked—and felt no tugs as a new season began. He had played exactly nine holes of golf since the end of Q School.

"I played with Loren Roberts and Vance Veazey [both tour players], and I was missing greens with short irons," he said. "I came home grumpy. I said to my wife, 'It's time to get out the dirt bike.'"

Of course, in six more years, the Champions Tour would beckon. "I won twice, but that's not enough to be fully exempt out there," Fehr said. "I hope by then I'll be really established at what I'm doing. I certainly wouldn't want to walk away from something good to go back to Q School again. I mean, enough is enough. I had my time. It's over."

FOR OTHERS, THE DECISION WASN'T as clear-cut. Jim Gallagher Jr. had missed at second stage in Kingwood by one shot. He would continue to do some TV work and play when he could as a past champion. Glen Day also had missed in Kingwood and was willing to split time between the Nationwide Tour and the PGA Tour. At forty, he wasn't close to considering himself finished with the game.

The same was true of Steve Pate, who may have been the most distinguished player to miss at second stage. Pate had six PGA Tour wins and had played on two Ryder Cup teams. He probably would have had a far more successful career if not for injuries and fluke accidents, including being injured when the car he was riding in en route to a Ryder Cup dinner in 1991 was in an accident. He was in another car accident in 1996 on his way home from playing in Phoenix and ended up with a broken hand, wrist, and cheekbone. Later that year, he tripped on a dock and broke his left wrist. "I guess you could say my biggest weakness as a player has been clumsiness," he said, laughing.

Pate made a remarkable comeback from his injuries, winning again in 1998 and then making his second Ryder Cup team in 1999 when he finished 13th on the money list. That year also included a fourth-place finish at the Masters after he birdied seven straight holes in the third round.

Early in his career, Pate had earned the nickname "Volcano" because of his temper. If the tour didn't make fines a state secret, it undoubtedly would have been Pate's record that Tiger

Woods broke when he became the most fined player in tour history fairly early in his career.

When Pate was angry, it didn't take a microphone for people to hear his profanity. At forty-four, he had a completely different demeanor and couldn't remember the last time he had been fined for on-course behavior.

"That's probably one of the reasons I don't play as well," he said in a rare serious moment. "It isn't that I don't care. I do. I want to play good golf. But I don't burn anymore the way I once did. Maybe it's because, with all I've been through, I think I'm lucky to be able to play. Hell, I must be crazy. I actually *like* Q School."

Pate first made it through Q School in 1984, a year after graduating from UCLA. "That was so long ago, they still made us do classroom stuff," he said. "It was kind of a wink-and-nod thing, because we all knew it was useless. We weren't there to be teaching pros. Still, we had to do it."

Beyond the lack of classroom time, Pate noticed one key difference when he returned to Q School in 2002. "There's no comparison in the quality of play," he said. "When I was in Q School in the '80s, second stage was pretty much a walk in the park if you could play at all. You might be playing for twenty-five spots, and there were thirty guys in the field who could actually play — if that. My first year, I think I shot 73–72–75 the first three rounds in good conditions, and I was in the top ten. Now you're playing for nineteen or twenty spots, whatever it is, and everyone out there can play. I'm sure they still get the occasional ringer at first stage, but not second. A lot of good players go home empty at second stage nowadays."

Like most of the fortysomething players still trying to compete, Pate found the distances the younger players hit the ball almost shocking. But he had learned to adapt. "Sometimes it can work to your advantage," he said. "I played with a kid at second stage last year on a really windy day who was losing his mind out there. I didn't mind hitting a five-iron from 110 yards if that was the shot. He was trying to hit nine-iron or wedge, and there was just no way. He ended up missing by a couple of shots, and he should have made it easily.

"I look at some of these kids, and I swear I think it's 1984 and I'm looking in a mirror. I'm having fun — I really am — and they can't draw a breath. That was me back then. I understand the feeling. I know now that if I don't make it through Q School, it isn't going to change my life or my career. I've had my career. Anything good from here on is a bonus."

Pate still played for one reason: he liked it. He enjoyed seeing old friends who were still playing, and he didn't mind spending time with younger players either. When he started to play the Nationwide Tour, he was taken aback at times by just how young some of the players were. "My daughter's eighteen," he said. "Sometimes I find myself playing with guys who could be dating her."

If there was one thing that bothered Pate about falling from stardom into the netherworld of "past champion," it was having to ask for — and frequently not get — sponsor exemptions. When he first failed to make it through Q School at the end of 2002, Pate figured he would be a lock to get sponsor exemptions most places as long as he asked nicely.

"I'm thinking, 'I've won six times. I've been on two Ryder Cup teams. People know who I am,'" he said. "I wrote all the letters, tried to say all the right things. I think I might have gotten four or five spots."

Pate was no doubt hurt by tournament directors' memories of him as an angry young man who frequently didn't "play the game" the way tour players are taught to play it: be kind to sponsors; be kinder to pro-am partners; say the right things about the golf course, the people running the golf tournament, and the volunteers.

"It's true, I didn't play those games," he said. "But I'm in my forties now; it's been a while since I was that guy. But I guess people have long memories."

Four years later, Pate was still writing letters asking for sponsor exemptions. "The letters are a lot shorter now," he said. "And I can't tell you the last time someone said yes."

That was why Pate was at Q School. He didn't want to have to ask anyone for favors. He just wanted to play golf. Which was why he would head back to the Nationwide Tour in 2006 without complaint. "It's competition; it's golf," he said. "That's enough for me."

AT THE OTHER END OF THE SPECTRUM from Pate, at least in terms of making a career for himself, was Ryan Gioffre.

Pate had made his first Ryder Cup team and finished sixth on the money list at the age of twenty-nine. Gioffre was thirty and still believed his best golf was ahead of him. "I've always been a late bloomer," he said. "The first year I went to first stage of Q School, I had absolutely no chance because I didn't think I had a chance. I'm not sure why I felt that way, because I'd had a good college career. Now when I go to first stage, I not only expect to get through, I'm hoping to win."

Gioffre is another in a long line of Wake Forest golfers. He and his older brother, Sean, had driven from Greensboro to Pinehurst every weekend as kids to take lessons from Ken Crowe, a well-known teaching pro. Living in North Carolina less than thirty minutes from the Wake Forest campus, Gioffre grew up wanting to play there. "I could have gotten a full ride from either North Carolina or South Carolina, but I had my heart set on Wake," he said. "I guess it's a little bit like a basketball player wanting to go to Duke or North Carolina.

So I went to Wake on a partial scholarship and worked my way up."

By his senior year, the late bloomer was an all-American, and he graduated cum laude in 1998 with a degree in sociology. He decided to turn pro not so much because there weren't other things he wanted to do, but because it seemed the right thing for an all-American golfer to do. After his bomb-out at Q School that first fall, he spent three years on the NGA/Hooters Tour, learning his profession. He learned how to travel and how to save money. And, like a lot of young players working their way up the ladder, he learned how to put together sponsorship groups to finance him until he started to make big money.

"My brother had done the same thing after he graduated from TCU, so he showed me the ropes," Gioffre said. "Eventually, I was able to put together a group of friends at home who backed me, and that made my life a lot easier."

His play improved steadily on the Hooters Tour, and he began making it through first stage at Q School. As is the case with a lot of good players, second stage became his stumbling block—until 2003. Playing second stage at the Deerwood Course, he started the final day right on the cut number and shot two under for the day. He knew that he'd beaten both players in his group and that it was unlikely that many players in contention had scored lower than he had. Still, he wondered.

"We had to walk in from the ninth hole, which was where we finished, so I had no idea what was going on," he said. "I went to the scoreboard and saw all the scores going up. I was at eight under. Everyone was saying the number was going to be six under, maybe five or seven, but no way would it be better than seven. I almost didn't want to listen. Finally, they put up the last group's scores and I stood there adding it up, and I could see six under was the number. I was almost frozen on the spot. I kept counting and re-counting to make sure I'd actually made it, that I wasn't dreaming.

"When I finally admitted to myself that I'd done it, I felt like I was taking a breath after holding it for three or four minutes. It was such a great feeling of relief to have done it and to know I didn't have to play the Hooters or mini-tours the next year."

The timing was also good because Gioffre had gotten engaged earlier that year and was getting married in May. He didn't play that well in the finals — "It was like the first time I was at first stage," he said. "I just couldn't make myself believe I was good enough to make it" — but he was on the Nationwide Tour the next year. He made the cut the week before he got married and the week after he got married, but that was it.

"Again, it was me trying to learn and to convince myself I was good enough to play out there," he said. "I had trouble with the crowds, believe it or not. You get in front of ten thousand people, you really can't hear anything. But you have ten or fifteen people in your group, you hear everything. I remember one week I was right on the cut number on Friday, and I bogeyed the 16th hole. As I was walking to the next tee, I heard a guy say to his wife, 'That boy just hurt himself bad.' I wanted to turn around and say, 'Ya think?' I think I missed six cuts by a shot. That's why I want to at least get back there and see if I can do better. I always do better with experience."

After losing his Nationwide card at the end of 2004, Gioffre went back to second stage in Houston. He didn't play especially well the first two days but got on a roll the third day. After 10 holes, he was inside the cut line and feeling confident that he was going to make it back to the finals.

Then it started to rain — hard. It rained all afternoon, and it rained again the next day and the day after that. After two full days of torrential rain, the tour officials running the qualifier decided to call it off and let the 36-hole scores stand. It would take at least another two days to dry out the golf course—if there was no more rain—and the rules said that if 36 holes had been played, the qualifier was official.

Gioffre was crushed. The 10 holes in which he had played himself back into contention didn't count, and he found himself with no status again in 2005. Rather than play the Hooters again, he played on a couple of mini-tours in North Carolina because the traveling was easier and less expensive. He had sailed through first stage again and came back to Deerwood as confident as he had ever been. "I honestly thought I was going to walk through second stage and get my PGA Tour card at finals—I felt that good," he said. "I was psyched."

On the day before the tournament began, he was hitting balls on the range and realized he couldn't see the yardage flags very clearly. "I figured my contacts were blurry," he said. He took them out, cleaned them off, and still couldn't see. Sean, who was caddying for him, suggested they go see an eye doctor that afternoon. The doctor told him he had a swollen cornea. It would be better, he guessed, in three or four days.

Gioffre didn't have three or four days. You can't apply for an extension at Q School. He had to be on the tee the next morning. He and Sean discussed whether he should withdraw. That was out of the question. He had to at least try.

"There were times when I was literally closing my left eye when I swung," he said. "That's the toughest thing about Q School. No one wants to hear excuses. I could not have felt better going in there. At first stage, I made three bogeys in four days. I went from feeling as good as I could possibly feel to as bad as I could possibly feel."

Gioffre hung in for all four days but ended up tied for 56th, way outside the cut number. He had turned thirty earlier in the year and now faced another year of mini-tour golf. "I remember when I was first on the Hooters Tour, I would look at some of the guys out there who were thirty and think, 'What are they doing? If you're thirty and you're still on the Hooters or the mini-tours, it has to be time to give it up.' Now I'm thirty, and look where I am.

"The toughest thing about this year was coming home and telling my sponsors what happened. You hate to make excuses, and saying 'I couldn't see' almost sounds silly—even if it's true. I know they'll stick with me, because they're my friends and they still believe in me.

"Still, it's difficult when a fluke thing like that forces you to basically go back to the drawing board for another year. I'm going to try to play in some Monday qualifiers on the Nationwide Tour this year. I think if I can get into some tournaments, I can play well. I still feel like I can get better."

Spoken like a true late bloomer.

12

Six Days

The PGA Tour had spent a lot of time searching for the right East Coast site for the finals. In recent years, the finals have alternated between a California site and a Florida site. For a while, the tour included Texas in the rotation, but awful weather on several occasions had led to the decision to stick with Florida and California.

The West Coast site had been locked in for years: Palm Springs, where the weather is almost always perfect and there is an abundance of golf courses. Most of the time, one of the courses at PGA West served as the host course.

Florida wasn't as simple. To begin with, the courses there are a lot more crowded than in California, and finding a resort with two good golf courses that would be willing to give up its facilities for almost two weeks—time to prepare the course, practice rounds, and then six days of play—wasn't easy.

The tour had often used the Grenelefe Golf and Tennis Resort in Haines City. It wasn't far from Orlando, but it was nonetheless a remote place to ask players to spend ten of the more intense days of their lives. Still, the two golf courses and the resort's willingness to invite the tour back made it an oft-used site. When Grenelefe went out of business in 1998, the tour went searching again. For one year it tried Doral Golf and Country Club in Miami.

Doral had plenty of golf courses, but it was so spread out and so busy and noisy that the 1999 finals there were a disaster.

"We were just another outing to them," Q School coordinator Steve Carman said. "You can't have the finals feel that way for the players."

In 2001 Carman found what he thought was the perfect spot: the Orange County National Golf Center and Lodge, in Winter Garden. Located just off route 4, just one exit past the Magic Kingdom, Orange County National was both accessible and slightly remote. Leaving route 4, a golfer drove through dozens of orange groves until spotting the sign that said "Phil Ritson Way."

Ritson, a longtime teaching pro, had brought his golf academy to the open spaces beyond Disney World and helped open two golf courses on the site: Panther Lake, named after the lake it was built around, and Crooked Cat. Both boars and bulls had once roamed in the orange groves that were cut down to build the golf courses, it was said, but none had ever been seen prowling the two courses, just the occasional Florida alligator.

Orange County National is a sprawling facility that includes a modern, low-slung clubhouse, Ritson's golf academy (complete with classrooms), a number of motel rooms that snake around the putting green and the driving range, and a huge parking lot. The golf courses are like most in central Florida: relatively wide-open, with a lot of bunkering and not much water. They are both long—for Q School finals, Panther Lake played at 7,369 yards and Crooked Cat at 7,411—and they both played a lot tougher when the wind blew, which it often did.

The average golfer pulling into the parking lot at Orange County saw what was, in effect, a golfing Wal-Mart. It had everything the average golfer could want at reasonable prices without a lot of fancy amenities or romantic vistas. During the height of the winter season, an out-of-county resident might pay $150 to play—still relatively cheap by Florida resort standards—and off-season rates could be as low as $35 (and local residents got a discount on all fees).

"It had everything we had been looking for," Carman said. "Plenty of space, rooms for the players to stay on-site if they wanted, lots of room on the practice facilities, and, because both golf courses have front nines that come back to the clubhouse, no one teeing off on number 10 of either course had to be carted out to start or carted back when they finished. It was perfect."

What's more, since Orange County National is a public facility, there are no members to get upset about not being able to use their golf courses for nine days. Most of the golfers who play there on a regular basis have plenty of other places in the Orlando area to play while the finals are taking place.

The idea to bring Q School to Orange County National came from Bruce Gerlander. He had just taken over as general manager of the two-year-old facility when he saw "the Disaster at Doral" on TV in 1999. He contacted Carman, who was intrigued but had already made a commitment to Bear Lakes Country Club in West Palm Beach for the finals in 2001.

"My thought was, we were perfect because everything here is self-contained—the golf courses, the lodging, the practice facilities," Gerlander said. "To get our name out there as the host site for a PGA Tour event could only be good for us in terms of branding. Nothing carries weight with golfers like saying you have a PGA Tour event at your facility. For us, Q School was a great fit."

Carman tested the site in 2001 and 2002 by holding second stages there. Second stage is an entirely different animal than finals, with less than half the number of players, but it gave the tour a chance to work out any bugs and to establish a force of volunteers—always key at Q School—before the finals arrived in 2003. In 2005 the tour paid $150,000 for the nine days—a relatively cheap price—and also picked up the tab for the players' food. Given that the tour made close to $500,000 in entry fees each year, that wasn't too hefty a price to pay. The tour and Orange County National already had a verbal agreement in place for 2007.

"I think it's been great for both sides," Gerlander said. "I know the tour's happy, and having the event has definitely increased our profile across the country. Imagine getting six days of advertising on national TV (Golf Channel) and being paid for it. It's the proverbial win-win."

For the players, there was no win-win. It was either win—get your PGA Tour card—or lose. The Nationwide Tour was a consolation prize but *not* the holy grail.

THE GROUP OF 165 PLAYERS who began gathering amid the orange groves of Winter Garden was at the very least an eclectic one.

There was one major champion—Larry Mize, who had finished second at the second stage in Panama City. In addition to Mize there were twenty-one players who had won at least once on the PGA Tour. There were players like Jeff Hart, who was playing in the finals for the fifteenth time, and Michael Allen, back for the twelfth time. "I just consider this my winter vacation," Allen said.

There were thirty-nine players who were in the finals for the first time. Some were just out of college—players like John Holmes, Nick Thompson, and Jeff Overton, who had represented the United States during the summer in the Walker Cup before turning pro. Others, like thirty-year-old Nick Malinowski, were amazed to be playing in the finals. Malinowski had been to the finals in 2003 and 2004—as a caddy for Kris Cox, a close friend from mini-tours. He had been a mini-tour player since turning pro after playing at the University of Texas. Like all the players in the field, Malinowski had to fill out a biographical form, since all of them would appear in either the Nationwide or the PGA Tour media guide in 2006. When Malinowski got to the question about "greatest thrill in golf," his answer was simple: "This week."

A total of sixty-five players had made it through the first two stages to reach the finals. For each of them, getting to the finals was a major achievement, since they had gone from no status at all when they started the three-stage grind in October to knowing they had a job playing golf the next year, regardless of what happened in the finals.

Although securing a spot in the top 30 and ties, which would grant the player access to the PGA Tour, was the ultimate goal for everyone teeing it up at Orange County National, a lot of players would be happy to finish in one of the next 50 spots and have full playing privileges on the Nationwide Tour. Everyone after that would have conditional status on the Nationwide — from conditional number one to conditional number seventy-five or so, with those finishing at the back of the field unlikely to get into many events early in the year.

"If you finish low, you have to hope that you'll play well when your chances come," Ryan Gioffre said, remembering his year as a conditional player. "That's the only way to get into a lot of tournaments before the end of the year."

Of course, for some players, anything short of making it to the PGA Tour would be a huge disappointment. For the forty-two players exempt into the finals, the only reason to show up was to get full access to the big tour for 2006. Most of them had either been on tour in 2005 and finished between 126th and 150th on the money list or had finished between 22nd and 36th on the Nationwide Tour. (Normally, players 21 to 35 are exempt into the finals, but because Jason Gore had been given a "battlefield promotion" to the PGA Tour for winning three Nationwide events, his third-place finish on the Nationwide money list didn't count among either the top 20 or the top 35.) In some cases, the

Nationwide players and the 126th to 150th PGA Tour players had been only two or three shots away from retaining or receiving their playing privileges without going through the six-day grind of the finals.

Perhaps no one in the field faced more pressure than Bill Haas. In a sense, that was extremely unfair. Still one of the youngest players in the finals, Haas was only twenty-three and had graduated from Wake Forest just eighteen months earlier, in the spring of 2004. But his golfing pedigree, combined with the success he had already had, made him one of the most visible players on the premises. His father was Jay Haas, a nine-time winner on tour, a two-time Ryder Cup team member, and one of the most popular players in golf. Jay had been playing successfully on tour for nearly thirty years (he made the Ryder Cup team in 2004 at age fifty) and is one of the tour's brightest, funniest, and most engaging people.

Because Jay had gone to Wake Forest with Curtis Strange and had been Strange's closest friend on tour, Haas and Strange were often compared with each other by the media. Strange was mercurial: charming one minute, angry the next. Not someone to be trifled with after a bad round, he frequently stormed straight to the range, his face red with frustration, after he had played poorly. He was also the game's best player in the late 1980s, winning seventeen tour titles while becoming the first man to win back-to-back U.S. Opens (1988 and 1989) since Ben Hogan (1950 and 1951).

In 2005 Haas received the Jim Murray award from the Golf Writers Association of America. The award, named for the late great *Los Angeles Times* columnist, is given annually to a player who has a history of being cooperative with the media. In his acceptance speech, Haas said, "I guess you could call this the 'Curtis blew us off so we'll go talk to Jay award.'"

It was a funny line, though self-deprecating, since Haas had done plenty to merit being interviewed about himself during his career. The next morning, the first day of the Masters, Haas's cell phone rang early.

"I heard you nailed me last night," Strange said.

"Nailed you good, Curtis," Haas answered.

Strange laughed. It was virtually impossible for anyone to get angry with Haas.

Jay's second son, Bill, has many of the same qualities. He has an easy smile, and even though he is often quiet when in the company of the pros he grew up around, he has a lot of confidence in his golf game—although golf wasn't always his favorite sport.

"I actually liked basketball more than I liked golf right into high school," he said. "If I hadn't been 5-4 as a freshman, it might have been my main sport instead of golf. If I'd known I was going to grow [he is now a lean 6 feet 2] I might have kept playing basketball."

He and his older brother, Jay Jr., learned the game of golf from their father. They also took lessons from Billy Harmon, their father's close friend and occasional caddy, and from their great-uncle Bob Goalby, the 1968 Masters champion. When Bill was a high school senior, he was recruited to go to Wake Forest by his uncle, Jerry Haas, who had played on tour for several years.

As it turned out, Bill was a better player than Jay Jr. Even though Bill's number one goal as a kid was to beat his brother—who was three years older than he—in everything, it became awkward when he became the Haas son whose golf everyone talked about.

"I know that was tough for Jay, and it's still tough for him at times," Bill said. "He's a very good player, but I've never sensed that he absolutely loves it. My sense has been it's something he's done because he has natural ability, and it didn't get hard for him until after he turned pro."

Jay Jr., who went to Augusta State, had played most of his professional golf on mini-tours. He hadn't signed up for Q School in 2005 because he wasn't sure if he still wanted to play golf.

Bill had great success at Wake Forest. He was an all-American as a sophomore and reached the semifinals of the U.S. Amateur, played that year at Oakland Hills Country Club outside Detroit. With his father and mother, Jan, following him around (something Jay didn't do that often, because of his schedule and not wanting his kids to feel any more heat than they already did because of their last name), Bill lost on the 18th hole to Ricky Barnes, who would go on to win the tournament the next day. If he had won that match, Bill would have qualified for the Masters, since both finalists in the U.S. Amateur are invited to Augusta. That would have made him and his father the first father-son combination to play in the Masters together. Davis Love Jr. and his son Davis III had both played, but not at the same time.

"The funny thing is, the Masters never crossed my mind until I shook hands with Ricky and it suddenly occurred to me, 'He's going to the Masters, and I'm not,'" Bill said. "The match was fun because we were both playing good golf. I tried to focus on that aspect of it."

So did his father, who was disappointed, too, but found himself enjoying being told what a fine player and nice young man his son was. "I thought I'd be a wreck out there watching," he said. "I know from talking to Jan and others that watching is harder than playing. But I actually enjoyed it."

Bill could have turned pro right then and received a boatload of money from sponsors. But he wanted to play on the Walker Cup team the next summer, and he was enjoying college. Unlike a lot of college athletes who are pushed to turn pro, he didn't need the money, so he saw no reason to rush.

He was an all-American twice more, finished second in the NCAA championships as a senior, and was voted the college golfer of the year. He also did something his father hadn't done—graduate from Wake Forest with a degree in religious studies. He chose his major because he met a professor early on whose view of religion from both a historical and a spiritual perspective fascinated him.

Once he graduated, there wasn't any doubt about where he was headed: the PGA Tour. Titleist instantly signed him to a five-year contract that would be worth at least $500,000 a year once he was on tour and about $200,000 a year if he wasn't. As a decorated college player with a famous last name, he was a natural for tournament directors when they started handing out sponsor exemptions. It seemed very possible that he might make enough money to avoid Q School completely, going the Tiger Woods/Justin Leonard route. He made six cuts in nine tournaments (earning an extra start beyond the eight sponsor exemptions he was allowed by tying for ninth at the Deutsche Bank Championship), but the $359,000 he earned was well short of the $605,000 he needed to match the money made by the 125th player on the money list—which would have given him a get-out-of-Q-School card.

Disappointing, but hardly a disaster. Going to Q School wouldn't hurt him. "Everyone says it's a rite of passage," he said. "I just looked at it as an opportunity."

It turned out to be an opportunity lost. He made it to the finals in 2004 but came up short of his PGA Tour card and headed for the Nationwide Tour. Another disappointment, but not a big deal. "I wanted to be on the big tour," he said. "I had played out there enough in '04, thanks mainly to my dad, to think I could play with those guys. But I also knew a lot of very good players had played on the Nationwide and considered it a good learning experience, so I tried to look at it that way. Plus, there were a lot of guys in my age group who were going to be playing there, so I knew it would be fun."

Bill Haas might very well have made the top 21 on the Nationwide money list, but he decided to play six PGA Tour events for which he was offered sponsor exemptions, and he played in only twenty-one Nationwide events.

"Looking back now, you can say I made a mistake," he said. "If I had played those six weeks on the Nationwide, I'd have my card right now. And if I don't make it this week, I'll probably kick myself once or twice about it. But my attitude has always been that if I'm good enough, I'm good enough. Obviously, I didn't anticipate [the Nationwide tournament in] Miami being canceled by a hurricane. I was rested for that tournament and think I would have played well."

He smiled. "When people bring that up, I like to tell them I don't think I was the person who suffered the most because of the hurricane."

Haas had taken the week before Miami off after playing six straight weeks. "I was completely burnt — toast," he said. "You play too many weeks in a row, you start to hate every hotel, you hate the people you're around, you hate everything."

When Miami was canceled, he went into the Nationwide Championship in 21st place on the money list — holding the last spot that would get him on tour. That week, perhaps for the first time in his golf career, Haas let the pressure and expectations get to him.

"I'm not sure why, but I felt as if I was going to let a lot of people down if I didn't play well enough to get my card that week," he said. "My family, my friends, my sponsors — I knew they were all expecting me to get my card. I was, too. I don't like to fail people, and I let it get to me that week."

He played decently the first two rounds, shooting 70–71, but fell to 74–75 on the weekend. He ended up tied for 24th place — three shots away from the number he needed to hang on to 21st

place. Two players passed him, and he ended up 23rd for the
year. What's more, for the first time in his life, he couldn't bring
himself to face the postround music, stalking away from a handful of writers who wanted to talk to him after his rounds on Saturday and Sunday.

"Bad week all the way around," he said, relaxing on the last
practice day before the finals began. "I played poorly; I behaved
poorly; I really didn't do anything right. I hope I learned from it.
I hope I've learned from everything that's happened in the last
year. I'm trying to take the approach here that whatever happens, happens. If I make it, it's because I'm ready for the tour. If
I don't, it's because I'm not."

He paused, took off his cap, and ran his hand through his
dark, thinning hair. "If I'm being honest with myself, though, I
want to be out there with the big boys," he said. "I've played with
them. I'm ready. I just have to earn the right to prove it."

THE LAST DAY OF NOVEMBER, the first day of the 2005
Q School finals, dawned warm and breezy. Most of the players
had already noted that almost any wind would play havoc with
their shotmaking, since there were almost no trees on the golf
course to block the gusts. A lot of them teed off in the morning
wearing jackets, with temperatures starting out in the 60s and
warming through the day.

The tour pairs players for the first two rounds, re-pairs them
for the next two rounds, and then re-pairs them again for each of
the last two rounds. Neither golf course was considered to be
noticeably easier than the other, so the first-day scores would be
a fair reflection of where players stood in the field.

The finals are a marathon. Until 1998 there was a four-round
cut, which meant that the pressure to get in gear after a bad

opening round or two ratcheted up quickly in the third round, because half the field — about 180 players in those days — would be cut after 72 holes.

In 1993 three young players trying to get their tour cards for the first time got off to poor starts and found themselves outside the cut number going into the fourth round. Jim Furyk shot 69 to make the cut on the number (two under par), as did Steve Stricker. Both went on to get their cards — Stricker easily after a fifth-round 65, Furyk on the number. The third player, David Duval, shot 67 in the fourth round and thought he had rescued himself by going from four over par to one under. But the cut slid to two under late in the day, and Duval went home.

"I can still remember standing in front of the scoreboard and watching them move that scissors [used to denote the cut line] from one under to two under and feeling sick to my stomach," Duval said. "I really thought I'd saved myself on the last few holes, and then I found myself heading down the highway.

"As disappointing as that was — and I mean it was *really* disappointing — it might have been the best break I ever got. I think playing a year on the Nike Tour was good for me. I was under the radar, I learned how to win [he won twice in '94], and when I came to the tour the next year, I was more mature and ready to handle what came next."

Furyk and Stricker were both ready for prime time in 1994. By 1996, Stricker had won twice and finished fourth on the money list. Furyk became one of the most consistent players in the game — a perennial Ryder Cupper — and won the 2003 U.S. Open. Stricker's career has been more of a roller coaster. After his big year in 1996, he switched equipment companies because he was offered a lot of money, and he struggled for years to find a driver that he could consistently hit fairways with. He fell out of the top 100 on the money list in 1997, then rebounded to finish 14th and almost win the PGA Championship in 1998. He won the Match Play championship in 2001 but continued to struggle in 2004 and 2005. In '05, he managed to get into twenty-one tournaments on his status as a past champion and as a good guy (a number of tournaments gave him sponsor exemptions) but he finished only 162nd on the money list, sending him back to second stage at the age of thirty-eight.

"It's been incredibly frustrating," he said. "I feel as if I'm fighting my swing all the time. A lot of times I don't know where the ball is going off the tee." He smiled. "Right now, it doesn't matter. I've got to figure out a way to get the ball in the hole for six days and then figure out something long-term. This isn't the time or the place to be looking for a magic swing thought."

Or maybe it was. To some degree, everyone teeing it up on that first morning was looking for some kind of magic, whether it was in his swing or in his putter or in some luck provided by the golf gods. No one really cared how he would get to the finish line as one of the anointed thirty-plus; they just wanted to get there.

"At Q School, the worst thing you can do is worry about the scoreboard every day," said Tom Byrum, another veteran past winner on tour who was playing the finals for the ninth time. "This is the ultimate grind. You put your head down and hope when you pick your head up six days later, you've played well enough to be back on tour."

He smiled. "It's all very simple when you think about it."

Of course *not* thinking about it was probably the key to their success.

BEFORE THE END OF DAY ONE, the tournament had lost its first player.

Pat Bates had thought seriously about withdrawing before he teed it up on Panther Lake that first morning. "I really didn't want to play," he said. "I think deep down, I thought it was wrong for me to play. But I had never quit anything in my life, especially in golf. I've shot 82 the first round of a tournament and kept going even though I knew I couldn't make the cut. I've always thought quitting was wrong. But when I got out there, my heart just wasn't in it. I realized that, in a way, I didn't want to make it because I would have felt guilty all next year if I had."

Bates's sense of guilt dated back to second stage in Panama City, Florida. Bates was not only a Q School veteran; he was a veteran of strange happenings in Q School. He had first played in 1991, shortly after graduating from the University of Florida. With his brother caddying for him, he shot 69 the first day. The next day, he shot 83.

"Back then, I was very long and very wild," he said. "When I started hitting it crooked, I really hit it crooked."

Thinking he was probably out of contention, Bates went back to his hotel room, planning to sulk. His brother would have none of it. "Come on," he said. "We need to go back to the golf course and figure something out."

They went. What they figured out was that Pat was long enough with his one-iron that if he hit punched one-irons off every tee and left his driver in the bag, he could play the golf course quite well. Fifteen years later at Royal Liverpool, Tiger Woods used the same strategy, hitting one driver in four days while winning the British Open. Bates isn't Woods, but he shot 70–68 the last two rounds with the driver safely tucked into his bag and made it through on the number.

At second stage that year, he was warming up before the third round on a frigid morning, hitting range balls that felt rock hard. "It isn't like on tour, where you practice with new balls," he said. "Finally, I hit a shot that went maybe 100 yards and then swerved straight left. Okay, no big deal. Next one goes 100 yards and swerves straight right. Now I know something is wrong. I looked at my driver and put my finger on it, and the entire face caved in."

In 2005, a caved-in driver wouldn't have been that big a deal at second stage. There would have been at least one equipment manufacturer's truck on-site, and at worst Bates could have borrowed a driver from one of them. In 1991, there were no trucks and no reps. Pat Burke, a longtime tour player, tried unsuccessfully to find an extra driver Bates could use.

"Essentially, I was out of luck," he said. "It wasn't as if I couldn't play without a driver. I'd done it at first stage. But this was a golf course where I needed the driver. Plus, it freaked me out."

He missed at that stage and spent two years playing in South Africa. In 1993 he made the finals for the first time, making a 50-foot putt on the last hole at second stage for birdie when he was trying to two-putt, thinking he needed par to make it on the number.

He was third on the Nike Tour money list in 1994, which put him on the big tour in 1995. He had a miserable year there, finishing 206th on the money list, and found himself back at second stage in 1996, where he lost in an eight-for-five play-off to get to the finals.

"I three-putted for bogey to knock myself out," he said. "It was just about dark by then, and I had to walk back into the clubhouse from the second green. It might have been the longest, loneliest, most depressing walk I've ever made in my life."

The sudden turn in his career surprised Bates. He had been on an up escalator through 1995, and now he was in reverse. He had even had a shot at becoming a movie star during that year on tour. One of Bates's talents is imitating other people's golf swings. He can be Jack Nicklaus one minute, Corey Pavin the next, and Jim Furyk soon after that. Gary McCord, the CBS announcer, was impressed by Bates's act. When McCord was hired as a consultant for the movie *Tin Cup,* starring Kevin Costner and Don Johnson, one of his assignments was to find a stand-in for Costner during the scenes in which he had to swing a golf club. Remembering Bates's talent, McCord called him and asked if he'd like to be in the movie.

"I asked him if I would have to cut my hair," said Bates, who has always worn his light brown hair long. "He said yes. I figured it would be worth it to be in the movie."

Sadly, his movie career was never launched. Working with McCord, Costner was able to come up with a swing that looked good enough that there was no need for a stand-in. "It wouldn't have worked for me anyway," Bates said. "They were filming in November. By then, I was back at Q School."

He pieced his career together nicely after the downer of the lost play-off, finishing 20th on the Nike list in 1997 after starting the year with only conditional status as a past champion. Ironically, his game really began to improve after he had neck surgery in 1999 to correct a condition that had bothered him since college. Following the surgery, he was never able to hit the ball as long as he once had, which forced him to learn more about the subtleties of his game. Bates's father-in-law, Doug Tewell, the very successful Champions Tour player, who was never a long hitter himself, explained to him that shorter didn't necessarily mean not as good.

"The surgery was really tough," he said. "My vertebrae [were] actually too straight, and they went in to fuse [them] in such a way that [they] would be more normal. But my spinal cord got damaged, and I woke up with no use of my left hand and unable to walk. To this day, my hand is only about 70 percent, and I can't count to three with my fingers. When I first got well enough to play again, I was freaked-out because I couldn't hit a ball more than 240 off the tee. That's when Doug talked to me about learning the game and my game better. I became a smarter, *straighter* player, and it helped."

He returned to Q School in 2000 and, sure enough, was involved in another strange incident. He was back at Bear Lakes Country Club, the scene of his initial second-stage success in 1993, and he shot even par the first day. On the second day, he was three under and probably, he guessed, in the top five for the tournament when he got to the 15th tee.

"I had four holes left, all downwind," he said. "I was looking, I thought, at a very good day."

It had rained a lot that fall, and the tees at Bear Lakes were sandy and slippery. Bates teed his ball up at 15, but as he took the club back and began his downswing, the ball began slipping off the tee.

"I don't even know for sure if I noticed it or not," he said. "Either way, I was committed to the swing, and I probably would have hurt myself if I stopped. The ball fell off the tee; I swung through and completely missed the ball. Meantime, the ball plopped into a little hole on the tee box."

Bates looked at the other players in the group for help. One of them, Mathias Gronberg, another veteran who was also back at Q School in 2005, suggested they call a rules official. "I remember Mathias saying, 'I can't imagine you can't re-tee, but we better be sure.'"

Normally, of course, if a ball falls off the tee, even if a player is addressing it at the time, he simply re-tees, since the ball isn't in play until the player has actually taken a swing at it. That, as it turned out, was Bates's problem. Mickey Bradley, a Nike Tour rules official, drove up when called and asked Bates to describe what had happened.

"Well, the rule book defines a swing as swinging through the ball with the intent of hitting it," Bradley said. "Pat, did you swing through with the intent of hitting the ball?"

"Yes, I did," Bates said.

"Pat, I'm really sorry," Bradley said. "But the ball's in play."

Already lying one and now playing out a hole, Bates ended up making double bogey. Still in shock, he bogeyed the next hole and ended up shooting even par again. "I never recovered," he said. "I missed by two shots. All the years I've played golf, watched golf, I've never seen anything like that happen—not before, not since. It's the kind of thing that you know will *only* happen at Q School. And the karma was perfect: I made double bogey, and I missed by two. That's Q School in a nutshell."

Bates not only recovered from that flukish incident, but he exploded in 2001, winning three times on what was then the Buy.com Tour to earn an instant promotion to the PGA Tour. He kept his card the next two years—finishing 123rd on the money list both times—but dropped to 168th and back to the Nationwide Tour in 2005. With his neck troubling him again (a bulging disc this time), he didn't play very well in 2005 and found himself back at second stage ("where most of my weird stuff has happened in the past") in Panama City.

He arrived feeling healthy, having worked with a chiropractor who had cracked his neck and alleviated a good deal of the pain, and began the last round in a fairly comfortable position—a couple of shots inside the cut line at three under par. That comfort level went away on the second hole when he hit his second shot into the water and made triple bogey. Then he three-putted the third hole to be four over par for the day after only three holes. Experience kicked in. He calmed himself down and holed an eight-iron at the sixth hole for an eagle to get himself back on track and back in contention. He was now, he guessed, right on the cut line.

"I just needed to play steady and confident from that point on," he said. "I didn't need to be spectacular. I just didn't need to make any more mistakes."

He parred the next four holes and hit his second shot at the 12th to 25 feet. His birdie putt was about three feet short, and he walked up to mark his ball. As he picked up the ball after putting down his coin, the ball slipped out of his hand and landed squarely on the coin.

"I saw the coin shudder," he said. "I wasn't sure if it moved a tiny bit or didn't move at all. I was confused. The guys I was playing with didn't see it happen, so I wondered if I should call for some kind of ruling. But I knew if I did, we'd back up the whole golf course waiting for someone to get there and then get the ruling. I wish now that I had just known the rule. I've never liked gray areas in the rules. I don't think I'm a fanatic or anything, but if I think it's gray, I'm usually going to lean toward penalizing myself. For some reason, at that moment, I didn't do it. I put the ball down, putted out, and kept playing."

Bates birdied 16 and 17 to remove any doubt about whether he would be going to the finals. He ended up tied for 10th place, two shots inside the number. "At the time, I was relieved that I'd come back from four over the first three holes to finish the day even and move on," he said. "But when I got home, the more I thought about what had happened, the more it bothered me."

Bates pulled out a rule book. The only reference he could find to what had happened was a notation that said if a player's coin moves "while [he is] in the process of marking his ball," there is no penalty. But was he still in the process of marking? He could find no reference in the rules to what had happened to him. He wondered if the coin had, in fact, moved. He went so far as to go on a putting green and re-create what had happened. "The coin moved seven times out of ten," he said. "I wasn't thrilled with those odds."

Although he doesn't talk about it unless asked, Bates is deeply religious and a regular attendee at the weekly Bible studies that take place on both tours. He was extremely disturbed by the notion that his desire to make it back to the finals might have overshadowed his desire to do the right thing. As soon as he arrived at Orange County National, he sought out Brian Claar, someone he had played with on both tours through the years, who had now become a rules official.

Claar had been a solid player on the tour for many years. Although he had never won, he had finished second three times and had kept his tour card for twelve consecutive years before slipping into the golf netherworld in the last few years of his career. He was a professional pilot, who frequently flew his own plane from one tournament to another. In fact, he had been in the air, flying from his home in Houston to a tournament in Tampa, on the morning of September 11, 2001.

"We were somewhere over Kentucky when I suddenly got a call from one of the towers telling me I had to land the plane immediately," Claar said. "I was with Mike Heinen [another pro who lived in Houston], and we were baffled. I asked the tower what the problem was, if there was weather ahead we didn't know about or some other problem. The guy just came back and said, 'I'm ordering you to land right *now*. Do *not* ask any more questions.' To say it freaked us out is a major understatement."

Of course, when Claar and Heinen landed, all their questions were answered as soon as they saw a TV inside the terminal.

Bates found Claar working on the setup of the golf course during one of the practice rounds. He had become a rules official three years earlier, even though he still had full status on the Nationwide Tour. "I was in the finals in 2002 and decided not to go," he said. "It was time, and I wanted to convince the rules guys I was serious about not playing anymore. They weren't going to hire me if they thought I was going to run back and try and play midway through the year."

Bates told Claar what had happened to him in Panama City. Claar gave him good news and bad news in his response. The good news was that both the rules of golf and the thick book filled with rules-based decisions always said that when in doubt, the player should be given the benefit of the doubt. So, if there was doubt in Bates's mind about whether the coin had moved, he was entitled not to call the penalty on himself.

The bad news was that although the rules did not specifically address what had happened to Bates, there was a decision based on the specific instance that Bates had been involved in. The decision said that if a player accidentally drops his ball on his coin after marking and the coin moves, he must penalize himself one shot.

Bates was crushed. He didn't know for sure that his coin had moved, but there was a good chance that it had. That meant he should have penalized himself, and by not doing so, he had signed for an incorrect score on the last day of second stage. To him, the "benefit of the doubt" notion was very shaky grounds on which to hang his hat. "At best it was gray area," he said. "Like I said, that doesn't work for me."

His instinct was to withdraw immediately. The results for second stage were now official, and nothing could be done to change them. Bates believed, based on what Claar had said, that he should have been disqualified because he had signed for a 72 in the last round when, in fact, he should have penalized himself and signed for a 73. The fact that a 73 would still have been good enough to make it to the finals was meaningless to him.

"What bothered me the most was the way I handled it at the time," he said. "I asked myself why I didn't tell someone right then, why I didn't get a ruling. I could rationalize not asking right away by saying I didn't want to hold up play, but what about when I finished? I knew, deep down, I should have checked with someone before I signed my card. Did I get carried away by the moment, by the pressure, by wanting to get through so bad? I don't honestly know. What I do know is that I don't think I could have lived with myself on tour during '06 if I felt there was [any] doubt as to whether I had gotten there fairly and squarely. I don't think I would have slept at night."

Bates decided not to make a decision while he was still upset. But during the first round, he simply couldn't focus on playing good golf. It was almost as if he wanted to play himself out of the tournament. After he finished his 81, he found rules official Jon Brendle, a good friend who also attended the tour's Bible study sessions. Bates told him he was withdrawing and why.

There may be no one on tour who is more about following the rules to a T than Brendle. He is a former pro—he and fellow rules official Mark Russell were both pros at the Disney World golf courses for several years—whose respect for the game, its traditions, and doing things the right way knows no bounds. Brendle has been known to lecture players at length for misbehaving on the golf course because he feels they damage the game when they act out in public.

Now Brendle told Bates he was being too hard on himself. "Sonny [born and bred in North Carolina, Brendle calls all good friends Sonny], you don't know if the coin moved. If you're playing by the rules, *they* say—not me, not you—the rules say you are supposed to give yourself the benefit of the doubt if you simply can't be sure."

Bates understood what Brendle was saying, and he knew that if Brendle believed he had been wrong, he would tell him. But it was all too much for him. He asked Brendle to officially withdraw him from the field and decided to pack and go home.

"It was as hard as anything I've ever done in golf," he said later. "But as soon as I did it, I started sleeping again."

On a different level, Bates's story is similar to one involving Davis Love III in 1994. Playing the second round of the Western Open, Love was paired with Tom Watson and Mike Reid. On the 13th hole, Watson asked Love to move his ball mark because it was in his line. Love moved his mark, Watson putted, and then Love putted out to finish the hole. Walking to the next tee, it occurred to Love that he couldn't remember if he had moved his ball back to the original spot. He asked Watson and Reid if they had seen him move it back, and neither was sure if he had or hadn't.

Love was torn. He honestly couldn't remember. He decided to give himself the one-shot penalty required for failing to move his ball back. As a result, he missed the cut by one shot.

At the end of the year, Love was 33rd on the money list — less than $5,000 out of 30th place. In those days, the top 30 on the money list automatically qualified for the Masters. (It is now the top 40.) If Love had made the cut at the Western, he would have made enough money to make the top 30 even if he had finished dead last. Instead, he began 1995 needing to win a tournament before April to qualify.

At one point that winter, a friend asked him how he would feel if he ended up sitting out the Masters because he had called a penalty that he might not have deserved. His answer was immediate. "How would I feel if I got in the Masters and won it and then had to wonder the rest of my life if I cheated to get in?"

The golf gods took care of Love. He won in New Orleans the week before the Masters, finished second to Ben Crenshaw, and slept soundly when it was over. Pat Bates would now sleep soundly, too. One could only hope that at some point, the golf gods would treat him as well as they had treated Love.

13

"This Isn't a Sprint"

PAT BATES'S 81 TIED FOR HIGH ROUND of the day with Mike Perez, the twenty-six-year-old younger brother of PGA Tour member Pat Perez, a talented player known more for his temper than his play, even though his play was often exemplary. In two years on the Nationwide Tour, Mike Perez had never finished higher than 35th in a tournament and had made only a little more than $8,000.

The day-one leader was forty-six-year-old Michael Allen, the man who always scheduled his vacations around appearing at Q School. Playing Panther Lake, which actually played a full stroke harder than Crooked Cat on the first day (most players said it was because of the wind), Allen shot an eight-under-par 64 to lead everyone in the field by two shots. Several other veterans were at 66: Greg Kraft, who had been plagued by injuries throughout his career; South African Gavin Coles; and Franklin Langham, who had been back and forth between the two tours for fifteen years. The only player in the 66 group who hadn't been on the tour before was Ryan Hietala, a thirty-two-year-old who had once worked on an oil rig. Hietala, who was 6 feet 5 and 230 pounds, could hit the ball for miles. He had finished 34th on the Nation-wide money list and was in the finals for the fifth time.

"Maybe I'm more relaxed because I know I have a job next

year," Hietala said, referring to the Nationwide. "I'm not protecting anything. All I can do here is improve myself by getting to the tour."

Allen was as close to laid-back as anyone could be under the circumstances. "Maybe because I've been through it so many times, I'm better at preparing," he said. "This is the only event I play in where I actually write down what I'm going to do each day: how long I'll putt, how long I'll hit balls, what time I want to get to the golf course." He smiled. "Maybe if I tried that on tour, I wouldn't have to come back here anymore."

Tom Byrum, another Q School veteran, also started well, shooting 67. "I don't even want to know where I stand until the last day," he said, sounding weary with five rounds left to play. "This isn't a sprint. You just keep your head down and see where you are at the finish."

Byrum was forty-five and had won one tournament in twenty-one years on tour, the 1989 Kemper Open. As luck would have it, that was also the year that his older brother, Curt, had his only win on tour (the Hardee's Golf Classic), making them the first pair of brothers to win on tour in the same year since Dave and Mike Hill did it in 1972. Curt had been plagued by injuries that forced him to retire by the time he turned forty. He was also at Q School, but his view was a lot more comfortable than his brother's: he was on the Golf Channel TV tower, working as an analyst.

Bill Haas started solidly, shooting a 68 that left him in a tie for ninth place. His mom, Jan, walked every step of the way with him. She and her husband, Jay, had made a deal that she would take the first three days and he would take the last three so neither of them would have to endure all six. "I think Mom probably called him from the course about a dozen times today," Bill said with a smile.

Joe Alfieri, whose late rally at Lake Jovita had left his father in tears, was in the group at 69, along with John B. Holmes, the ex–University of Kentucky player who had played on the Walker Cup team during the summer of 2005 along with two other finalists, Nick Thompson and Jeff Overton.

The name John Holmes is one that almost invariably makes anyone over the age of thirty smirk. Twenty years ago, there was a porn star named Johnny "Wad" Holmes, the nickname existing for reasons that were obvious to anyone who had seen him perform. Holmes had died of AIDS at the age of forty-three in 1988 but remained a semilegendary figure, especially since his life was the basis for the movie *Boogie Nights*.

The fact that John B. Holmes hit the ball about as far as anyone on or off the tour had led to all sorts of jokes about his "length." During an interview early in the week, Rich Lerner, the normally straitlaced Golf Channel reporter, asked Holmes, "Has anyone tried to give you a nickname yet?" All of this would lead Holmes to a new name early in 2006, J. B. Holmes, after CBS analyst Gary McCord gently suggested it would make his life easier to be known just by his initials.

THERE IS AN OLD ADAGE among tour players that one cannot win a golf tournament during the first round, but one can *lose* a golf tournament during the first round. At Q School, that wasn't really true, because there was so much time to rally from a poor start. There were twenty-eight players at three under par or better after the first round and another twenty-one who were tied at two under. If it had been day six, the tour would have awarded forty-nine cards, but everyone knew the field would spread itself out as the tournament moved on.

Garrett Willis, Mike Hulbert's caddy at Lake Jovita, was among those at 70, as were veterans Bill Glasson, Neal Lancaster, and

Esteban Toledo. Peter Tomasulo, the youngster out of the University of California who had played his way onto the Nationwide Tour during 2005, also was at 70.

Ron Whittaker, the newly expectant father, was one shot further back at 71, along with Tommy Tolles, Blaine McCallister, and many others. B. J. Staten, who had been convinced he had knocked himself out of the finals with his quadruple-bogey/bogey finish in Houston, was in the group at 72, as was Larry Mize, who had to be the most watched man in the finals.

Everyone in golf knows Larry Mize. Anyone who has paid attention to the sport for more than fifteen minutes has seen a replay of Mize's remarkable 140-foot chip-in on the 11th hole at Augusta in 1987. That shot beat Greg Norman on the second hole of a play-off when it looked as if Norman, safely on the green in two, was about to win. The fact that Norman had never won the Masters made the moment that much more significant to golf historians and fans.

Mize was twenty-eight at the time, and the shot, the replays, and the aura of being a Masters champion—who had actually grown up in Augusta and had worked a Masters scoreboard as a teenager—made him a star. He didn't win again for six years, then won twice in 1993 and almost won a second Masters in 1994 before finishing third behind José María Olazábal and Tom Lehman. Mize was a model of consistency, if not greatness. He finished sixth on the money list after his Masters victory and had four other years when he was in the top 20.

He remained exempt for twenty straight years until a horseback riding accident at the end of 2001, in which he suffered a concussion and injured his shoulder, changed the arc of his career. Since then he had struggled. He had gotten into eighteen tournaments in 2005 as a past champion and had finished 193rd on the money list. He had gone twenty-three years—from 1981 to 2004—without going to Q School. In 2004, he had gone back to second stage and missed. This year, he had easily made it through second stage, finishing second in Panama City.

"There was one embarrassing moment there," he said. "I've almost gotten used to hearing 'Mr. Mize' and 'yes sir,' because I'm forty-seven and [have] been around a while. But after the last round, Gary Christian [one of his competitors] said to me, 'Mr. Mize, if I go home without your autograph, I'll never forgive myself.' I was glad he waited until we were finished playing."

Mize had taken his fall from golfing grace with the kind of good humor that anyone who knew him would have expected. He didn't complain (Larry Mize *never* complains) or bemoan the injury that had clearly affected his game. He still rode horses, following the proverbial "get right back on" rule, and never acted as if Q School was somehow beneath him because of his status as a Masters champion. A lot of players who have won majors and then lose their status later in their careers refuse to go back to Q School, choosing instead to rely on sponsor exemptions given to them because of who they had once been.

"I've done all right with that, getting some extra tournaments," Mize said. "This year, I wrote to every tournament director where I figured not to get in off my [past champion's] number, and I got six sponsor exemptions. Next year, who knows, it might not be as many. I don't want to have to rely on it. I want to have full status and make my schedule at the start of the year without having to beg people to give me spots."

Mize remembered playing with one young player the previous year at Q School who had said to him, "Mr. Mize, it just isn't right for you to be here. You should play on tour for as long as you want to." Mize laughed, remembering his reply: "That's not the way it works in golf. If you want to keep playing, you have to earn it."

He admitted that filling out the Q School application had been difficult. "I guess I never really thought I'd have to do it again," he said. "I know there are guys who don't want to do it, and I understand why. In a perfect world, I wouldn't be here. I asked Bonnie [his wife] what she thought, and she said I should do it."

He smiled. "It's different," he said. "It's been a long time since I changed my shoes out of the trunk of my car because I don't have an assigned locker in a locker room. Golf's a humbling game. You have to accept that, or there's no point in being here. Coming here and complaining doesn't do anyone any good."

Mize knew his presence in the finals would make him a media target. He knew he would be asked to talk every day. He was fine with it. "I haven't done that much talking the last few years," he said. "Every time someone interviews me, they ask me about the chip-in and then apologize for asking again. I say, 'Don't apologize. That's one thing I'm very happy to talk about.'"

Mize sometimes wonders what his life would have been like if he had been able to win a second Masters in 1994. But he also understands how fortunate he is to have won in 1987. "To this day, winning that tournament has a positive effect on my life," he said. "It affects me financially, it affects the way people look at me, and, to some extent I think, [it affects] the way they treat me.

"For a long time, I worried about whether I was worthy of being a Masters champion. I'm not sure I completely got past that until '94, when I almost won it again. I remember being at Turnberry [the British Open] that year and thinking to myself, 'Do you need to prove that victory?' The answer was no."

He looked up and down the range and waved a club at the other players practicing around him. "I've gotten an awful lot out of the game," he said. "I still want more, but I consider myself very lucky. For this week, I'm no different than anyone else out here. I'm trying to accomplish the same thing they're trying to accomplish, and all of us know it won't be easy."

Actually, Mize wasn't exactly the same as everyone else. As

he talked, Jeff Martin, a club pro from Rhode Island, stood a few yards away hitting balls. Martin had gotten into second stage by virtue of finishing 10th at the PGA Club Professional Championship. The top 20 finishers in the event qualified for the PGA Championship and got a pass to second stage. Martin had played well at second stage and was thrilled to be in the finals, even though he knew he had almost no chance to make it to the tour. He had shot a respectable first-round 74, which left him in a tie for 118th place.

When Mize paused, Martin walked over, hand extended. "Mr. Mize, I just want to say hello," he said. "I was in the seventh grade when you chipped in. I still remember it like yesterday. It's a thrill just to be able to hit balls next to you."

Mize shook Martin's hand and thanked him for bringing up his happiest golf memory. The two men chatted—as equals, guys who had just finished the first round at Q School—for a couple of minutes.

For Mize, it was a pleasant reprise, something he had done before and would do again. For Martin, it was a moment he would tell all his friends about when he got home. Maybe he would even get a picture taken with Mize: Q School companions.

One a club pro. One a Masters champion. Peers for a week.

GIVEN THAT SEVENTY-ONE PLAYERS had broken par and ninety had shot even par or better, those who had failed to do so weren't feeling very happy with themselves. It was way too soon to panic or even be overly concerned. It just meant some extra time on the range and, perhaps, the smallest bit of self-doubt. Younger players might find a bad opening round disturbing; older ones tend to roll with it.

Brian Henninger had been to seven finals. He had gotten through one year when the last round had been washed out by rain and he was sitting on the number after five rounds. He had missed another year after shooting 65 the last day to get to what he thought was the number, only to see it go one shot lower late in the day. "I still get an empty feeling in the pit of my stomach when I think about that one," he said.

Opening with a 74 wasn't going to freak him out. "The golf course is going to give up some low rounds," Henninger said, hammering balls on the range late in the afternoon. "I'm capable of going low; I always have been. I just have to find a way to make some putts."

Henninger had played full-time or part-time on the PGA Tour since 1993. In 1992 he was the first player in the history of the Hogan Tour to win three times in the same year, but that was before the creation of the so-called battlefield promotion, which would have moved him straight to the tour.

He had won twice on tour—both times on the same golf course outside Jackson, Mississippi: in 1994 the tournament was called the Deposit Guaranty Golf Classic; in 1999 it was called the Southern Farm Bureau Classic. He had been in the two-tour netherworld for several years and had only started to come to grips with that status in 2005.

"This year was the first time I started going out of my way to shake hands with guys on the Nationwide," Henninger said. "I spent a lot of time thinking I was too good to be on that tour and there was no reason to get to know anyone, because I wasn't going to be around that much. This year it occurred to me that, like it or not, this is where I'm playing most of my golf, so I might as well try to enjoy it and get to know the guys I was playing with there.

"The interesting thing is, when you've been on the PGA Tour for a while, guys on the Nationwide are a little bit intimidated by you—not on the golf course, but in the clubhouse or on the range. They sort of wait for you to make the first move. This year

I finally started to make the first move. I'm sure it made them more comfortable, and it made me more comfortable, too."

Henninger was forty-three with three kids, but at 5 feet 8 and 150 pounds, and with a classic baby face, he might have been mistaken for someone's kid brother tagging along to watch. He went to Southern California as a tennis player and ended up walking onto the golf team. In spite of his size, he had always been an excellent ball-striker. The issue with him had been putting. When he made putts, he was as good as just about anyone. The problem was finding a way to make them consistently.

"I must have a hundred putters in my basement," he said. "I'm always fooling around, looking for one that will work. I'd probably be better off if I stuck with one and just tried to build some confidence in my putting stroke."

In 1994, on the day before the BellSouth Classic, Henninger's good friend Paul Goydos had given him a putting lesson, urging him to keep his back straighter when standing over the ball. Henninger practiced in front of the mirror in his hotel room that night and finished second to John Daly in the tournament, rolling in an eagle putt on the 72nd hole to make enough money to get himself back on tour full-time. Eleven years later, he was trying Goydos's tip again, searching for the magic of that long-ago week in Atlanta.

He would be the first to admit, however, that he wasn't the same player now that he had been then. His game wasn't all that different, but his attitude was. "I was very cocky when I first got out here," he said. "I'm not sure I respected my peers as much as I should have. I've certainly learned that lesson over the years.

"Back then, I had this hunger to prove to everyone how good I was. People would look at me and say, 'That guy's on the tour?' because I was little and looked young. Now I really don't care anymore about that stuff. I just want to enjoy doing what I do—whichever tour I do it on. I'd like to be a mentor to some of the younger players, because I've seen a lot and learned a lot. I would enjoy that.

"When B. J. [Staten] found out he had made the finals after that collapse in Houston, I was so happy for him that I almost started crying myself. I liked the fact that he cried. I think any man who can cry that way must be a pretty good guy. I'm rooting for him here. That's the funny thing: I want to do well here, obviously, but there are a bunch of other guys I'm rooting for to play well, too. Some are guys in my age group, like Steve Stricker and Grant Waite and David Sutherland—guys I've known for years. Then there are some of the young guys I've met on the Nationwide, like B. J. and Chad Collins."

He shook his head. "I'll tell you one thing: I'm glad I'm not starting out now. I don't think I could hit it far enough to compete consistently. These kids have so much more game than we did when we were young. It's almost scary.

"I think the one thing I have going for me now is that I understand this event. You can't sit around and figure out what it's going to take or worry about anyone else but yourself. A few years ago, I shot 38 under par at second and third stage combined, and I didn't make the tour. I was 25 under at second stage—won by 12 shots—and 13 under at the finals, and missed by one. Think about that: I averaged almost four under par for ten rounds of golf—averaged!—and it wasn't good enough.

"That's golf. That's Q School." He smiled. "I guess that proves why Q School is like life: there is absolutely no guarantee that it will be fair."

IF THERE WAS ONE THING that frustrated Henninger and a number of players on the first day, it was the pace of play. There is nothing on earth slower than the pace of play at Q School, with the possible exception of the time it takes to get to a human voice when calling any government office.

"Generally, the unwritten rule on tour is, if you've got a putt of 18 inches or less, you walk up and finish," Henninger said. "Here, you see guys inside a foot marking their ball. We were out there more than five and a half hours today, and we all know it's only going to get worse as the week goes on."

Rules officials can put players on the clock at Q School, especially if they lag behind the group in front of them. But groups rarely lag behind, because *everyone* plays slowly. Backups of two or even three groups on a tee are not uncommon. Stories about players losing their minds while waiting for twenty minutes to tee off, especially later in the week, are part of Q School lore.

"It's amazing the stories that come out of Q School," David Sutherland said after shooting a frustrating 76 on opening day. "I played in the British Open a few years ago, at St. Andrews no less. I think since then, maybe three people have said to me, 'What was that like?' I get asked all the time what Q School is like. I think it may have something to do with the fact that a lot of people, especially low handicappers or anyone who ever played college golf, sits back and thinks, 'I wonder how I would do.' Of course, the answer for most of them is they wouldn't make it out of first stage. But they don't really know that.

"Q School is like a brotherhood." He laughed. "In fact, it may be the one thing guys like me have on Tiger and the handful of other guys who never had to go. If you're sitting around during a rain delay in the locker room and you really want to get a good conversation going, just start telling Q School stories. Just about everyone in that room will have a story that's sad or funny or poignant or outrageous.

"It's like being initiated into a fraternity. It may not be fun at the time, but it bonds you with people in ways very few things can. It is also a complete meritocracy. You don't make it through because you have a guaranteed contract. You make it through because you play well enough—period. Look at my brother [Kevin]. He went to Q School eight times before he made it. Now he's a millionaire, because he stuck with it and because he was determined to really make it once he was out there. I remember in 1996, when we both made it, we were rooming together at La Purisima. We got back to the hotel afterward—Kevin made it on the number by holing out from the fairway at 15—and he looked at me and said, 'You realize, don't you, that we haven't done anything yet.' That may be why he's done as much as he's done.

"To me, what's neat about Q School is, it is completely up to me at this point in my life if I want to enter. No one calls me in and says I'm being cut or I'm being put on waivers. If I want to try, I can try. I'm the one who decides when it's time to quit, not anyone else."

Sutherland's presence at Q School was something of a conundrum. Part of him was ready to move on with his life. He would turn forty in February and had two young sons at home. In conversation, he appeared to be every bit as passionate—if not more passionate—about Civil War history and politics as he was about golf. He talked about getting a high school teaching job—history or English—or a coaching job. He had filled in as a cohost on a morning drive show on the all-sports radio station in Sacramento, his hometown.

He and his brother had learned the game there from their father, Bill Sutherland, an Air Force pilot who had flown F-111s. There was a nine-hole, par-three golf course right near their house outside Sacramento, and Kevin and David had paid 75 cents a day to go around and around until their father decided it was okay to take them to a real golf course.

Neither was a star in high school, and both were walk-ons at Fresno State, but they were determined to keep improving and make it to the PGA Tour. Kevin was thirty-one when he finally made it in 1995, but he had to return to Q School a year later. Both he and David made it through that year, and both were steady presences on the tour until injuries began to plague David in 2001.

Now, by his own admission, David was searching for his second act—and was well-read enough to understand that phrase—but a piece of him still wasn't quite finished with golf. He'd had both wrist and shoulder surgery in 2001 and had come back. After a second wrist surgery and seven cortisone shots, and after being told by doctors in 2005 that he'd be lucky ever to play even recreational golf again, he was back once more. He had a condition in his wrist known as synovitis, which meant that the joint was chronically inflamed.

"The doctor told me I should start thinking about finding a job," he said. "Having the wrist fused was a possibility. Even now, if I hit balls for thirty minutes, it swells. I ice it and take Advil. I know, even if I make it back to the tour, that I haven't got twenty to twenty-five tournaments in me. No way. I'd like to be able to say I retired as a member of the PGA Tour. That's one reason I'm here. If I made it back, I'd play as much as the wrist allowed, get a cortisone shot every six weeks, and take twelve to fifteen Advil a day when I was playing. That's the only way I could do it. If I make the Nationwide, I might play a little, but probably not much.

"I have to admit, though, that I was surprised at second stage by how good it felt just to be back in the heat of competition. I mean, it had been a long time since I came to the back nine on the last day of a tournament and knew I had to really grind to get what I wanted. It was work, but it felt great because I felt like I was a golfer again. That's what I told my wife when I got home. Even if I had missed by one shot, I would have walked away saying, 'So that's what real players do to compete.' I felt like a real player again."

The bonus came on the 18th hole of that final day. Like

any veteran player, Sutherland was pretty sure he knew what the number would be, and he was right on it. "I had made a 10-footer for par on 17, and I knew I couldn't make worse than par on 18 and still get in," he said. "And then I proceeded to drive it in the rough. Bayonet [the second-stage golf course at Fort Ord, California] is a tough golf course. Difficult, gnarly rough. No give. I hacked it out of there and put my third shot about 10 feet from the hole. Do-or-die putt, and I made it."

Even after he had signed his card, Sutherland wasn't certain he had made it. Nevertheless, he left the golf course to go get lunch. He called back after lunch and was told he was in. "I did that for several reasons," he said. "One, I don't like hanging around scoreboards. Two, there are going to be guys who just miss, and I don't enjoy watching them try to deal with the disappointment. And three, I'm not going to say it wasn't important — I mean, I really worked for it — but if I hadn't made it, I was going to be okay. For me, being there and being competitive was what it was about. The same thing is true this week. I'm going to give this everything I've got. I got here early to get to know the courses, and I'm ready to grind for six hours a day for six days.

"But I'm comfortable with where I am right now. I know, best case, I've got one more year left in me. I've got a wrist that makes opening the refrigerator difficult and picking up my kids with one arm impossible. I understand where I am."

He smiled. "The good news is, I feel like a golfer again — one way or the other — and I like the way that feels."

14

Cold and Wind and ... Cold

THE CONDITIONS HADN'T BEEN EASY the first day, but they had been mild enough to allow more than half the field to shoot even par or better. Things turned tougher on the second day. The weather was cold—somewhere in the 50s when the early groups teed off at 8 a.m.—and the swirling wind made it feel even colder. The more difficult conditions, combined with some players needing to play some catch-up, ratcheted up the tension just a bit for everyone.

Brian Claar was patrolling the front nine of Crooked Cat in his Rules Cart early in the morning, huddling in a Windbreaker to stay warm, when he heard someone calling his name. He was surprised to see Brian Henninger walking toward him. If Henninger had wanted a ruling, he would be standing on a specific spot. Clearly, this was something else. Claar and Henninger were friends, contemporaries who had played on tour together for a number of years. Claar was fairly certain this wasn't a social call.

"Hey, Brian," Henninger said, his normally friendly voice filled with sarcasm. "Nice setup on number one. Did you guys happen to notice we're playing in a *hurricane?*"

Claar knew exactly what Henninger was talking about, and he shuddered. The first hole at Crooked Cat was playing dead into the wind, and the tee had been moved back as far as possible, perhaps because the course had played a full shot easier than Panther Lake the day before. With the tee back and the wind up, it was almost impossible for many, if not most, players to reach the fairway, even with a good drive.

Henninger hadn't been that upset about shooting 74 on the first day, but when he walked onto the first tee to begin the second round and found the fairway virtually unreachable, his normally calm demeanor disappeared. He was even less calm when he walked off the first green with a bogey. Claar, sitting on a cart path to the left of the second fairway, was in the wrong place at the wrong time.

"My heart sank when I heard Brian," he said. "I told him I was sorry, I hadn't done the front nine setup, and he let me have it again. I knew right away it was going to be a long day. When Brian Henninger gets upset like that, you know a lot of guys are going to be upset."

There were, in fact, numerous complaints to rules officials that day about different aspects of the setup on both golf courses. Jon Brendle made the mistake of sitting down at lunch with Grant Waite, another normally mild-mannered fellow, and found himself getting an earful in between mouthfuls about a waste area on Panther Lake that Waite thought was unfair and unplayable. Waite almost never raises his voice. But he was leaning forward in his chair, his face filled with anger and frustration as he spoke. "Jon, you guys don't understand," he said. "We're out here playing for our lives."

"No you're not, Grant," Brendle said. "You are not going to die if you don't finish in the top 30 on Monday. Your family isn't going to go hungry either. I know this is important, and I know you guys are under a lot of pressure, but let's not make this bigger than it is. For *your* sake, don't make it bigger than it is."

Waite cooled off a little. "Maybe I exaggerated," he said. "But you know what I'm saying here. All we want is a fair course setup."

"And all we want to do is give it to you," Brendle answered.

The consensus among the players was that the tee at Crooked Cat number one had been a mistake. The rules officials conceded that it might have been "borderline."

"You can't let it ruin your day," Brendle said. "It wasn't as if the fairway was unreachable. I had guys tell me they reached it, so it wasn't impossible. The one thing I've learned about working this week is to not take anything guys say to me seriously. They just aren't themselves."

Brendle had heard about the mini-tirade Henninger had directed at Claar. "That's what I'm talking about," he said. "I mean, Brian Henninger yelling at people? Come on. Brian Henninger? That's a different person."

"My evil twin," Henninger said that night. "Sometimes I think you need to become your evil twin playing in this thing."

Henninger had shot 73 in the second round on a day when the average score at Crooked Cat had gone up just about one shot per round from the day before. Panther Lake, where the wind seemed a little less difficult, had scored almost exactly the same.

Clearly, another thing that had gone up was the tension level. "It's only going to get worse, I suspect," said Steve Stricker, one of the mildest-mannered men on tour under most circumstances.

Stricker had come off the course that afternoon frustrated after a second straight even-par 72. That left him smack in the middle of the field—tied with eighteen other players in 73rd place, three shots away from where the cut would have fallen if it had been day six. Forty-two players were at three under par or better, and those who were not under par knew that although the time to stop saying "plenty of golf still to be played" hadn't arrived yet, it wasn't that far off.

Stricker was angrier with himself than with the course setup. He knew that he was lucky to be as close as he was, because the golf courses, though not extremely hard, had enough danger in them that someone hitting the ball all over the place—the way Stricker was—could easily put up a high number. He had watched Ryan Hietala, one of the players in his group, go from 68 the first day to 78 the second.

"I think I made a mistake deciding to stay here," Stricker said, referring to the room right behind the putting green where he was staying for the week. "I'm starting to feel like I'm in *Groundhog Day*. I wake up every morning, eat the same breakfast in the same place, walk to the range to warm up, play, eat lunch in the same place, practice, and then go back to the room." He smiled. "I feel like I've been here my whole life."

He had been there only five days, including the practice rounds. There was no doubting that the marathon aspect of the event wore on everyone, especially when you threw in what was at stake. Jon Brendle was correct that no one's life was at stake, but the quality of the next year of their lives was hanging in the balance. Everyone knew that one blown shot—whether on the opening Wednesday or the closing Monday—could radically alter their lifestyle for twelve months, and possibly beyond.

"You just can't allow yourself to think that there can be a one-shot difference between playing for $5 million a week versus $500,000 a week," said Bob Heintz, who had been on the right side of the cut line by one shot at Lake Jovita. "If you start to think that way, you won't be able to hold a club. What's more, we all know the stories about the guys who double-bogeyed the last hole to miss by one and never got back. Or that poor guy [Jaxon Brigman] at Doral in '99.

"It's the elephant in the room all week. You go back to your room every night and sit there and say, 'I'm not thinking about it.'"

A number of players produced good bounce-back rounds on

day two. David Sutherland recovered from his god-awful 76 to shoot 69 and move to within four shots of the cut line. Nick Thompson, the young Walker Cup player from Georgia Tech who had won the first stage at the TPC Tampa Bay and then cruised through the second stage in Kingwood, had put a nervous 74 behind him and produced a 67 that put him right on the number at 141. He was smiling as he hit range balls late in the afternoon.

"I played poorly the first round at Tampa and then had a really good second round there when I had to have it," Thompson said. "I felt pretty confident I could do it here, too. Of course, doing it as opposed to thinking I could do it is pretty nice."

B. J. Staten went from 72 to 68 and was feeling a lot more relaxed at his first finals than he had felt on day one. Larry Mize also played better, going from 72 to 69. Bubba Dickerson rebounded with a solid 70 after an opening 73. "Last year, I played my way from inside the number to outside," he said. "This year, I'm trying to do the opposite."

Some players who had played well on day one went backward on the second day: Heintz went from 68 to 74; Bill Haas followed his 68 with a 72; Tom Byrum had good reason not to look at the scoreboard after following his 67 with a 73; and Tommy Tolles, after an okay 71, shot a not-so-okay 74.

The leader was still Michael Allen, who added a 68 to his 64 in the first round and led the field by a whopping six shots at 12 under par. John Holmes was one of five players tied for second after a second straight 69, and Peter Tomasulo was one shot behind that group after a confident 70–69 start.

Two players in the field were virtually guaranteed to spend the entire week with smiles on their faces. One was Jeff Martin, the club pro for whom making the finals was roughly the equivalent of playing in the last group of a major with Tiger

Woods. He was at 153, tied for 157th place and enjoying every minute of the experience.

The other player who couldn't stop smiling was Bob May. He *had* played in the last group of a major with Tiger Woods and had come within an eyelash of beating him. That was in the 2000 PGA Championship, when May shot a final-round 66, including a 15-foot birdie putt on the 18th hole to force Woods into a three-hole play-off. The two men finished at 18 under par for the championship, which at the time was the all-time lowest score (to par) ever shot in a major.

"My luck, I have the week of my life, and I'm head-to-head with the best player in the world," May said, smiling. "Still, it's a great memory. I know people were waiting for me to fold that last day, and I never did. I'll always feel good about that."

In fact, Woods had to make a six-footer of his own on top of May's birdie at the 18th to force the play-off. May went par–par–par in the play-off. Woods went birdie–par–par. "The good thing for me was that I could look back and honestly say Tiger won it," he said. "I didn't lose it, throw it away. He was just that much better than me. Doesn't exactly make me the Lone Ranger."

Everyone knows that missing at Q School by one shot changes the next year of a player's life. But the argument can be made that there is no difference in golf quite like that between first and second place in a major—especially if that player is unlikely ever to be in that position again. "You always think there will be another time," May said. "But, obviously, there's no guarantee."

In many cases, a close loss in a major proves to be a so-called journeyman player's one moment in the sun. Ed Sneed bogeyed the last three holes of the 1979 Masters, lost to Fuzzy Zoeller in a play-off, and never contended in a major again. T. C. Chen's double-hit at the 1985 U.S. Open led to his losing to Andy North by one shot and never again being a factor in an important tournament. Mike Donald lost a 19-hole play-off to Hale Irwin in the 1990 U.S. Open after leading the entire weekend and was back at Q School two years later. Jean Van de Velde led the British Open by three shots on the 72nd tee in 1999, made triple bogey, and lost to Paul Lawrie in a play-off. He also lost his playing privileges a couple of years later.

May's story wasn't that different. He had been a phenom as a kid growing up in California, qualifying for the Los Angeles Open in 1985 at the age of sixteen. He went on to Oklahoma State where he was a three-time all-American, and then scuffled to get regular work on tour after turning pro in 1991. His breakthrough year was 2000, when he made more than $1.5 million and finished 29th on the money list.

The highlight for May was that near miraculous weekend in Louisville when he matched Woods shot for shot until the very end. A week later, May was having dinner with some friends in Reno, the next tournament stop. When he asked for the check, he was told it had already been taken care of.

A man named Tim Kissinger walked over to the table and introduced himself to May. "I just wanted to say thank you for the great show you put on last week," he said. "It was good to see someone stand up to Tiger in the last round of a major."

May enjoyed the notoriety. "We all love recognition, especially for something good," he said. "I think people enjoyed seeing me play that well under that kind of pressure. I just wish I had been able to build on it."

May played decently the next year, finishing 94th on the money list, but ended up back at Q School after dropping to 138th in 2002. He started 2003 solidly, making six of his first seven cuts, and had made nearly $135,000 when he arrived at the Byron Nelson Championship in May. He had a good week and came to the 18th tee on Sunday in 35th place. As he hit his drive, he felt a pain in his back.

"At first I thought it was just a tweak," he said. "I pulled something maybe. I figured I needed some rest."

He didn't hit any balls for the next two weeks. When he tried to, figuring he would play the following week in the Memorial, the pain was worse. That was when he got worried. The next year was filled with tests and rehab and rest—everything but golf. After all the testing, the doctors finally told May that if he wanted to play golf again, he would need surgery. The spinal nerve canal in his back was too narrow—a condition he was probably born with—and all the years of swinging a golf club had pinched it so much that it needed to be opened up for him to play again.

"They said if I wasn't a golfer, it wouldn't be that big a deal," he said. "But that's what I am—a golfer. In the end, I felt I had no choice."

The surgery proved to be more difficult than the doctors had thought. It took more than three hours to complete the procedure. Before the operation, they had told May that he might need as much as four weeks of bed rest. That turned out to be wildly optimistic.

"It was ten weeks," May said. "I had to sleep in a special bed down on the floor because I couldn't get in and out of a regular bed. I had to wake my wife up to roll me over at night. It was really a miserable experience. I spent a lot of nights lying awake, thinking, 'I'm never going to play golf again. What am I going to do?'"

His misery was exacerbated by the fact that his PGA Tour health insurance didn't cover his surgery. The insurance company claimed that his back problem was a preexisting condition, and thus the company wasn't liable. The Mays have two young children and had no idea when, or if, Bob would work again. May sued the insurance company on the grounds that the back condition never would have become as serious had he not been a professional golfer. At the end of 2005, he was hoping for some kind of resolution in 2006.

In the meantime, he slowly progressed. The surgery was in April 2004. He started walking—gingerly—in midsummer and underwent extensive rehab. He couldn't start hitting golf balls again until June of 2005. "The first time I went out with a club in my hands and hit a few balls was an amazing feeling," he said. "I had honestly wondered if I would even make it that far back."

He began playing golf soon after that, but Q School was his first tournament since that day at the Byron Nelson more than two and a half years earlier, and it would be the first time since then that he had walked 18 holes. "Believe me, I thought about that as much as the actual playing," he said.

Because he had played in only seven tournaments in 2003, he would be able to play in at least fifteen tournaments—as a non-exempt player, since he had finished 138th on the money list in 2002—on a medical exemption in 2006. If he could make $353,000 in those fifteen tournaments, that money would be added to the $135,000 he had made before his injury in 2003 and give him enough money to equal the amount made by the 125th money winner, which would make him fully exempt again.

May knew all those confusing numbers by heart, but he wasn't really thinking about them when he arrived at Orange County National. He felt as if he had come home after a long trip in the wilderness. A lot of the older players knew he had been hurt, although they didn't know the extent of his injury. Some of the younger players remembered the PGA play-off and wondered where he had been. Others had no idea who he was.

"Which is fine," he said, smiling. "A couple of the guys who live near me came and saw me while I was out," he said. "John Solheim [the president of Ping] came and saw me and checked in with me constantly. But that was probably about it. Out here, you're out of sight, you're out of mind. I understand that.

"All I can say is this: I may be the only guy in history to be thrilled to be at Q School. I'm savoring every minute."

May shot 75 in the first round, but he wasn't unhappy, because the walk felt fine, his back felt fine, and his biggest complaint was his putter. He could live with that. The second day, he shot a bogey-free 69 to put himself in contention.

"I'd love to get through here and not have to worry about making the money on the medical," he said. "But I'm fine either way. I'm playing golf again. I have my college degree [in early childhood care and development], and I know if I had to, I'd find something else to do.

"But I don't want to do that. I'm a golfer. I want to play golf. I think I can honestly say there's not a guy out here this week who appreciates the chance to play more than I do. If the worst thing that happens to me is a three-putt or a bad swing, believe me, I can live with that."

ONE OF THE OTHER COMEBACK STORIES on the second day belonged to Steve Wheatcroft. He was the twenty-seven-year-old mini-tour player who had played so well on the last day at Lake Jovita and then found himself besieged by caddies who had noticed he had no caddy while he played second stage.

"There was one guy who called me every day," he said, laughing. "These guys are pretty smart. I don't know how he got my cell, but he kept calling it. I finally told him I had someone. He still called a couple more times just to make sure the guy hadn't fallen through. I told him I had a friend who was going to do it for me, but if something happened I'd call him. I can't imagine what it might be like if I somehow get through here."

Not surprisingly, Wheatcroft had played a nervous first round, shooting 77. But he had put his nerves behind him to bounce back with a 69 in the second round.

"It's still a little bit hard for me to get used to the idea that I'm actually playing here," he said. "I still catch myself staring at some of these guys, because I've seen them on TV. I've really had to work to tell myself, 'Don't just be happy you're here.' Realistically, I know I'll be happy if I leave here with full status on the Nationwide. But I know I need to go all out to try to get a spot on the tour. That has to be my attitude."

Wheatcroft was one of those unlikely golf stories. He had learned to play mostly because he grew bored on visits to his grandparents' house watching the grownups play cards. "There were clubs, so I just went out in the backyard and slapped the ball around," he said. "For a long time, my baseball swing was better than my golf swing."

His golf game was good enough in high school that he was recruited by a number of small, nonscholarship schools. "All D-3 and NAIA," he said. "Nothing D-1. But I visited Indiana, just to see the school, and fell in love with the place. I decided, one way or the other, I was going to go there."

He sent an e-mail to Indiana golf coach Sam Carmichael asking if he could walk onto the team in the fall of 1996. When he didn't hear back, he wrote Carmichael repeatedly—eleven times by his count—and still heard nothing. Since he lived in Washington, Pennsylvania, Wheatcroft decided to drive to Ohio State one weekend when Indiana was there to play in a tournament. Carmichael was apparently impressed with Wheatcroft's doggedness. He told him if he got into school, he could try out for the team as a walk-on. Wheatcroft got in and, after being redshirted for a year, ended up as the number one player on the team his last three years.

"By my last couple of years, I was starting to beat guys who were turning pro," he said. "It made me think if I could keep getting better, I might have a chance."

He played mini-tour golf after graduating, but his game didn't take off until he decided to give up the draw he had played for years and learn to hit a cut off the tee, the thought being that he would have more control over where the ball was going. He had injury woes—a broken finger and a popped disc in his neck—that slowed him down.

But in 2005 things began to come together. He made $108,000 playing the Grey Goose Gateway Tour in Florida, and, for the first time, he cruised through first stage. He played well enough at Lake Jovita that, even with his hands shaking on the 18th green, he qualified for his first finals.

Like everyone else in the field, Wheatcroft woke up on Friday morning and knew the chance to go low was going to be there for the third round. The weather had warmed considerably, and Thursday's biting wind had turned into a comfortable breeze. There was little doubt that anyone shooting even par on a day like this was going to lose ground.

The players were re-paired after the first two rounds, just as they would be in a regular tournament, the difference being that no one was cut and the pairings would stand for the next two rounds, with everyone again switching golf courses after the third round. Wheatcroft had jumped from a tie for 152nd after the first round to a tie for 105th following the second, putting him well within shouting distance of 80th (which would make him fully exempt on the Nationwide) and only five shots outside the PGA Tour cut line. Granted, there were a lot of players to climb over, but there was also a lot of golf left to play.

Wheatcroft was in the second-to-last group off the first tee at Panther Lake, meaning the conditions were just about perfect by the time he, Keoke Cotner, and Brett Bingham arrived for their 10 a.m. tee time. From the beginning, Wheatcroft felt as if he was in one of those zones golfers occasionally get to where he simply couldn't hit a bad shot. Every drive found a fairway; every iron found a green.

"It's the oldest lament in golf," he said later. "If I could have only made a few putts."

Even not making putts, his ball-striking was so good that he was three under par through 10 holes. As he made the long walk from the 10th green to the 11th tee, Wheatcroft caught himself wondering if he might be able to put up a low number and really make a move on the field.

The 11th is a par-three that can play as long as 228 yards. On this day, the rules staff had moved the tee up so the hole was playing 193 yards. Wheatcroft wasn't sure whether to hit a four- or a five-iron, but with the pin on the front right of the green and the wind apt to blow the ball to the right, he decided on the five. As soon as the ball was in the air, he knew he had hit a good shot — he just didn't know if he'd picked the right club. When he saw the ball land eight feet from the hole and begin rolling right at the flag, he heard himself shouting, "Go in! Go in!"

The ball listened. Wheatcroft saw it disappear into the hole and threw his arms into the air. At that moment, his threesome had a gallery of zero. Thus, as Steve Carman often notes, a hole in one at Q School was greeted by total silence, except for the high-fives Wheatcroft received from Cotner and Bingham and from the caddies.

Wheatcroft was now five under par for the day and, having once been five-over for the tournament on the first day, was three under for the tournament — and straddling the PGA Tour cut line. Visions of courtesy cars and corporate sponsors danced briefly in his head.

At the 12th, a long par-four, he hit a near perfect second shot to within eight feet and had a good chance to get to six under for the day. "Right then, I was just trying to stay in the moment, as they say," he said. "I told myself, 'Don't think beyond getting to six under. If you get there, then try to get to seven under.'"

He didn't get to six under on 12, missing an eminently makeable putt. As the three players walked to the 13th tee, they noticed their gallery had swelled — to one: a man Wheatcroft didn't recognize but knew instantly had to be an agent, because he was wearing a suit. No one who wasn't an agent was going to be caught dead walking the golf course in a suit on a day this hot and sunny.

"That guy an agent or something?" he casually asked the other players, both of whom were more experienced than he.

"You bet," came the answer.

At second stage, when a new face pops up, the caddies swarm. At the finals, the cache ratchets up: agents and equipment reps begin appearing.

Wheatcroft hit the 13th green in regulation — he had now hit all 13 greens — and missed another birdie putt to stay at five under for the day.

"I think I can honestly say I wasn't nervous at that point," he said later. "I was hitting the ball so well, I felt great after the hole in one. Maybe, in the back of my mind, I understood what kind of an opportunity I had. I was a little bit baffled, because usually putting is my strength."

Wheatcroft finally missed a green on the 14th, which led to his first bogey of the day. Then he bogeyed 15 before calming down to par the 16th. He was still in good shape, especially with the par-five 18th still left to play. A par and a birdie would put him in at 68 and move him past quite a few people. On the tough over-water par-three 17th, he hit his tee shot onto the green but left himself a long birdie putt. "Four putts later, I tapped in for a double bogey," he said later, forcing a smile.

Angry with himself, he bogeyed the 18th, meaning he had played the last five holes at five over par, wiping out everything he had accomplished in the first 13 holes, including the hole in one. By the time he holed out on 18, the lurking agent was nowhere in sight.

"It's frustrating," he said. "Talk about a missed opportunity. I had a chance to go *really* low today—maybe seven or eight under—and instead I finish at even, spinning my wheels."

He shook his head. "It's easy to say, 'Well, I'll get 'em tomorrow.' That's not the way the sport is. Whatever I had going today might be there tomorrow—or it might not be. There's no way to know."

On a day when Wheatcroft had thought he was going to pass at least half the field, he dropped from a tie for 105th to a tie for 111th. He walked directly from the scorer's trailer to the putting green. He didn't feel much like eating right at that moment.

IT WASN'T A COINCIDENCE that an agent showed up to stalk Wheatcroft when he made his early move on Friday. It is on Friday afternoon that agents, equipment reps, and teachers start to show up. They leave their offices on Friday, bring their cell phones with them, and head to the finals—in part to check on investments already made, in part to look for new blood (like Wheatcroft) that may pop up on the radar.

Most players who make the finals already have an agent and have some deals in place. Many deals are what are called "split" deals—if you make it to the PGA Tour, you get paid a lot more money for the next year than if you play on the Nationwide. This is due partly to the galleries you will be playing in front of if you make the PGA Tour, but more to the potential you have to show up on network TV (as opposed to the Golf Channel, which televises the Nationwide Tour).

It might be argued that no one on-site was more nervous heading into the weekend than Mac Fritz, the longtime Titleist rep who made many of the company's decisions on whom to sign and for how much. Almost two years earlier, when Bill Haas graduated from Wake Forest, Fritz had won a bidding war for him and signed him to a five-year Titleist contract that guaranteed him $200,000 a year regardless of where he played his golf and at least $500,000 a year if he made it to the PGA Tour.

Haas had been close to making the tour almost since getting out of college, but he hadn't quite made it yet. Titleist could live with one year on the Nationwide Tour—a lot of young players go through that—but a second year out there was almost unthinkable for Fritz and, more important, for his boss, Wally Uihlein. They *wanted* him on the PGA Tour, even though it cost them $300,000 more a year, because the payback of the added exposure would more than compensate for the extra money spent up front.

Haas had started well, with a solid first-round 68, but the next two rounds, 72–73, had not been as good. He had dropped into a tie for 48th place at three under par, two shots outside the PGA tour cut number, which was now at five under, with a total of thirty-five players at five under or better.

Jay Haas would arrive the next day to take over as the designated parent for the rest of the tournament. No doubt he would be nervous watching his son play—almost as nervous, perhaps, as Mac Fritz.

THE SCORES WERE, AS EXPECTED, lower on Friday in the relatively benign conditions. Both golf courses played to scoring averages that were under par, and no fewer than forty-two players broke 70. Michael Allen wasn't one of them, shooting 71, but he still had a three-shot lead on the rest of the field.

The low round of the day was produced by Joe Alfieri, the mini-tour player from Tampa who had come through with a 68 on the last day at Lake Jovita. Alfieri shot 64, the kind of number

Steve Wheatcroft had thought himself capable of at one point during the day, and made the jump from a tie for 54th to a tie for 5th.

It was also a good day for the '06 Walker Cup team: John Holmes shot his third straight round in the 60s (68) and was tied for second place at 10 under par; Jeff Overton shot 69 and was two shots farther back; and Nick Thompson also shot 69 to move up to a tie for 19th at six under par.

A number of the veteran players appeared to be stuck in neutral. Steve Stricker and Dan Forsman both added 73s to their 72–72 starts and headed for the range looking for something to get going. Bob May couldn't continue the momentum after his 69 and also shot 73, the same score produced by David Sutherland. Brian Henninger might have been the most frustrated of the veterans after shooting a 71 that he was convinced should have been three or four strokes better.

"I'm sure there are fifty guys saying exactly the same thing tonight," Henninger said. "The golf courses were there to be taken today, and a lot of guys took advantage. Those of us who didn't have to feel like we missed a big chance. The days are starting to run out for those of us who are behind. You can only say 'Tomorrow is the day' for so long before there aren't any tomorrows left."

One player who was feeling no frustration and not worrying about time running out was Peter Tomasulo. He had played steady golf for three days — 70–70–69 — not spectacular, but good enough to put him inside the cut number, with no reason to believe he wasn't going to play even better the last three rounds.

Getting better had been Tomasulo's history as a golfer, dating back to his boyhood, when he first played the game with his three older brothers and his dad, Joe, a pathologist at Long Beach (California) Memorial Medical Center. Joe Tomasulo was never a great player, about a 13 handicapper, but he loved to play, and he taught his sons to love golf, too.

"He was a very laid-back guy," Peter said. "About the only time I saw him angry [was] when [my brother] Nick and I would get upset on the golf course or with each other—which happened. We were both pretty hot-tempered and competitive. When we did lose it, that was the end of the day for us. I can remember some long walks back to the clubhouse after I'd lost it. Dad just wouldn't tolerate that kind of behavior."

Nick and Peter were the two brothers who got truly hooked on the sport. Peter was also a gifted soccer player, playing both sports through high school. He was a good enough winger to be recruited by colleges for soccer as well as for golf. He was also a good student—something expected of all six Tomasulo children—with a solid grade point average and a combined SAT score of 1,350. A lot of his drive, both in the classroom and in sports, came from one thing: he wanted to make his dad proud.

"He never pushed any of us—neither of my parents did," he said. "That's why he would get upset when Nick and I lost our tempers. His attitude was, if you couldn't enjoy yourself on the golf course, you shouldn't be on the golf course."

During Peter's junior year in high school, Joe Tomasulo started to feel sick. The doctors ran a battery of tests. The results were shocking: Never a smoker, he had lung cancer.

"I remember being very scared when he told us," Peter said. "He went through all sorts of treatment—chemo, radiation, some experimental stuff at UCLA. He and my mom didn't really talk to us that much about what was happening, but we could see it was bad."

None of the treatments helped. Just before Christmas in 1998, during Peter's senior year of high school, Joe died. Seven years later, Peter readily admitted that he thought about his father every day.

"I've tried to use his absence to make me better at what I do," he said. "I always wanted him to be proud of me, and now I feel even more strongly that way. I was lucky there were other people to push me and help me along the way, but I definitely feel his absence all the time. I'd like for him to see what I've done."

Peter didn't think that he was good enough to be recruited by a big-time golf school. But a friend of his named Han Lee, who was on the team at the University of California, Berkeley, convinced Steve Desimone, the golf coach there, to take a look at the slender kid with the determined face. Based on Lee's recommendation, Tomasulo's attitude, and his grades and SAT scores, Desimone offered him a partial scholarship (books only), which he quickly accepted.

In his first college tournament, Tomasulo finished fifth, which shocked him and his coach. By the end of his freshman year, he made honorable mention Pacific-10. During the next summer, he first thought he might have a chance to be a pro when he qualified for the Long Beach Open as an amateur and found himself in the last group after two days.

"I was surprised to be there," he said. "A lot of guys who have played on the tour play in that event every year. I was nineteen years old, and here I was competing with guys who were a lot better than the college players I'd been playing against."

He hung in through the weekend and finished fourth. (Doug Garwood, who won the tournament, landed on the PGA Tour in 2005.) From that point forward, Tomasulo was focused on turning pro when he graduated from college. He was a first-team all-American as a senior, then decided to remain amateur through the summer of 2004 to represent the United States in a team match against Japan and to play in the U.S. Amateur.

"It was at Winged Foot, and I really wanted to play there," Tomasulo said. "Plus, I know that doing well in the Amateur gets you noticed by equipment companies and sponsors, and I thought it was a great chance to get myself noticed."

He laughed. "There was just one problem. I was awful. It was the worst tournament I played in three years. I just tried too hard, which rarely works well in golf. I wanted to go out with a bang as an amateur, and I wanted to get people's attention. Instead, I just went out."

Tomasulo failed to survive the 36 holes of stroke play that led to sixty-four players advancing to match play. He turned pro after the tournament was over, but did so without any of the sponsor endorsements he had hoped for.

He went to first stage at PGA West in Palm Springs and promptly shot 78 the first round. "I was clueless about the whole thing," he said, shaking his head. "I had serious doubts about whether I belonged, and I was shaking with nerves at the start. Everyone who had been through it told me, 'Just don't make any big mistakes.' So I tripled the fifth hole. I really thought I'd shot myself out of the thing on the first day."

He was fortunate that the conditions were tough—lots of wind—and the scores high. The next day, under similar conditions, he shot one under par and passed a lot of people. When the week was over, he had made it through—on the number.

"Big confidence boost," he said. "The problem was, because I was one of the last guys in, I didn't get to go to second stage where I wanted to in California."

Instead, he was sent to Kingwood, Texas, where the golf course had been saturated with so much rain that the rules officials were forced to play three holes from the 150-yard markers to the greens because the rest of the fairways were under water. That made the course into a par-68 and left the players feeling as if they were in some kind of miniature golf event. The only thing lacking was a windmill.

"I shot one under the first day, and all my buddies back home were saying, 'Hey, 67, great score,'" Tomasulo said. "And I had to tell them it wasn't that great. The next day, I shot three or four over, and that *really* wasn't great."

He thought he had rallied on the third day when he posted an early 63 (five under), only to watch helplessly as another round of storms swept in and drowned the course completely, forcing officials to call off the rest of the tournament and declare the 36-hole scores final.

"That left me out," Tomasulo said. "Now I had to figure out where to play in '05."

The easiest route would have been a mini-tour; California is rife with them. But an old college friend, Tim Hewitt, who had gone to work for TaylorMade, recommended that he try to qualify for the Canadian Tour, even though the money wasn't as good as some mini-tours or the Hooters Tour. Hewitt told Tomasulo that most of the Canadian events were played on good golf courses that were set up to be difficult, which would be good experience for him. What's more, the travel had the feel of a real golf tour, which also would help him down the road.

Before he went to the Canadian Q School in Texas in February, Tomasulo qualified for the AT&T Pebble Beach Pro-Am. (The players call this "four-spotting," since there are four spots available during a Monday qualifier prior to every tour event. They also call it "Mondaying," as in "I Mondayed at Pebble Beach.") He made the cut and played on Sunday with Steve Pate, Matt Kuchar, and Jason Bohn — all experienced PGA Tour players.

"We teed off on the 10th, which is a tough hole under any conditions," Tomasulo said. "It was early in the morning, and the wind was blowing. All three guys made birdie. As we walked to the next tee, Jamie [Mulligan, his teacher in Long Beach, who was caddying for him] said to me, 'Welcome to the NFL, kid.'"

Tomasulo didn't shrink from the big-league experience, finishing 50th. He tied for first in the Canadian Q School and was third on the Canadian money list when he Mondayed for a Nationwide event in Wisconsin. He took a week off from the Canadian tour to win the Long Beach Open, beating his pal John Merrick down the stretch, and then got into the Alberta Classic on the Nationwide Tour because of his ranking on the Canadian money list. He shot 61 in the second round and held on down the stretch to win by a stroke.

Suddenly, he had gone from no place to play at the beginning of the year to a full exemption on the Nationwide Tour. "It all happened so fast," he said. "I almost wasn't paying attention to what was going on. I was just playing really good golf, having a good time, and starting to make some money."

He got into his second PGA Tour event of the year at the Canadian Open and finished tied for 24th. By the end of the Nationwide season, even playing in only nine events, he was 35th on the money list.

"Getting into the top 35 was a big deal," he said. "Instead of going to second stage and trying to grind through it, I got invited to the Callaway event and had four days that was nothing but fun."

The Callaway event, a year-ending exhibition event, is held at Pebble Beach—which was where Tomasulo had started his year ten months earlier. He had come a long way to return to the same place. A month later, he arrived in Florida full of confidence, convinced that the finals were just another step toward the spot on the 2006 PGA Tour he was destined to fill.

The only seed of doubt he had was his putting. Since the Miami tournament had been canceled because of Hurricane Wilma, he hadn't putted on the Bermuda grass greens prevalent in Florida—and at Orange County National—all year. Bermuda greens feel different than bent grass greens, especially to pros who notice subtleties that other golfers don't. Still, he arrived early, spent a lot of time on the putting green, and teed it up on Wednesday not even thinking about what the number might be. Whatever the number was, he was convinced that he would be inside it. After three days, sitting two shots inside the cut line, he felt exactly the same way. His swing felt great, and he was feeling a little more comfortable on the greens each day. It would be fun, he thought, to open the season at the Sony Open in Hawaii—a long way from the qualifier for the Canadian Tour in Texas.

THREE MORE PLAYERS DROPPED OUT of the tournament after the third round: Tom Scherrer, Jim Carter, and Joe Daley. Not coincidentally, all three were near the bottom of the field, and all three already had some status for 2006. Scherrer was a past champion on the PGA Tour and had finished 22nd on the Nationwide list in 2005—one spot from reclaiming a place on the big tour. Carter was a part-time golfer at the age of forty-four and still retained his status because he had won on the PGA Tour. Daley had finished 24th on the Nationwide list in 2005, so he would have full status there in 2006. He was 13 over par and had, according to the tour, reaggravated a neck injury.

Daley, of course, would always have an unfortunate place in Q School lore because of his two-foot putt on the 17th hole at PGA West in 2000, which somehow bounced out of the cup. Two days later, he missed making it back to the tour by one shot. Now he was forty-five. An unusual golf story, he had quit his job as a credit manager at the age of thirty-two to take a shot at making it to the tour. He had made it to the PGA Tour for two years in the late '90s and had been a solid Nationwide player since then.

The end of the third day is when players begin to pay attention to where they are on the leader board. Those at the top claim they have no idea where they are, but they do. Everyone makes a mental note of where the cut line is and begins to calculate where it might fall at the finish. Three days in, the number was five under. The weather report for the next three days was hot and breezy, which meant that the number was likely to fall somewhere between 10 and 12 under: double the five under, take off another stroke a day if the conditions remain relatively calm, and you get 13 under.

"But you have to take into account the choke factor," said David Sutherland as he stared at the scores on Friday afternoon, as if doing so might change his 73–218 (two over par, tied for 111th) into a better number. "Monday afternoon, there will be guys who are going to have trouble drawing the club back because they'll know they're close to the number and they're scared to death."

He smiled. "Boy, would I love to be one of those guys."

15

Beginning of the End

EARLY THE NEXT MORNING, Hiroshi Matsuo sat inside the clubhouse relaxing before he went out to the range to warm up. His relatively late tee time — 9:40 on Crooked Cat — had been pushed back even further because a frost delay had moved the first tee times from 8 to 8:30.

"Right now is when this tournament really starts to be a grind for everyone," he said. "We're all conditioned to play four rounds of tournament golf. Today we're playing the fourth round, but we've still got two days to go when we're done. And you can make the argument that you need to be at your freshest and best on the sixth day, because that's when everything is ultimately decided."

Matsuo was in that large group of players who knew the time to say "There's plenty of time" had passed. At two over par with 54 holes to play, he wasn't by any means out of contention for a PGA Tour card, sitting seven shots outside the number. But he also knew that he probably needed to go low at least twice to have a chance.

"There's a part of you that says you can't change your mindset — the goal is a PGA Tour card," he said. "I look at the younger players out here, how prepared and serious they are, and I wonder sometimes what kind of player I'd have become if I'd been that prepared coming out of college eleven years ago. Who knows? Maybe I'd have burned out if I'd taken that approach, and I wouldn't be playing now.

"I know the younger guys who are sitting where I am are all thinking they're going to shoot 65 today. I would certainly *like* to shoot 65 today, but realistically, I have to start thinking that, at worst, I want to be totally exempt on the Nationwide. For me, that would be a step in the right direction, because this time I'd be ready, I think, to handle the travel and the life. The first time [in 2000], I wasn't ready for any of it."

Matsuo has had what would best be described as a love-hate relationship with golf for as long as he can remember. When he was a child, his father, who immigrated to the United States after attending college in Japan, was an assistant pro at Westchester Country Club. Since his mother also worked and the family couldn't afford a babysitter, young Hiroshi began going to the golf course with his father on a regular basis before he was three.

Later, when the family moved to Florida, Matsuo played baseball, football, and golf before figuring out that golf was his best route to college — which turned out to be Auburn. "I spent a lot more time working on enjoying myself than on my golf in college," he said. "When I graduated, I really didn't have any particular desire to try the tour. I played some mini-tour golf, had no luck at Q School, and decided in 1996 it was time to move on. For one thing, I didn't think I was good enough. For another, I had my father's restaurant business as a fallback."

It wasn't until he met Olin Browne, the longtime touring pro, during an outing at Bear Lakes (Matsuo's home course), that he even started to think about giving pro golf another shot. "Olin and I hit it off right away," he said. "We became friends, stayed in touch. In the fall of '99, he called me and said, 'Where are you going for first stage?' I hadn't even given it any thought. He said to me, 'Is the dream still there — to play on the PGA Tour?' I thought about it, and the answer was yes. On the other hand, I was making pretty good money doing what I was doing."

Matsuo decided to talk to his wife, Tammy, to see what she thought. Given that she was about to have their first child, her opinion was important. "She just said, 'Go for it. You need to find out if this is in your system or out of your system.' So I signed up and decided to give it one more shot."

That shot had now lasted six years. He got through first stage that year by birdieing the last two holes to make it on the number, then did the exact same thing to make it through second stage. He played well at Doral in the finals but came up two shots shy of making the PGA Tour. That left him fully exempt on the Nationwide. He didn't play poorly there—his highest finish was a T–4 at Odessa—but the travel, especially with an infant either in tow or at home with her father missing her, was difficult. Still, he had shown enough potential that he wanted to keep trying.

"The next few years were frustrating," he said. "I just couldn't get through second stage. It didn't matter how I played. If I played well, I missed by one or two. If I played poorly, I missed by one or two."

The only good news was that he was making a decent living on mini-tours. Two years in a row, he was the leading money winner on the Gateway Tour in Florida. He even qualified for the 2003 U.S. Open, again giving him hope that he could play with the big boys. By 2005 he was thinking it was time to rethink—again. He turned thirty-six in June. He had worked hard to get himself into better shape than he had been ten years earlier.

"Lake Jovita was huge for me," Matsuo said. "That first time, in '99, when I made it through second stage, I wasn't even thinking about what a big deal it was. Now it had become the biggest deal. I was lucky that I built enough cushion the first three days that all I had to do the last day was stay out of harm's way."

Often players who have struggled to get out of second stage find it difficult to peak again for finals. Matsuo appeared to be having that problem. "I don't want to sit here and think I've already done my job just being here," he said. "But I wouldn't be human, I don't think, if the thought hadn't crossed my mind. I just need to go out today and make as many birdies as I can and see where that puts me."

Ron Whittaker had arrived at Orange County National under very similar circumstances — only more so. "Hey, I was retired for about an hour, remember?" he said, thinking back to the day at second stage when he believed he had missed the cut by one shot. Whittaker had gone seven years without making it to the finals after spending 1996 on the PGA Tour. Having turned thirty-four in August, he had told his wife before starting Q School that if he couldn't make it out of second stage this time, he needed to think about putting golf in the rearview mirror.

Now, given a last-second reprieve at second stage, he appeared completely relaxed playing the finals for the first time since 1997. "I've still got my Ambien and Pepto-Bismol," he joked.

He had started slowly, shooting 71–73 the first two rounds, but a 67 on the third day had vaulted him from way back to on the number and given him a shot of adrenaline and confidence. "On the one hand, you can say I'm playing with house money here," he said. "But the way I'm playing, the way I'm hitting the ball, the way I feel mentally, it would be foolish not to be going after the big tour card. I know I'm good enough. I was good enough ten years ago, and I'm a better player now than I was then." He smiled. "Of course, back then I was just a kid, and my nerves were kind of numb. They definitely aren't numb anymore. That last day in Houston, I felt sick the whole day because of what was at stake. I'm not feeling that way right now, but we'll

see how it goes Monday coming down the stretch if I'm in position to get back to the tour. That will be the test."

ONCE THE FROST BURNED OFF on Saturday, the temperature
warmed quickly. The conditions were similar to those on Friday:
hot, with less breeze than on any of the first four days. "They're
going to have to go low to keep up today," Jon Brendle said as he
watched the early groups head out on Panther Lake from his Rules
Cart. "This is one of those days when a player has to think birdies."

Brad Klapprott was thinking birdies as he warmed up on the
range. He had started the tournament well, shooting 71–70 the
first two days before losing a little bit of ground with a third-
round 73. But he was feeling confident as he took out his driver
to finish his preround routine, thinking he now had his bad
round behind him and was ready to produce a round in the 60s.

Klapprott was another thirtysomething player (thirty-six to
be exact) for whom being in the finals was a big deal. He had
spent one year (2002) on the Nationwide Tour but had spent
most of his career making a living on mini-tours. His golf back-
ground was unusual. Growing up in the small town of Keokuk,
Iowa, he had access to two 9-hole golf courses but no driving
range. When he wanted to practice, he hit balls in the direction
of barges sitting on the Mississippi River. He went to the University of Iowa, was all–Big Ten as a senior, and decided to pursue a pro career. Married to a family practice doctor and with
two young children, he was hoping to put off any decisions by
making it to the tour. Three shots from the cut line on Saturday
morning, he believed this was the best chance he had ever had.

All that changed in an instant on the driving range. As he
bent over to pick up a tee, he felt a sharp pain in his back. It had
happened before, a shooting pain that usually indicated he had
pulled something. "The best thing for me when it happens is to

get some heat on it and get some rest," he said. "It usually goes away in a couple days."

Klapprott didn't have a couple of days or a couple of hours. What he had was about ten minutes to get to the first tee at Panther Lake. "I knew I was in trouble right away," he said. "All of a sudden, just standing up had become a challenge. I knew I wasn't going to be able to swing the club the way I needed to in order to play well. It was an awful feeling."

Klapprott asked one of the volunteers on the range to radio for a rules official. Vaughn Moise, a veteran PGA Tour official, was dispatched to meet him as he headed for the tee. Klapprott told Moise what had happened. He wanted to know if he withdrew what kind of status he would have on the Nationwide Tour in 2006.

Moise felt for Klapprott, but there was nothing encouraging he could tell him. All four players who had withdrawn thus far—Pat Bates, Tom Scherrer, Joe Daley, and Jim Carter—had some status based on past performance. Scherrer and Daley would be fully exempt because of what they had done on the Nationwide in 2005. Carter had a PGA Tour victory, and Bates had past champion status on the Nationwide. Klapprott had none of that. He would go to the bottom of the Nationwide conditional list if he withdrew at that moment.

Once he heard that, Klapprott made a decision to try to play. He explained the situation to the other two players in his group, Fran Quinn and John Merrick. Both were sympathetic. Back problems plague a lot of golfers. To have an injury suddenly crop up midway through Q School finals was a nightmare no one wanted to contemplate.

Klapprott was in obvious pain right from the start. On a lot of shots, his hand came off the club because he couldn't grip it trying to follow through. Shots frequently flew low and short—the kind of shot you might expect from a 10 handicapper, not from someone with a shot at the PGA Tour. Every time Klapprott had to tee a ball up, he squatted to a crouching position. He did the same thing whenever he had to mark. Watching from his cart on the front nine, Brendle shook his head sadly.

"This is tough to watch," he said. "The poor guy basically has no chance. He can't swing the club, and he doesn't want to quit. I feel for him."

When Klapprott finished the front nine, shooting 40, Brendle stopped him en route to the 10th tee — a long walk for anyone; especially long for someone who was hobbling. "Is there anything I can do for you?" he asked.

Klapprott's face was a mask of pain. "I've asked my dad to go out to my car and get me a jacket," he said. "I think it would help if I kept it warm."

"I'll take him out there," Brendle said. "I'm also going to go see our physio guy to see if there's anything he can do for you."

Klapprott thanked him and headed for the 10th tee. Brendle returned a few minutes later with Scott Knolling, a physical therapist who worked in the exercise trailer that most of the players used. Knolling got to Klapprott right after he bogeyed the 10th hole.

"There's nothing I can do for him right now," Knolling said after examining Klapprott's back. "If he can finish the round, I might be able to help him for tomorrow with some ice and electrostim. Based on the way he's walking, he's not going to hurt himself by continuing to play. But he's going to be in a lot of pain the rest of the way. He's got guts, but I'm honestly not sure he can make it."

Klapprott ended up hitting a number of shots with one hand before the long day was over. He did make it, shooting 80, a miraculous round under the circumstances. "I had to hit shots out of the rough at the third and the seventh, and I tried to swing hard to get the ball moving," he said. "The pain was so bad I almost quit then. After that, I swung one-handed whenever I thought I could.

"I'm proud of myself for hanging in there and finishing. Fran and John were great. They tried to encourage me the whole day. This is very tough to take, but at least maybe I'll have a chance tomorrow and Monday if I can get something done between now and the morning."

Klapprott's chance to make the PGA Tour had disappeared the moment he felt the tug in his back. He had gone from 62nd, three shots out, to a tie for 146th, 14 shots from the cut line, which had moved to eight under par in the benign conditions. Realistically, all he could do the last two days was improve his position on the Nationwide.

When he signed his card, Brendle was waiting to give him a ride straight to the exercise trailer, where Knolling was waiting. "Least I can do," Brendle said. "He seems like a good guy. Never whined at all. And even if he was a terrible guy, I wouldn't wish what happened on him. No one deserves that."

THOSE WHO WERE HEALTHY took full advantage of the warm, windless conditions. The low scores of the day were a pair of 64s turned in by Scott Hend, a two-year tour veteran trying to get his card back, and Nick Thompson, the Georgia Tech grad who was part of the Walker Cup contingent. Thompson's round tied the Panther Lake course record, which was held by Ty Tryon, who had set the record during second stage in 2001 en route to making the tour at age seventeen.

Thompson's Walker Cup teammate John Holmes shot his fourth straight round in the 60s (67), putting him in a tie for third place with Tom Byrum. They were one shot behind Michael Allen and D. A. Points, who led the field at 16 under par through 72 holes.

Holmes was beginning to get a lot of attention for his ability to hit the ball several miles off the tee. He wasn't especially pleased by his newfound fame, making a face when he walked out of the scorer's trailer Saturday and was told by a PGA Tour official that a number of media members wanted to talk to him. He agreed to talk to Rich Lerner of the Golf Channel, but only after Lerner had given his word that he would not tell him where he stood in the golf tournament. "I don't want to know anything," he told Lerner.

That was fine with Lerner, although it occurred to him that Holmes might add up the fact that he was 15 under par and had reporters waiting to talk to him, and guess he was pretty high up on the leader board. If that didn't work, being in the second-to-last group off at Crooked Cat the next day (the leaders would play Crooked Cat in the fifth round, Panther Lake in the sixth) might also have been something of a giveaway.

Jeff Overton, the third Walker Cupper in contention, was one of the few players who lost ground, shooting a 74 that dropped him from three shots inside the number to two shots outside. The margin for error for everyone was rapidly shrinking as the days and holes dwindled.

In all, 106 of the 160 remaining players broke par for the day, 67 of them breaking 70. "Guys were being aggressive," said Brian Henninger, whose 67 jumped him into contention at three under par. "The conditions dictated it, and so did the day. If you were behind and you didn't make a move today, chances are pretty good you don't have a move in you."

A lot of players finished the day with renewed hope. David Sutherland also shot 67 and was at three under along with Henninger. Steve Stricker and Dan Forsman each shot 69 and were one shot farther back at two under. Bubba Dickerson, who had vowed after his opening-round 73 to play his way from outside the number to inside the number, did just that, shooting 66 to jump to eight under, which was right on the cut line at the end of the day. Grant Waite was tied with him after a 67. Bob Heintz, who had struggled in rounds two and three, found his game and produced a 68 that left him one shot outside the number at seven under. There were now only thirty-one players on the number or better.

"Today it's okay to be one shot out," Waite said. "Even tomorrow it's okay. Just not Monday."

Tommy Tolles, who had scraped through the first two rounds in one over par, shot a second straight 69 to get to within striking distance at five under. "Boy, am I glad this is six rounds and not four," he said, grinning.

Bill Haas, with his dad following—and being followed constantly by the Golf Channel cameras—shot 69. It was a decent round, but he didn't gain a lot of ground on a day when thirty-nine of the top fifty-one players shot 69 or better. Still, Haas was only two shots outside the number.

"I'm doing fine," Jay Haas reported when asked repeatedly how he felt. "What matters is how Bill's doing."

Bill insisted that he felt fine, too, his confidence returning after two tough days.

Mac Fritz of Titleist continued to look a little pale.

Ron Whittaker continued his confident play, shooting a 66 one day after his 67, jumping him into a tie for 10th place at 11 under par. "Oh, God, do I wish it was Monday," he said, a big smile on his face as he relaxed on a cart after a postround practice session. He was tied with, among others, Peter Tomasulo, who had played his best round of the week, shooting a 68 that did nothing to sway his belief that he would be going home to Long Beach with his PGA Tour card. Tomasulo's buddy from Long Beach, John Merrick, hadn't let Brad Klapprott's struggles affect his game, shooting a 69 to move to seven under.

B. J. Staten was no doubt wishing the same thing as Whittaker after a 65 jumped him into seventh place at 13 under. "I have never felt so good on a golf course as I do right now," he said as he ate lunch after his round. "I'm actually looking forward to the next two days."

Some players who had needed a big move failed to get it. Hiroshi Matsuo shot 71—a respectable round, but not close to what he needed. He moved from a tie for 111th to a tie for 104th. "Where have you heard this before?" he said, forcing a smile. "I hit it great but couldn't make anything."

Perhaps from Steve Wheatcroft, who posted a second straight 72 and was two shots back of Matsuo. Bob May, after his second-round 69, couldn't get anything going, shooting a second straight 73. He admitted to feeling weary, having walked 72 holes in four days after not having walked anywhere near that much in almost three years.

Word of Brad Klapprott's injury spread quickly among the players. Just as players in team sports don't like to talk about players who have been cut, golfers don't like to discuss players who are injured. "It's almost as if talking about it means it can happen to you," said David Sutherland, who knew plenty about injuries. "The problem is, whether you talk about it or not, it *can* happen to anyone, anytime."

A lot of the players had no idea who Klapprott was, especially those who had been on the PGA Tour in recent years. But they all felt for him.

"There is no worse nightmare than getting hurt during Q School," Grant Waite said. "Any other week of the year, you get hurt, you say, 'Okay, as long as it isn't serious, I've got next week. Or the week after.' You get hurt at Q School, it's, 'Well, I've got next year.' Next year feels like a lifetime away. Especially now, when you're so close you can almost touch it."

———

ONE PLAYER WHO FELT CLOSE ENOUGH to touch it was Johnson Wagner. He was in the finals for the fourth straight year, but for the first time, he felt as if he belonged—not only in the finals but also on the PGA Tour.

"I know I'm ready for it now," he said after shooting 68 on Saturday to get to eight under par, right on the number. "I've become good friends with Bob Heintz, and he keeps telling me that my game is good enough for the tour. Now it's up to me to give myself that chance."

Wagner hadn't started out to be a golfer. He was considerably bigger than most golfers, 6 feet 3 and a solid 230 pounds. He had an easy smile and a friendly manner that made his size easy to forget. His first love, growing up in Nashville, had been hockey. He was the starting goalie and captain of his high school hockey team as both a junior and a senior, and if he'd had a chance to go to college as a hockey player, he probably would have done so.

But he was meant—or so it seemed—to be a golfer. His grandfather, M. T. Wagner, was a member of the U.S. Golf Association's executive board, and from the beginning, Johnson could hit a golf ball a long way. He went to Virginia Tech on a partial golf scholarship, figuring he'd play golf or pro football. "I had the size for football," he said, laughing. "But I liked golf better. No one hits you."

His parents moved to New York while he was in college because his father got a job teaching computer science at West Point. Wagner played a lot of golf in New York, winning the prestigious Metropolitan Open twice—first as an amateur, then in his first tournament as a pro in 2002. He rose steadily from that point on, finishing 120th in his first year on the Nationwide Tour in 2003, then 42nd, then 36th.

Normally, a 36th-place finish would have consigned him to second stage, since only those who finish between 21st and 35th are exempt to the finals. But because of Jason Gore's promotion, the 21st player on the list went straight to the PGA Tour, the 36th player straight to the finals.

"I should probably write Jason a thank-you note," Wagner joked. "He certainly made November a lot more pleasant for me. I think going back to second stage is really tough when you feel as if you're right there, ready for the PGA Tour. You have to tell yourself that second stage is not beneath you. I've seen guys struggle with that."

Wagner was living Steve Stricker's *Groundhog Day* existence during Q School week. Katie Winn, who had been his girlfriend since college, had volunteered to make the short drive from their home in Jupiter, Florida, to keep him company and lend support during the week. But Wagner had asked her not to come. "I just didn't want any pressure to do anything—go to dinner, watch TV, not watch TV, talk," Wagner said. "I don't know if that's the best approach or not, but right now it feels like the right one to me.

"I remember the first year I was in the finals [2002], I was just so thrilled to be here, I never hit a good shot all week. I think I finished 130th, never had a chance. I sit home at night and see these Walker Cup kids [Johnson was only two years older than "kids" like John Holmes and Nick Thompson] talking about how they don't feel any pressure and they're having a good time here, and I think, 'Wow, I'd love to feel that way.'

"I feel like I've come a long way since that first year here. I'm a better player. I'm better prepared. I'm sleeping well. I feel comfortable."

He sighed. "I'm forty-eight hours from realizing a dream. That's it—forty-eight hours."

At that moment, he certainly wasn't alone.

16

Go Low or Bust

THE ATMOSPHERE ON SUNDAY MORNING was officially tense. With two rounds left, just about everyone was feeling the jitters.

Those who stood inside the number, even if they were well inside the number, knew there was still a lot of golf left before they could take a deep breath and start to celebrate. "There's still half of a normal golf tournament left," said Tom Byrum, sitting comfortably in a tie for third place. "You can't afford to let up even a little bit."

Those outside the number, especially those a few shots or more outside, knew there were no more tomorrows; they needed to make a move today. The penultimate round of any golf tournament is known among the players as "moving day," because if you don't make a move then, there aren't enough holes left with only one round to play.

"Sitting here now, five shots outside the number with two rounds to play, I know I've got work to do," Brian Henninger said. "But it's work I know I'm capable of doing. If I'm still five shots out tonight, I'll know I need something approaching a miracle to get my card back. I don't want to feel that way."

On Saturday night, almost everyone in the field went to bed thinking there was still a chance. Realistically, anyone within 10 shots of the number still had a chance. "You can shoot 66–66 on these golf courses," said Jason Buha, a former PGA Tour member who, thirty years old and about to become a father for the second time, was doing the "how long do I keep grinding?" dance. "I'm seven shots out. If I went 67–67, I'd take my chances at 11 [under]. I'm sure a lot of guys are thinking that way."

A lot of guys were thinking that way, because elite golfers always believe they're one round away from finding something on the range or the putting green and going low. Buha fit into that category. He had an economics degree from Duke, and more and more, he found himself wondering if he was putting that degree to good use. He had made it to the big tour twice (2000 and 2003) but had failed to crack the top 150 on the money list either time. He'd had his worst year ever on the Nationwide in 2005, leading to discussions with his wife—and with himself—about his future.

"After I had missed seven or eight cuts in a row, I was ready to quit—I mean really ready to quit," he said. "I sat down with my wife [Ashley] and asked her what she thought. I said, 'I know I can get a decent job, but if I want a good job, I probably need to go back and get an MBA.'

"She told me I needed to stop thinking like that; it wasn't time for that yet. She said I needed to be nicer to myself, to stop beating myself up—which I tend to do—and said, 'Jason, if you quit now, you'll have the itch again within six months.'

"She was right. I still love doing this. I tried to ease up on myself and went back to some old things that had worked. I went to second stage [in McKinney, Texas] and played good golf on a hard golf course. It was a great confidence boost.

"The funny thing about Q School is, you can walk on the range the first day and know exactly who the first-timers are. Ignorance is bliss. They're all just jacked to be here. The other thing I can do is walk on the range and tell you exactly what day of Q School it is. First day, everyone's got their head up, ready to say hello; most guys are smiling. By the fifth day, everyone's got their head down. If you see a buddy, someone you're close to, you *might* get a hello. But that's it. There's no one around here talking about going to the movies tonight. We're all well beyond that."

Or, as Hiroshi Matsuo put it, "By the fifth day, even the funny guys aren't funny anymore."

THE LEAST AMUSED PERSON on the grounds early that fifth morning was Bill Glasson. Not that Glasson was a hold-your-sides guy to begin with. He was a tough, forty-five-year-old, twenty-two-year tour veteran who had won seven times and been through surgery almost as often. He had been on and off the tour because of injuries for most of the past ten years, dating to surgery in 1996 to repair a detached muscle in his right forearm.

Glasson would frequently refuse requests to go into the interview room when he was contending in a tournament, but he would willingly talk to anyone who approached him in the locker room or outside the scorer's tent. "He doesn't mind talking," said Wes Seeley, a former tour media official. "He just doesn't like talking in the setting that we offer."

Which was fine with most writers, who preferred the informality of the locker room anyway. Glasson first made it through Q School in 1984, then returned twenty years later. In 2005 he'd had to go back to second stage. He never complained.

On Sunday morning, he was sitting comfortably in a tie for eighth place at 12 under par and had a 9:50 start time on the 10th tee at Crooked Cat. He arrived on the tee in plenty of time, except for one problem: he was on the wrong golf course. He had misread the schedule and thought he was playing Panther Lake. As soon as he saw three players on the tee and realized that none of them were B. J. Staten or Robert Garrigus, the players he was paired with, he knew he had a problem.

He raced across the property to the 10th tee at Crooked Cat, arriving a few seconds after his name had been called by the starter. Under the rules, that meant he had arrived late for his tee time. Which meant that when he teed his ball up, he was hitting three, docked two shots for being late. Glasson made no excuses for the screw-up and was able to take it in good humor later in the day. "I would call it a rookie mistake," he said, "except for the fact that that would be an insult to all rookies."

A rookie might have let the two-shot penalty ruin his day. Glasson kept his cool, dealt with the double bogey he made on the 10th, and then calmly shot 70, which allowed him to remain in a tie for eighth place when the day was over.

Things were a little more heated in the group that teed off at number 10 on Crooked Cat at 8:30. Johnson Wagner was paired with Briny Baird and Matt Hansen. Wagner was right on the cut line; Baird and Hansen were one shot outside at seven under. Perhaps hoping to lighten the atmosphere a bit, Wagner jokingly remarked as the group walked off the third green that he still owed Jason Gore a thank-you note for getting him into the finals without having to go to second stage.

Baird was not amused by the remark. "I've got Jason Gore to thank for my being here, too," he said.

"I walked right into it," Wagner said later. "I didn't realize."

What he didn't realize was that Baird had finished 126th on the PGA Tour money list—exactly one spot and $2,545 (one more birdie or one less bogey)—shy of the coveted 125th spot, which would have sent him back to the tour with fully exempt status in 2006. The reason Baird was 126th and not 125th was Jason Gore, who, after his promotion to the PGA Tour in August, had continued his hot play, winning a tournament and finishing the year with $871,545—good for 94th on the money list.

Someone had to be knocked out of the top 125 because of Gore, and it was Baird, a thirty-three-year-old tour veteran who hadn't won on tour but had finished 22nd on the money list in 2003 with more than $2.2 million.

Now, thanks to Gore, he found himself struggling at Q School and paired with someone who was as delighted by Gore's success as he was distressed by it.

"If they're going to stretch the Nationwide list when something like that happens, they should stretch the PGA Tour list, too," Baird commented. "They shouldn't let you guys [numbers 20 to 35 on the Nationwide list] straight into the finals anyway."

"That's really not fair to say," Wagner said.

Baird said nothing in response. The next time the two men spoke was when they shook hands—briefly—at round's end. Wagner had shot 69; Baird 71. Wagner was still right on the number, which had gone to 11 under with the conditions again almost perfect for scoring. Baird was now three shots outside the number.

Wagner wasn't upset with Baird; he understood his frustration. "I just wish I'd known," he said. "I'd have kept my mouth shut."

There really wasn't a lot of talking going on around the two golf courses. By now, there were actual galleries—perhaps a couple of hundred people following certain groups. Q School is covered daily in the *Orlando Sentinel,* and since the Golf Channel is located in Orlando and the city is a haven for golfers escaping the cold weather, people were well aware that it was going on, that it was free, and that few places on the golf courses were roped.

Jay Haas politely signed autographs most of the day as he walked with Bill's group. Not surprisingly, Bill Haas was getting a lot of Golf Channel time, as was John Holmes, who was emerging as the star of the tournament, playing better each day. He shot 66 on Sunday, his fifth straight round in the 60s and the fourth straight day he had gone one shot lower than the day be-fore. That left him tied for first place at 21 under par with D. A. Points, the only other player in the field who had been in the 60s every day. Michael Allen fell out of the lead with a 70 but was still sitting very comfortably in third place at 18 under par, seven shots inside the number.

By the end of the day Sunday, there were 30 players at 11 under-par or better, with another 44 within six shots of the num-ber. Of those 30, probably only 5 were almost certain to stay in the top 30: Holmes and Points, at 21 under; Allen at 18 under; and Alex Cejka and Nick Thompson at 17 under.

"Can't think that way," said Thompson, who had come a long way since shooting 75 in the first round at the TPC Tampa Bay in October. "You can't go out there and play safe or protect. That's when you get into trouble. Someone is going to do that tomorrow — I just hope it isn't me."

Ron Whittaker was one more night of Ambien and Pepto-Bismol away from making it back to the tour after shooting 70. He was tied for 10th with, among others, Bubba Dickerson and Joe Alfieri at 13 under par.

The best round of the day might have been the 67 turned in by Bill Haas. He had finally gotten turned around the previous day with a 69, but he knew that he needed a very good round on Sunday to be in solid position going into the final day. No one had a bigger gallery than Haas, in part because of his last name, in part because people had seen him play on the tour, and in part because his dad was in his gallery.

"This is one of those times when you find out a little bit about yourself," he said. "I've played with some pressure on me before, and some of the time it's gone well, some of the time it hasn't gone so well. Today, it went well."

Jay Haas hadn't had the chance to watch his son play in important situations that often because he was frequently playing himself on those days. Bill enjoyed having him there, mostly because he felt that there was at least one person watching who understood exactly how he was feeling as the round went on. He knew he wasn't going to hear any cheering from his dad—or any moans or groans either.

"The great thing about Dad is, he's there to talk when I want to talk, but he isn't going to be waiting for me when I come off 18 with a shot-by-shot critique or with swing tips," Bill said. "He's been through everything I've ever been through and lots more. So if I ask for help, he's there with it. But he isn't going to hammer me with it."

Right from the start on Sunday, Haas looked more confident than he had all week. He was finding fairways consistently and firing at flags. Before the day was over, he had six birdies and just one bogey. "I knew with the conditions the way they were that going one or two under wasn't going to do me much good," he said. "I was three under on Saturday, and I went from two shots outside the number to two shots outside the number. I was running in place. I knew if I started the last day a couple shots outside, I would still have a good chance. But I didn't want to do that. I was hoping to get some cushion."

He didn't get any cushion, but he did get right to the number, which jumped to 11 under by day's end as low scores continued to pile up. One reason for the scores was the conditions, but another reason was that a lot of players were taking the same approach as Haas: the time to be cautious had passed. Most players start out repeating the Q School mantra: "Don't make a big number." By day five, if you are outside the cut line, you can no longer be cautious.

Haas's 67 jumped him into a nine-way tie for 22nd place. Among those at 11 under were Johnson Wagner, B. J. Staten, and Peter Tomasulo. The last two had played disappointingly, with Tomasulo shooting 72 and Staten 74 on a day when Crooked Cat played to an average score of 70.5 and a total of forty-nine players in the field broke 70. Staten readily admitted that nerves had come into play during the day.

"I certainly know exactly what's at stake right now," he said. "I looked at where I was after yesterday's round [seventh], and it was almost hard to comprehend. I would hope this will bring me back to earth a little, remind me that, okay, I have to go out there and really grind tomorrow."

He smiled. "I guess it's fair to say I can't stand prosperity. Every time I seem to have a cushion, I go backward. Well, now I don't have a cushion. I'm right on the number. Maybe that's just what I need."

Tomasulo had never had a cushion. He had been steady all week — the first four days, he had been no higher than 70 and no lower than 68 — so he still felt comfortable being where he was. "In an ideal world, we'd all like to be where John Holmes is," he said. "But it isn't that simple, I guess. No one ever said Q School is supposed to be easy."

A number of players moved into contention with low rounds on Sunday, notably Marco Dawson, who had been on and off the tour for close to twenty years. Dawson was forty-two and had come back to play in 2005 after back surgery. He had started 76–73 the first two rounds, but his 64 on Sunday jumped him from a tie for 80th to a tie for 31st. It wasn't that surprising to see some of the veteran players getting in gear on Sunday. All of them understood how to come from behind, and none of them had much interest in making sure they secured full-time Nationwide privileges for 2006.

"It isn't as if you're protecting anything out here," Dan Forsman said after a 67 moved him to seven under par and a tie for 48th place, four shots from the cut line. "I'm here to try to get my job back — period."

Larry Mize felt the same way. After a decent start (72–69), he had faded a little the next two rounds with 74–70. On Sunday he pieced together a 69 to get into contention at six under par. Mize was one of the players in the field who was regularly drawing a gallery that went beyond friends and family. He was easily the most recognizable name in the field because of his status as a Masters champion. Some people who had made the drive out to watch the "kids" play were shocked to see Mize on the course.

"One guy yelled at me, 'Hey, Larry, you don't deserve to have to go through this,'" Mize said, laughing. "I said, 'Unfortunately, I *do* deserve it.' I guess he didn't know I had to play my way through second stage just to get here. Heck, I *earned* it."

Mize had grown accustomed to playing in qualifiers. His Masters victory had given him a ten-year exemption on tour and five-year exemptions into the other three majors. But beginning in the late '90s, he'd been forced to play qualifiers for both the U.S. Open and the British Open. When he showed up in 1997 and 1998 to play British Open qualifiers, his presence stunned the British fans, who were not accustomed to seeing American stars show up to play if they weren't exempt. In fact, some American players skipped the British Open even if they were exempt.

Mize failed to qualify for Troon in 1997 but did qualify for Birkdale in 1998. His willingness to try so charmed the British fans that he became a crowd favorite.

"When I first had to start qualifying for majors again it was tough," he said. "I remember one year during U.S. Open qualifying, I was in a play-off for the last couple of spots, and I hit my tee shot into a bunker. I got down in the bunker and looked up, and there were all these people standing right there peering down at me from a few feet away. That took some getting used to. I hadn't played a lot of golf for a long time without ropes between the fans and me. But after a while, I didn't mind it. For the most part, people have been very supportive."

It would be difficult to know Mize and not want him to succeed. He is soft-spoken and modest, a deeply religious man, but one who doesn't wear religion on his sleeve. Jim Mackay, who has been Phil Mickelson's caddy for the past fourteen years, caddied for Mize earlier in his career and says very succinctly, "I have never met a better human being than Larry Mize."

Character doesn't give you a pass through Q School, although it may help you deal with its vagaries. After Mize played on Sunday, he sat at a table in the dining area with his agent, Jim Lehman (Ryder Cup captain Tom Lehman's brother); his caddy, Tim Tallman; and a couple of friends. "This time tomorrow, there will be a lot of celebrating going on in here," he said with a knowing smile as he surveyed the crowded room. "Those who aren't celebrating won't be anywhere to be found. They'll all be down the road licking their wounds. Regardless of what happens to me, I feel good that I've hung in and competed.

"Of course, in the end, no one cares if you competed. They want to know if you succeeded."

THE END OF THE FIFTH ROUND meant that a lot of players had to face up to the fact that they weren't going to get a 2006 PGA Tour card. Hiroshi Matsuo shot 71 for the second straight day and was 10 shots outside the cut line. His realistic goal for Monday would be full Nationwide status. The same was true for Steve Wheatcroft, who had not been able to bounce back from his awful finish in the third round. He was 12 shots outside the number after shooting 71 on Sunday. Other veteran tour players also had fallen back: Jim McGovern, Mike Springer, and J. P. Hayes were all too far back, as were other experienced players such as Esteban Toledo, Perry Moss, Franklin Langham, and Jeff Hart. All had been fully exempt tour players at various times in their careers and now faced a return to the Nationwide Tour in the latter stages of their playing lives.

Blaine McCallister and Notah Begay III, both multiple past winners on the tour, were still alive but on life support, sitting at three under par. Brian Henninger hadn't been able to maintain his momentum after his fourth-round 67. He shot 71 and was at four under, as was Steve Stricker. David Sutherland and Tommy Tolles were each a shot better than that, clinging to hope for a low round on Monday. David Peoples, another past winner on tour who had also battled injuries, was at six under, and Bob Heintz, after a 72, was at seven under and in need of a low final round.

"All the people that you're talking about — the veteran guys — have absolutely no interest in going back to the Nationwide," Heintz said. "We've all been there, done that. I didn't have to play Q School at all this year, and I'd be exempt on the Nationwide. Where I'm sitting isn't bad if I can get something going tomorrow, because the one thing I can guarantee is that the number isn't going three more shots under par tomorrow. Not the last day of Q School. It's 11 now; I'd say there's a good chance it will be 11 tomorrow. Maybe even 10 if the wind blows a little. So my approach has to be that I don't need to shoot 65. In the 60s, yes, absolutely, and I know I can do that."

He smiled. "Of course, it will help a lot if I can sleep tonight."

He wouldn't be the only one worrying about being sleepless in Orlando. Even the rules officials were feeling jumpy as the tournament wound down. "You wouldn't be human if you said the last day isn't tough to watch," Jon Brendle said. "You feel great for the guys who make it, because you know what they've gone through and what it means to them. But there are always sad stories. For whatever reason, those are the ones you tend to remember."

Brad Klapprott had been the saddest story of the fourth day because of his back miseries. After lots of ice and electrostim he felt well enough to play Sunday, and he played better (73) than the day before. But the 80 had ruined his chances even to get full status on the Nationwide. His round Saturday moved him up two spots, to a tie for 144th, still 11 shots outside the cut line for full status on the Nationwide. His conditional number, however, was improving. Two more players, Phillip Price and Aaron Barber, dropped out after the fifth round, meaning 159 players would tee it up for Monday's final round.

By late afternoon, the driving range at the far end of the parking lot was packed. So was the putting green. A lot of players were searching for something—anything—that might jump-start them the next morning. Even though it seemed as if most of the players in the field were on the range, it was quiet, the thwacking sound of balls being hit the only consistent sound.

David Sutherland leaned on his driver and looked around him for a while, shaking his head. "You know, at this point, the chances that any of us are going to find something out here [are] close to zero," he said. "You don't come to Q School looking for your golf swing, and you certainly don't go looking for it before the last round."

Why, then, was everyone out here, the hot sun still beating down on them, when they could be in air-conditioned hotel rooms watching football?

Sutherland laughed. "Because we would all sit there and stare at the TV, and if you walked in an hour later, most of us wouldn't know the score or who is playing," he said. "And most of us are big football fans. The Cowboys and Giants were on inside when I was eating lunch, and I swear no one was watching. That's a big game.

"Right now, none of us wants to go back to our rooms because we're just going to sit there and stare into space and worry about tomorrow. In a different way, everyone is at a crossroads in our lives tomorrow. We're all going off in one direction or another, and only a handful can be pretty sure right now what that direction is. If you think about it, that's a pretty scary thought."

He teed up another driver. "Which is why we're out here. Out here, we don't have to think."

Johnson Wagner insisted he was happy to think about golf. "I'm going to go home and think I'm one round away from being on the PGA Tour," he said. "I've never been in that position before. I expect to sleep like a baby."

No doubt most of the players would sleep like a baby that night: a baby with colic.

17

Final Countdown

THOSE WHO WERE ABLE TO SLEEP past sunrise the next morning awoke to the sort of day every golfer dreads when facing an important round: a day when the wind would blow.

By 7 a.m., it was already getting gusty. It wasn't cold the way it had been on the second day, but it was windy enough that playing conditions would be much tougher than they had been the previous three days.

"Wind and nerves," Brian Henninger joked. "A perfect combination."

Most of the leaders would play Panther Lake, although a few players who had jumped up the leader board the previous day would be at Crooked Cat. The players were re-paired after the fifth round, but everyone switched golf courses one more time. The players with the lowest scores at Crooked Cat were Dan Forsman, Jeff Klauk, and Cameron Beckman, who all began the last round at seven under par. That meant the top forty-seven players in the field were at Panther Lake.

One of the myths of golf and the PGA Tour is that every last-day pin position is the toughest one available. When golfers refer to a "Sunday pin," they mean the flag has been placed in the most difficult spot the rules officials can find on a green—the spot where they expect it to be during the tournament's last round.

In fact, pin positions are usually divided up over the four days: four greens will have the toughest spots on Thursday, four on Friday, and then five each on Saturday and Sunday. And picking the toughest spots is always subjective: one man's Sunday pin might be another man's easy pin.

The pin placements on Monday were identical to what they had been on Sunday in order to ensure that all the players faced conditions as close to identical as possible (one half of the field on Sunday and the other half on Monday on each course). But regardless of pin positions, the wind would make the courses play very differently. As Jon Brendle made his early-morning tour of Panther Lake, checking the tees and greens and bunkers to make sure they were as pristine as possible, he paused at the top of the hill behind the 17th green. He pointed at the flag, which was located on the back/left of the green, on the upper plateau of the two-level green.

"Now yesterday, that wasn't that hard a pin," he said. "You pick the right club, maybe an eight-iron, and just make sure you don't pull it in the bunker, and you're fine. Today, with that wind, given the pressure these guys are going to be feeling when they get to this hole..." He paused and shook his head. "If you make par on this hole today, when you really need it, you've earned your card. And a birdie? Hell, I'll drive to your house and hand you the card in person."

He got into his cart and said, "I don't envy any of these guys today."

A LOT OF PLAYERS might have envied Brendle and the rest of the rules staff, sitting comfortably in their carts as the day got under way. Not only was it windy, but it was also humid, making conditions both difficult and uncomfortable.

Orange County National had a New Year's Eve afternoon feel to it as players gathered in the clubhouse one last time to sip coffee or eat a Danish before going out to warm up. A large chunk of the PGA Tour staff was now in town. Sid Wilson, vice president of player relations (the PGA Tour is awash in vice presidents) was there to greet those who would be heading to the tour in 2006. On this day, his job would be relatively pleasant. He would congratulate the qualifiers, focusing on the newcomers to make sure they understood there was paperwork they needed to pick up before they left. Then there was a party that night and an orientation session the next morning on matters ranging from insurance to investments to dealing with pro-am partners and the media.

Most weeks on tour, Wilson spends Tuesday and Wednesday on the range and in the locker room listening to player complaints on everything from the quality of the golf course to the quality of the food to the pace of play in the Monday pro-am. He is also responsible for organizing player meetings and for convincing players to serve on the Policy Board or the Players Advisory Committee (PAC). Players shy away from both jobs because they require a lot of time and have very little influence, since Commissioner Tim Finchem controls five of the nine votes on the Policy Board and since many PAC recommendations—if they aren't in concert with the commissioner's ideas—go unheeded.

Paul Goydos, a many-time Q Schooler who had served on the PAC for several years, remembered a 16–0 vote against giving full exemptions to foreign players who played in the Presidents Cup. Two weeks later, the policy board, at Finchem's behest, voted in favor of the exemptions. Goydos resigned from the PAC soon after.

One of Wilson's other jobs is to formally notify players when they are subject to a fine and to deal with any appeals. The PGA Tour treats fines as if they are matters of national security, but the players—even the very rich ones such as Tiger Woods—resent them. Woods, who is frequently fined for using profanity on the golf course, has complained that the system is unfair because he rarely hits a shot that isn't captured by a TV camera and a nearby microphone.

The best reaction to a fine in tour history may have come from Jay Haas, who is as mild-mannered as anyone who has ever played the game. On a hot afternoon in Milwaukee, Haas had a terrible third round, going from in contention to near the back of the pack. On 18 he slapped a miserable chip that ran all the way across the green, summing up his day. As he walked to his ball, thinking all sorts of dark thoughts, someone standing nearby shouted, "Boy, Haas, you really suck."

For once, Haas couldn't keep his frustrations in check. "Fuck you," he said, looking directly at the heckler.

The next day, after he finished his round, Haas found rules official Wade Cagle waiting for him. "I knew just what it was about," Haas said. "I wasn't that upset about it, [but] Wade was a little pale.

"'I got a note, Jay,' Cagle said. 'I think it's a mistake, but I have to ask you about it. A fan claims you said "Fuck you" to him. He misunderstood, right? You probably said "Thank you," and he didn't hear you right.'

"'No, Wade,' I said. 'He heard me exactly right.'"

Paul Goydos probably held the record for most unusual fine. He was nailed for yelling at a telephone answering machine. Even Wilson, who has spent a good deal of time through the years arguing about anything and everything with Goydos, had a tough time keeping a straight face and maintaining the tour's strict "we don't comment on fines" policy when that story came up.

Goydos was leading the World Series of Golf after the first round, which had been played on Friday because of rain on Thursday. Both the second and third rounds were scheduled to be played Saturday in order to ensure a Sunday finish for TV. Goydos played miserably all day Saturday and went from being in one of the last groups to being in one of the first.

"The only consolation in the whole thing for me was that it meant I could get an early flight and get home on Sunday night instead of staying until Monday, which I would have had to do if I played late," he said. "So I called the tour travel office to change my flight."

He got a tape informing him that the office closed at 4 p.m. on Saturday. Since he had been in the last group, Goydos hadn't finished until six o'clock. "I just started screaming into the phone, 'What do you mean you close at four o'clock on Saturday? We play until six o'clock on Saturdays! We don't need you in there at ten in the morning. We need you at six at night!'" He smiled while telling the story. "There was probably at least one profanity in each sentence. Maybe two."

Thus Wilson had to write Goydos a letter telling him he was being fined for yelling profanities into an answering machine.

The tour did change the travel office hours after the incident, however. "Didn't cost me a cent," Goydos said. "Bunch of guys got together and raised the money to pay my fine."

The last day of Q School would be far more pleasant for Wilson than a typical day on tour. None of the men he would be dealing with would have very much to complain about. The person who wouldn't have as easy a day was Wilson's Nationwide Tour counterpart Marty Caffey. He would be dealing with a number of players who had just had their hearts broken and who, in many cases, would be going to a tour they had no desire to play.

"You learn to tread lightly," said Caffey, like Wilson a southerner who rarely let anyone see him sweat. "For some of these guys, walking out of here today with their Nationwide Tour card is a big deal, and, to be honest, a lot of them are the ones who will have questions for me—the first-timers. The older guys are...different. I'll give them lots of space. If there's something I have to tell them, I will. And if they have to ask me something, I'll try to answer in a way that lets them know I understand that this isn't exactly the best day of their lives."

Jodi Herb, who works with Wilson and Caffey in the tour's Ponte Vedra Beach office, was also in town, set up at a table in a corner of the dining room. Each player would report to her at the end of the day for a set of instructions. The smaller and much happier group would be given information on the orientation session and the 2006 PGA Tour. The rest would be handed a schedule that told them their year would begin in Panama in February, rather than Hawaii in January. "Maybe that's the approach to take the last day—tell yourself you're just playing for a trip to Hawaii," Bob Heintz joked.

One PGA Tour official who was noticeably absent was Tim Finchem. It had become a tradition at the Nationwide Tour finals each October for the commissioner to present the "graduating" class of twenty with their PGA Tour cards after the last round. There was no such ceremony on the last day of Q School.

"It's probably something we should do," Finchem said when asked why there was no ceremony at Q School. "I guess the notion has been that the guys on the Nationwide play all year to get to that day, and it makes sense to have some kind of ceremony. But it's certainly just as big a deal for the guys who make it through Q School." There was no ceremony after Q School in '06, but Finchem did take the '07 rookies to lunch the next day.

The clubhouse scene on the last morning was borderline chaotic. Orange County National was now overrun with golf people. Agents and equipment reps were everywhere, either showing support for clients or looking to sign up new ones. Some players had broken down and asked their wives or girlfriends to come in for the last day. Many of the younger players who were in position to get to the tour for the first time were being followed around the golf course by buddies who wanted to be there for their pals' big moments.

Most of the important action would take place at Panther Lake, the golf course farther from the clubhouse. By comparison, Crooked Cat looked a bit like a ghost town, with only a handful of players in contention to make it to the big tour.

"Maybe a few of us can sneak up when no one is looking," said Dan Forsman, who would be in the last group going off the 10th tee at Crooked Cat. "If I could post a low number without anyone noticing, that would be just fine with me."

That wouldn't be likely, especially for a player as well known and liked as Forsman. If he did make a late move, the Golf Channel would certainly have a camera on him as he finished. Like a lot of older players, Forsman, who is about as cooperative with the media as anyone who has ever played the game, would prefer to play Q School in isolation.

"I think what they do by televising Q School is great for golf," he said. "But selfishly, I'd just like to be out there with no one watching when I play this tournament. This isn't like a regular tour event. This is so…" He paused, looking for a word. "Personal."

FORSMAN WAS RIGHT. Although every player in the field had some kind of support group—many of them walking the golf course to cheer the players on—the last day of Q School is very personal. Only the players know the hours and hours of work that have gone into getting to this moment—whether it is a twenty-two-year-old doing so for the first time or a forty-seven-year-old hoping to do it one last time.

Golfers often talk about the hours they spent alone on the putting green as kids and the times they would say to themselves, "This putt is to win the U.S. Open" or "Make this, and we'll have a new Masters champion."

That's a fantasy lived by a tiny handful of players. For most who become very good players—and no one who reaches Q School finals does so without being a very good player—the real dream is to play on the PGA Tour. If stardom comes with that, it is a huge bonus. Although the image of the PGA Tour is defined by players like Tiger Woods and Phil Mickelson, who can afford to fly from event to event on their private planes, the reality is Paul Goydos, screaming into an answering machine in the travel office because he wants to find a way to get home on a Sunday night.

Goydos has been on tour for fourteen years. He has won twice, first in 1996 at Bay Hill; been back to Q School three times since first getting his card; and been forced to sit out a year after hip and sinus surgery. He has been through a divorce and, at forty-two, has made a good living but is hardly wealthy, even after his win in Hawaii early in 2007.

His life is a lot closer to what life on the PGA Tour is like than that of Woods or Mickelson or Fred Couples or Davis Love III or Vijay Singh. It may not be exactly what the players going through Q School each year aspire to, but it isn't that far off. Most would happily sign on the dotted line for fourteen years on tour, more than $5 million in earnings, and two tournament victories. Yet the word often used to describe players like Goydos is "journeyman." It implies mediocrity, which is ludicrous. To play on the tour consistently for that long, one must be an extraordinary player.

Casey Martin, who became famous because of his lawsuit against the PGA Tour and managed to make it to the tour as a full-fledged player for one year, has trouble understanding why people look at players on the Nationwide Tour as failures. "Worst case, if you're on the Nationwide, you're one of the best 500 golfers in the world," he said. "If you're on the PGA Tour with any status at all, you're one of the top 200. That means you are well within the top 1 percent of people playing golf in the world. In almost any other business, that makes you a superstar—you're a CEO or some kind of stud at what you do.

"Not in golf. In golf, you're a journeyman or a minor leaguer."

There were a few players at Orange County National on the first Monday in December who knew what stardom felt like: Larry Mize, certainly; Bob May, briefly; Jay Haas—who wasn't playing—absolutely. A few others might someday know that feeling: Bill Haas, John Holmes, and Bubba Dickerson all had that kind of buzz. But most just wanted to make a living playing golf.

They wanted to be Paul Goydos. This was their chance to do it for at least a year and perhaps beyond.

18

Hawaii, Here We Come

I<small>T WAS APPARENT EARLY IN THE DAY</small> that Bob Heintz's Sunday call—that the number wouldn't go lower than 12 under, and might very well be 11 or even 10 under—had been a good one. The wind and last-day nerves would see to that. Pace of play had gone from slow to slower to slowest. Players were routinely marking one-foot putts and then looking at them from three sides. The rules officials weren't even bothering to time them.

"What's the point?" Jon Brendle said. "Everyone's keeping up because everyone's slow. The last thing you want to do today is put a guy on the clock and have him tell you that's the reason he missed his card. No one's going to play in 4:30 today if I go out there with a whip. So unless someone tells me there's a problem, I'm staying out of the way."

Because there were no computerized scoreboards around the golf course, players and spectators used different methods to keep track of what was going on. All discussion focused on two words: "the number."

Since no one was policing cell phone use, a lot of people were phoning home, where someone watching on the Golf Channel or sitting at a computer could tell them what the number was at that moment. Donna Caponi, the two-time U.S. Women's Open champion who was a walking commentator for the Golf Channel, was constantly bombarded with questions as she followed the threesome of Brett Wetterich, Peter Tomasulo, and B. J. Staten around the back nine.

"I swear, I'm more nervous now watching these guys than when I was playing," Caponi said at one point. "This is agony."

Jay Haas kept calling Jan for updates. He was staying as far from Bill as he possibly could, trying to be as unobtrusive as possible—which was impossible, because every time Bill made or missed a putt, the Golf Channel would cut to a shot of Jay's reaction. "This keeps up, they're going to have a shot of me throwing up on camera," he said, at least half-joking, as Bill struggled to get to the number.

All day, the number floated. "It's 10," Caponi told spectators at one point as she walked past. "But it may go back to 11. Remember, all these guys finish on 18, and it's playing straight downwind."

The 18th on Panther Lake is a par-five that is reachable on most days and was eminently reachable now with the wind blowing out of the west.

The 10th hole, also a par-five, plays in exactly the opposite direction, meaning the players were dead into the wind and had little chance to reach the green in two. Since the top 42 players in the field had started their last round on the first tee at Panther Lake, they all arrived at the 10th tee, about three hours after they'd started, knowing they had just nine holes left to rise or fall.

A few of the players, perhaps those in the last two groups, arrived at that tee—which was a long walk from the ninth green—knowing that if they remained standing for the last nine holes, they would have their cards comfortably. A couple, notably Johnson Wagner after a front-nine 40, arrived knowing that they had to find a way to go low on the last nine to be one of the anointed.

Most walked onto the tee—after a quick break to go to the bathroom or grab a drink or a snack—took a deep breath, and realized that, after six days (not to mention the practice rounds), everything they had worked for came down to nine holes.

Not surprisingly, the Golf Channel had picked the group of Wetterich, Staten, and Tomasulo for Caponi to follow. All three players had started the day right on the number, at 11 under. Each had a story to tell.

Wetterich was thirty-two and had made it to the PGA Tour three times. The first time, in 2000, he had injured a wrist and had surgery. The second time, in 2002, he had finished 174th on the money list. The third time, in 2005, after making it back by finishing 10th on the Nationwide money list, he made more than $576,000 but had finished 132nd on the money list, thus bouncing him back to Q School. Tour players like to point out that playing on the PGA Tour is one of the few jobs on earth where someone can make more than $500,000 in a year and get fired.

Staten was twenty-eight, still grateful that his late collapse in Kingwood had not cost him his first trip to the finals. Now he was on the verge of doing something far bigger than making it through second stage. He had played so well in the second, third, and fourth rounds (68–70–65) that not making the PGA Tour would be a huge disappointment. His fifth-round 74 had pushed him back to the cut line and ratcheted up the pressure again.

"When I first got here, I was hoping to get to the PGA Tour," Staten said late on Sunday afternoon. "But if you had said to me that I'd be fully exempt on the Nationwide, I'd probably have said, 'Well, that wouldn't be too bad.' Now it would feel like a huge letdown."

Tomasulo, the youngest in the group at twenty-four, had never given any thought to anything but a PGA Tour card throughout the week. He had been as consistent as anyone in the field—no round higher than 72, none lower than 68—and had started the final round brimming with confidence, even sitting squarely on the number.

The front nine did nothing to change that feeling. Tomasulo turned at one under par, which put him at 12 under, at least one shot inside the number. Wetterich and Staten were both at even par and still 11 under for the week. All three players walked to the 10th tee knowing that if they maintained their current position, they would be members of the PGA Tour before sundown.

Looking as if he was playing a buck nassau Sunday morning round at home, Tomasulo split the 10th fairway. Because of the wind, the ball landed well short of where most players had been driving the ball throughout the week. Neither Wetterich nor Staten looked nearly as calm, both sending their drives into the right rough — Wetterich with a push, the lefty Staten with a pull.

Staten's ball was found quickly, but it took a lengthy search, which included several dozen spectators, before Tom Reilly, Wetterich's agent, found his ball. "Now that gives new definition to client services," someone said.

Wetterich slashed his ball out of the rough and up the fairway. Staten wasn't nearly as lucky. Trying to play a punch shot from just in front of a small tree, he shanked the ball, sending it dead left — across the fairway, across the rough, and through a low fence running along the left side of the hole. He caught a huge break because there were no out-of-bounds markers.

"I'm just trying to make it interesting," Staten said as he marched across the fairway and through the rough to where his ball had finally stopped. He managed to get his third shot onto the fairway.

Tomasulo had been waiting through all of this. When it was finally his turn, he decided not to go for the green, with bunkers in front and the wind in his face. He hit a routine layup to about 80 yards short of the hole. After Wetterich hit his third shot to about 25 feet and Staten had pitched his fourth to about 15 feet,

Tomasulo marched up the fairway to his ball, figuring he was in good position to get up and down for a birdie and put himself at least a couple of shots inside the number.

As he approached the ball, he saw something he had never seen before in all his years of playing golf: his ball was lying squarely on a loose piece of sod that someone had not replaced after taking a divot.

"I had no idea how to play a shot like that," he said later. "Not only had I never hit a shot like it, I don't think I'd ever *seen* any-one hit a shot like it. I had no idea what to do."

He ended up chunking the ball, leaving it well short of the hole in the high grass in front of the green. All of a sudden, what had appeared to be a fairly easy birdie had become a tough par. His chip from the gunk squirted 12 feet past the hole.

Wetterich was able to two-putt for par. Both Staten and To-masulo missed their par putts and walked off the green looking a little bit stunned. Par-fives are supposed to be birdie holes for pros, even when playing into the wind. At worst, if a player hits a poor drive the way Wetterich did, he makes par. A six is unpardonable.

Tomasulo was shaken, doubt creeping into his mind for the first time all week. Staten was resolute. During the lengthy walk to the 11th tee, he glanced at his longtime teacher, Randy Smith, who simply nodded his head and said, "You're fine. Keep playing."

Smith knew a little bit about pressure. For many years, he had taught Justin Leonard, the 1997 British Open champion. He had walked with Leonard many times during major champi-onships. Now he said softly, "Never felt anything like this. Not during Troon [Leonard's British Open victory had been at Royal Troon in Scotland], not at any other major. Remember, Justin didn't have to go to Q School. This is tougher to watch than a major. At least there are four of them every year, not just one."

By now, the pace of play had slowed from a crawl to something approaching going backwards. As the three players approached the 11th tee, Fran Quinn, Jeff Overton, and Kevin Johnson were just getting ready to hit their tee shots to the par-three. As a courtesy, they hung back and waited until the players in front of them had hit their shots. Then they sat and waited almost fifteen minutes for the threesome in front to play the hole.

"The only thing that keeps you sane at that point is that you've been playing slow for six days anyway," Tomasulo said. "But right then and there, I didn't need to wait. It gave me time to think—which was the last thing I needed at that moment. I needed to just play."

By the time it was his turn to hit, Tomasulo had all sorts of dark thoughts racing through his mind: Was the bad break at 10 a harbinger, a sign? He was now at 11 under. Was that the number? Was it 10? Was it 12?

"All week I'd been in this really good zone, where all I thought about was the next hole, the next shot," he said. "I lost that for a while after the 10th."

The result was an awful tee shot, a three-iron that flew way left of the green. He was fortunate to be able to get his wedge shot over a bunker and onto the green. But his 15-foot par putt slid low for another bogey. Twelve was no better for either Staten or Tomasulo. Staten missed the green, and his chip rolled 10 feet past the hole. From there, he missed. Tomasulo found the green but three-putted from 45 feet. Both men were two over par for the day. More important, they were now at nine under for the tournament, and everyone knew that wasn't going to be good enough. Wetterich was playing the steadiest golf in the group, making one par after another at a time when par was clearly a very good score.

As they made the walk to the 13th tee, Donna Caponi walked over to Randy Smith and whispered, "The number's just gone to 10," meaning that at that moment, there were fewer than thirty players at 11 under or better. Smith nodded but decided to say nothing to Staten. "No sense putting numbers in his head right now," he said. "He just needs to play."

Almost as if reading Smith's mind, Staten blasted a perfect drive, hit his second shot to about 18 feet, and drained the putt. *"Yes!"* he said, pleased to jump off the bogey train with a birdie. Tomasulo had a similar chance to birdie, but his putt did a 360 around the cup and spun out.

The 14th was another par-five, normally a very good birdie chance. But the hole was 622 yards dead into the wind. Tomasulo almost hit his drive out-of-bounds and had to punch his second shot back to the fairway. He still had more than 200 yards to the green and found the front left bunker. From there he hit a gorgeous shot to four feet and saved par. Staten played the hole straight from the textbook: perfect drive, layup, wedge to eight feet, and a putt that was dead center. He was back at 11 under. Wetterich also made birdie to get to 12 under. Tomasulo looked pale.

Smith wandered off with his cell phone and called his wife at home for an update. "Exactly thirty guys at 10 as of this moment," he reported back. "Right now, these guys need to keep the fairway under their feet the rest of the way. In this wind, you miss a fairway, you're going to be lucky to make par. Look at Peter on that last hole."

The players were now smack in the middle of the back nine and could hear occasional cheers from those following the groups ahead and behind them. Smith said that his wife had told him the roar they had just heard behind them probably had come from Bill Haas's group, which was two holes behind.

Nerves were clearly frayed as the players waited on the 15th tee, a par-three with water on the left and in front. The last thing anyone wanted to do here was make a fatal mistake—and any mistake would be fatal this late in the day—by going left. Staten, trying to bury any thoughts about the 17th hole in Kingwood, kept his ball safely to the right, just missing the green. He chipped close and made the putt, a three-footer that on most days would be routine. Not on this day. He heaved a big sigh when the ball went in.

Tomasulo's tee shot was right at the flag, but it carried 40 feet past the stick. He carefully cozied his putt to 18 inches and happily took par, as did Wetterich.

Tomasulo was now running out of holes. Wetterich and Staten were relatively comfortable at 12 and 11 under, respectively. Staten was convinced that with the wind up, there was no way 11 wouldn't make it. "I thought 10 might make it, too," he said. "But I didn't want to take that chance. If I could get to 12, great, but I wasn't going to do anything crazy to get there."

Tomasulo was also thinking that 10 under might be good enough, but if he wanted to be certain, he had to get to 11. As the players made yet another long walk from a green to a tee, they crossed the group of Alex Aragon, Tommy Tolles, and Brett Bingham heading to the seventh tee (having teed off at number 10 to start the day). Aragon's body language made it clear that he was having a great round. He was walking five steps ahead of everyone and had a big smile on his face.

"He's six under for today," one of the caddies said. "He's got it to 11."

At that moment, Tolles was also making his move, having made four front-nine birdies to get to nine under. As the players and caddies crossed, Aragon's caddy pumped a fist at Tomasulo. "Come on P.T.," he said. "You go get 'em."

He put out a hand to offer encouragement. Tomasulo never saw him. "If a bomb had gone off at my feet at that moment, I probably wouldn't have noticed," Tomasulo said.

They were now waiting on every tee. Tomasulo knew it was now or never. Both 16 and 18 were downwind. If he could birdie both, he would go to the PGA Tour. His drive found the fairway at 16, and he had only a wedge left to the green. He flipped it to within 10 feet and finally made a putt, earning himself a high-five from Staten, who had safely made par. Wetterich missed the green and bogeyed, so he was now at 11 under, too. Tomasulo was at 10.

One group was walking off 17 as they approached; another one was waiting. Tomasulo decided to go to the bathroom, if only to kill a little time. Caponi, standing a few yards from the tee watching the players wait, shook her head. "I feel like I'm going to be sick," she said. "I can't imagine how they must feel right now."

It was a solid twenty minutes before they could take aim at the pin Jon Brendle had predicted would bring someone grief several hours earlier. Tomasulo, with the honor, took a long time deciding between an eight- and a nine-iron. He finally decided on the eight to make certain he could get the ball onto the upper plateau of the green. His hope was to start the ball safely to the right of the flag and let the wind move it toward the stick.

"I'd seen a guy get in the back left bunker on the first day," he said. "I knew it was almost impossible to get up and down from there. I just wanted to get the ball on the green, make par, and go for birdie at the 18th."

As soon as the ball was airborne, he knew he was in trouble. It started right at the flagstick and began drifting left, the wind pushing it toward the bunker he wanted to avoid at all costs. The ball took one big bounce and landed in the bunker. Tomasulo looked sick.

Staten hit the shot Tomasulo wanted to hit: the ball drifted left of the flag but stayed safely on the green. He carefully putted downhill from 20 feet, leaving himself with a knee-knocking four-footer.

"Oh, God," Smith said. "I don't think I can breathe."

Fortunately, Smith wasn't putting. Staten knocked it in for par.

In the meantime, Tomasulo, knowing he had to make par, tried to open the face of his wedge and somehow stop his bunker shot from running through the green. He couldn't do it. The ball squirted from the bunker, through the green, and almost into the water fronting the green. That was the moment when it first occurred to him that he wasn't going to get his card. His knees almost buckling, he tried desperately to hole his third shot but was lucky to get it within 15 feet out of the weeds in front of the water. When he missed the bogey putt, he knew he was done. Putter on top of his head, clearly in shock, he stood aside to watch Wetterich and Staten putt out. Walking to the 18th tee, he fired his ball into a waste area behind the tee and stood staring in that direction as if hoping he might wake up and find that it was Monday morning and he still had 18 holes to play instead of one.

Staten and Wetterich, both at 11 under, were delighted to have only one hole to play. Staten crushed his drive down the middle, shook his head, and said, "That's all I've got." Tomasulo's drive found the fairway, but it didn't really matter. He walked behind Staten and Wetterich, trying to find his composure.

Staten had hit his drive so far that he had only a five-iron left to the green. But as he got over the ball, the enormity of what he was about to do hit him. His hands started trembling. He tried to shake it off and put a smooth swing on the ball, knowing that even if he missed the green, getting down in three from there would be good enough.

"I almost shanked it completely," he said.

The ball flew to the left in the direction of a water hazard that was, for all intents and purposes, out of play. Staten almost brought it into play. The ball stopped no more than five yards from the water.

"This round is never going to end," Smith said.

Staten composed himself and hit a solid chip to about 15 feet above the hole.

"Oh, God, he's got a downhill putt," Caponi said. "I don't think I can watch."

Wetterich was comfortably on in three, with about a 10-foot birdie putt. Tomasulo was also on the green in three, but at that moment he seemed more concerned with catching the eye of his friend John Merrick, who was finishing on the ninth, which runs parallel to 18. When Merrick finally saw him, Tomasulo put his hands out, palms up, as if to say, "And?"

Merrick shook his head and pointed his thumbs down. Then he pointed at Tomasulo. Sadly, Tomasulo had to send the same signal back.

Staten took plenty of time over his birdie putt and hit it just the way he wanted to, the ball trickling to a stop about four inches from the cup. "I think," Smith said, breaking into a huge grin at last, "he can handle that one."

Staten tapped in. A moment later, so did Wetterich, and Tomasulo congratulated both of them. The number, they would soon learn, had gone back to 11 under but wasn't going to go any lower.

The three players made their way through what had now become a battery of fans — some just waiting to watch players finish, others there to see specific players. Staten and Wetterich were being pounded on the back. Tomasulo had become invisible. He walked into the scorer's trailer, signed his card, and then stood watching as Staten talked to Rich Lerner of the Golf Channel. Later, he would have absolutely no memory of standing there. "From the moment I shook hands until the moment I got to my car, I really don't remember anything," he said. "It's all a blank."

Staten was still a tad shaken by the near disaster on his second shot. But once the congratulations began, he moved into celebration mode. "It's one of those things," he said, "where no matter how many times you've dreamed it, the actual moment is even better. Much, much better."

ALL AROUND THE TWO GOLF COURSES, dreams and night-mares were being realized—often, as with Staten and Tomasulo, at the same moment in the same group.

While Tommy Tolles was fighting his way to 11 under, only to see all his work blown up when he drove the ball into the water on his last hole of the day, Alex Aragon, playing alongside Tolles, was having that magical day that everyone who begins the last day outside the number dreams about.

Like Staten, Aragon had played all three stages after finishing 212th on the Nationwide money list in 2005. He was twenty-six and had never played in a PGA Tour event in his life. Now, after shooting the low round of the final day (65), he was going to the PGA Tour as a full-fledged member.

Bob Heintz, playing in the same group with Tomasulo's friend John Merrick, also put on a late charge. After he birdied the sixth hole, he was at 10 under par with three holes to play. "In my heart of hearts, I knew I needed one more birdie," he said later.

He came close on each of the last three holes. But when his 15-footer on the ninth slid below the hole, something told him he had just missed getting back to the tour by one shot. "By one shot or three inches, depending on how you want to look at it," he said.

In the scorer's trailer, he was told the number at that moment was 11—but there were exactly thirty players sitting on that score.

"On the one hand, it's the last day of Q School, and people do choke," Heintz said. "But almost all the guys still playing who were at 11 were on the back nine, meaning they were finishing on the 18th, which was a birdie hole for everyone. And there were also guys at 10 who were finishing on that hole, too."

Heintz stood outside the scorer's trailer for a few minutes, watching the bedlam around him as players who had earned their cards celebrated. "I'm going to wait this out at the scoreboard like I did at Lake Jovita," he said. "I have a feeling the ending isn't going to be as happy this time."

Dan Forsman didn't even bother going to the scoreboard when he finished about an hour after Heintz. When he walked into the scorer's trailer, the volunteers working there confirmed what his gut had already told him: the last birdie chance he had missed on the ninth green at Crooked Cat had sealed his fate. Forsman is, by nature, an emotional man. He said his thankyous, then asked the volunteer who offered him a cart ride to the clubhouse if he would mind taking him straight to his car.

"Aren't you going to eat?" the man said. "You've had a long day out there."

"I don't feel much like eating right now," Forsman said. He didn't want to tell the man that he thought it might be tough to get any food past the giant knot in his stomach.

When he got to his car, Forsman changed into comfortable shoes, put his clubs in the trunk, and then sat leaning against his car for a solid thirty minutes. No more than 50 yards away, Peter Tomasulo was leaning on the trunk of his car, lost in thought just as Forsman was. One was twenty-four, with an entire career still ahead of him. The other was forty-seven, with most of a distinguished career behind him.

At that moment, they were feeling almost identical emotions: both disbelieving that all their work, all the hours, and all the emotion they had poured into the last six days had left them leaning on their trunks, with nothing to take home except a knot in their stomachs.

"I just kept looking around at places that had become so

familiar to me in the past week," Forsman said. "I'd spent hours on the driving range and the putting green working toward one thing, and I'd come up one shot short. Those two golf courses were my field of dreams, and now there was nothing left for me to do except go home. All the years I've played golf, I can't remember a more melancholy feeling than right at that moment."

OUT ON THE GOLF COURSE, a number of players were still hovering around the number. One was Bill Haas. He had watched the other two players in his group go in opposite directions as the afternoon wore on. All three players—Haas, Hunter Mahan, and Johnson Wagner—had started the day at 11 under par.

Mahan was only a week older than Haas, having turned twenty-three on May 17, but he already had two years' experience on tour, having made it all the way through Q School in 2003 after leaving Oklahoma State at the end of his junior year. He kept his card in 2004 by finishing 100th on the money list, but slipped to 131st in 2005, sending him back to Forsman's Field of Dreams.

His experience was clearly paying off on the last day. Even in the wind, he was in complete control of his ball all day, rarely in trouble, and sitting comfortably at 15 under par as they came to the final holes.

Wagner, who had given much thought to how close he was to realizing *his* dream, hadn't been able to hold his game together in the crucible of the last day. He was on his way to shooting 78, the second-highest score in the field all day. He would drop all the way to a tie for 70th place and leave devastated in a completely different way than Forsman and Tomasulo. For them, it had come down to one swing or one putt. For him, it had come down to one bad day.

"I still believe I'm going to be on the tour someday," he said. "I guess this wasn't my time. No one hands this to you. You have to take it. I didn't."

Haas was the one player in the group still very much on the bubble down the stretch. He had made the turn at 12 under, but like Tomasulo, he had started very poorly on the back nine. He hit his second shot hole high at number 10 but short-sided himself. He had a bunker between his ball and the hole and almost no green to work with. Trying to get cute, he dumped his wedge shot in the bunker and made a bad bogey from there. On 11, he crushed a three-iron, but it went over the green. He chipped back to within three feet but missed the putt to drop to 10 under.

At that point, Jay Haas called Jan at home. "She said the number is 10 right now, but they're saying it's almost certain to go to 11 because 18 is playing downwind. That means he's got no margin for error at all on these next few holes."

Bill was convinced the number was going to be 11. As he walked to the 12th tee, for the first time all week the thought crossed his mind that he might spend a second year on the Nationwide Tour. He pushed the thought away and made solid pars at 12 and 13, which brought him to the par-five 14th, a hole he normally would have been able to reach in two. But with the wind in his face, he laid up. He then hit a good wedge shot to about 10 feet, but his birdie putt slid below the hole.

"Bad move," he thought. "Now you can't afford anything even resembling a mistake the rest of the way."

Later, he laughed remembering that thought. "Of course, I went out and immediately made a dumb mistake on the next hole."

The mistake was his first putt. He had hit a five-iron on the tee and found the middle of the green, about 25 feet from the hole. Rather than just make his par and move on, he tried to make the birdie putt. He rammed the putt six feet past the hole, then missed coming back for his third bogey in six holes. Now he was well outside the margin of error. Assuming the number was going to be 11, he needed to birdie two of the last three holes or make an eagle at 18. That was possible, since the green was reachable in two, but the last thing Haas—or anyone— wanted was to stand on the 18th tee at Q School needing an eagle to get to the number. A birdie would be daunting enough.

Realistically, his best chance to make a birdie before 18 would be on the 16th, since it was playing driver–wedge for most players. Trying to bomb his drive, he pulled the ball just a tad, and it rolled into the edge of the rough on the left side. He still had only a pitching wedge left, but the ball skittered just off the green, leaving him with a 25-foot chip. Trying too hard—again— he chunked the chip. He was now looking at a 15-foot par putt, knowing that a miss would make it virtually impossible for him to make the tour.

It was at that moment that his father began preparing his consolation speech. "I started to think about what I was going to say to him," Jay Haas said. "I knew I wasn't going to say a thing right after the round was over, because I know from my own ex- perience that the last thing I want to hear when I've come up short of a goal on the golf course is, 'Hey, nice job' or 'You'll get 'em next year.' There just aren't any words that are more hollow than that.

"At some point, though, I figured we would sit down and I would say, 'You're still only twenty-three years old, and you've proven you're good enough to get out there and stay out there. I know it will be hard, but you need to go and play great on the Nationwide next year and just take Q School out of the equation completely.'"

Fortunately, Bill wasn't thinking about consolation speeches at that moment. He was well aware that if he didn't make the par putt, his chances were, realistically, done. "I figured if nothing else, I was due to make one," he said.

He was right. The putt went dead center, and he was still alive—albeit just barely—at nine under. He now had to finish birdie–birdie or par–eagle. His dad knew that, too, having checked with Jan, who confirmed that the number had gone back to 11 under.

Sitting on the 17th tee, waiting for the group in front to finish, Bill Haas was trying not to think about anything beyond the tee shot he was about to hit. Often, the most difficult thing for an athlete to do at a crucial moment is to stay in the present, not to let his mind wander to the glory or the consequences that may lie just ahead. It was okay for Jay Haas to think that way, but it would have been disastrous for Bill.

"All I could do at that point was tell myself I had to finish birdie–birdie," he said later. "I didn't even want to think about par–eagle. I had to believe I could make a two on the hole right in front of me."

Given the wind and the pressure and the treacherous pin placement, most players were hoping and praying for a three on the hole. Twenty minutes earlier, Peter Tomasulo had stood on the same tee believing if he could make a three, he would have a great chance to get his tour card. He had made a five.

Haas decided on a nine-iron, figuring the wind would give the ball an extra hop toward the pin if he hit it the way he wanted to—starting it right of the flag and hoping it would drift in. He wasn't playing for the middle of the green or to find the green safely. He knew he had to get close. Having a long putt was just about as worthless as missing the green. "Boom or bust at that point," he said.

As soon as the ball came off the club, he knew he had made a good swing and had hit the ball about as well as he possibly could. Now it was all up to the vagaries of the wind and the bounce. The ball landed just right and short of the flag and pulled up eight feet away from the hole.

"Tell you what," Jay Haas said, "I've seen Bill play a lot of golf. I'm not sure, given the circumstances, he's ever hit a shot that was any better—or, for that matter, as good—as that one."

Bill felt pretty good about the shot, too, but it would be meaningless if he didn't make the putt. Par after a pretty tee shot was no different than par after an ugly one.

He took his time looking the putt over—everyone was taking his time over every putt by now—and finally stroked it at the hole. For an instant, it appeared as if it might break away at the last moment, but it held its line and dropped into the cup as the couple of hundred people around the green roared.

Bill smiled—barely. Jay let out a sigh of relief. "Now," he said, "he's got a chance."

He had checked in at home one more time on the 17th tee, and Jan had told him that 11 under was almost certain to be the number.

Pumped up, Bill bombed his drive off the 18th down the left side, only to watch it slide into the rough just as his drive had done on 16. But the ball carried so far that he had only 194 yards to the hole. Downwind, with his adrenaline running amok, he decided on a seven-iron.

That was plenty of club, but coming out of the rough, he pushed the ball just a little. The ball easily reached the putting surface, but it hung out on the right side, a good 50 feet across the green from the hole location.

Walking up the right side, surveying his son's putt, Jay Haas said quietly, "That is not an easy two-putt."

Jerry Foltz, who did the postround interviews for the Golf Channel, had now walked down to where Jay was standing. Foltz was a Q School veteran himself, having been through the finals seven times, so he could empathize with the players and, no doubt, the fathers as well. The closest he had come to making the tour had been in his first finals at PGA West. He had arrived on the 17th tee one shot inside the number and, after one of those interminable last-day waits, had hit his tee shot into the water and made triple bogey. He knew the empty feeling of being "that close."

"The last thing in the world I wanted to do was stick a microphone in Jay's face after Bill had three-putted to miss by one," he said later. "If Bill didn't make birdie, the plan was to check with [producer] Keith Hirshland to see if he still wanted me to talk to Jay. I was hoping he would say no. Most of the time, Keith will let me make a call like that, and even though I knew Jay would do it no matter what, I really would have felt awkward asking him. I was probably pulling for Bill at that moment about as much as Jay was."

Probably not quite as much. Jay had now pulled his cap as low on his forehead as it would go, hoping no one could see his reaction as Bill lined up his eagle putt. "Just don't do anything crazy," he said in a whisper.

Bill didn't. The ball tracked across the green and pulled up about four feet short of the hole. "Little bit sidehill, too," Jay said. "He's got to be careful not to baby it, because it will slide off if he does."

There is no putt a golfer feels more pressure on than a sidehill slider from three to five feet that you *must* make. Players call anything from three to five feet under pressure "the throw-up zone."

Bill Haas was in the throw-up zone, with the next year of his life at stake. "When I walked up to it, I swear to God my first thought was, 'It's 10 feet!'" he said. "Then I realized that it was more like four. It just looked like 10 feet at that moment."

In the clubhouse, Mac Fritz of Titleist looked as if he might throw up *before* Bill putted. "That putt may have been more important to Bill and Jay than it was to me," he said later, "but I'm not sure."

The last thing Fritz wanted to do was go back and tell Wally Uihlein, the CEO of Titleist, that their million-dollar baby would be on the Nationwide Tour for another year.

Bill Haas wasn't thinking about any of that. "The only thing in my mind was to make sure and hit it, not let it get away from me," he said. "For some reason, I wasn't nervous. I really thought I was going to make the putt."

He didn't take too long to line it up, partly because he didn't want to overthink, partly because he knew exactly what the line of the putt was. He stroked the ball smoothly, saw it roll toward the hole, and, just before it got there, start to slide to the left. One more roll, and it might have missed. But it caught the corner of the hole and dropped in.

Jay Haas's knees buckled from relief and exhaustion. He didn't get a chance to watch Bill accept congratulations from Hunter Mahan and Johnson Wagner because Hirshland had ordered Foltz and crew into action as soon as Bill's putt dropped. Jay talked about how proud he was of Bill, how he had battled back on the last two holes, and how glad he knew Bill was that this was over. Foltz thanked him. The camera was turned off.

It was only then that Jay Haas let the tears come.

Q SCHOOL IS DIFFERENT from any other golf tournament in the world in that most of the final-day suspense is over long before the last groups finish. On Crooked Cat, the last threesomes on the course were those players who were so far back going into the last day that a low round wouldn't even get them full status on the Nationwide Tour.

Brad Lardon, who had gotten through the finals successfully

on four different occasions, shot 67 in the third-to-last group off the first tee at Crooked Cat and moved from 153rd place to a tie for 142nd. One of those he was tied with was Brad Klapprott, who never recovered after his back woes on Saturday. He shot 75 the final day.

On Panther Lake, the last groups were in a completely different mode. Only a collapse of biblical proportions would keep them from getting their cards. D. A. Points and Michael Allen both shot 74 in the final round and were still eight and five shots inside the number, respectively.

Ron Whittaker spent the day avoiding serious trouble, playing for the middle of greens and not taking chances. He shot 72, which left him at 13 under, in a very comfortable and satisfying tie for 13th place. He was finally able to trade in his Ambien and Pepto-Bismol for a beer. The champagne would come after he got home. One of those he tied with was Bubba Dickerson, who also shot 72 the last day after 66–67 in the fourth and fifth rounds had gotten him into a comfortable position. His plan to try to pick up his play and be more aggressive as the tournament wore on had worked. On the calm days, he had taken advantage and produced low scores. On the windy ones, he had been more conservative. On Monday, even par was more than satisfying.

Like Dan Forsman, Steve Stricker made a late move on the last day, finally finding some fairways with his driver and making some putts. But he had started from too far back, and shooting 67 only got him to nine under par, two shots outside the number. "At least I didn't come apart, which was entirely possible the way I was hitting the ball the first few days," he said. "It was disappointing, but when it was over, I actually felt better about my game than I had in a good long while."

Brian Henninger finished three shots farther back, at six under, but he also felt better after his last three rounds were under par following three straight days when he was over par. Larry Mize wasn't nearly as sanguine as Stricker or Henninger after shooting 76 the last day, dropping him from an outside shot to make the number (he had been six under par starting out) to a tie for 88th place at two under par. He would play in 2006 on his status as a past champion, a past Masters champion, and a nice guy. The last two credentials would probably get him into more events than his past champion status would.

"That's a long, grinding week," he said, forcing a smile. "I think it's fair to say it's a young man's event."

David Sutherland, who at thirty-nine wasn't as old as Mize but wasn't as young as most in the field, also had a bad final day, shooting 77 to finish at even par in a tie for 102nd place. "As it turned out, I needed to shoot 66 today to make the big tour again," he said. "That's the only number that mattered to me. If I'd shot 67, I'd probably feel worse than I do now after shooting 77, because I'd have to go home and second-guess ten different places where I could have saved one shot. I wasn't out here look-ing to get status on the Nationwide. Thirty-third would have been no different to me than 102nd. In some ways, 102nd might be better for me than 33rd or 43rd because it tells me I need to get serious about finding my next act."

Bob May finished one shot behind Sutherland but was pleased that his back had held up for six rounds. "If I can play six rounds here, I should be able to play four on tour," he said.

Steve Wheatcroft would be going to the Nationwide as a con-ditional player after finishing at three over par. He had never gotten it going again after his blazing start in the third round fizzled.

The cutoff number for full-fledged Nationwide status was four under par. There were 46 players between 10 under and four under, and full status went to the next 50 players after the

PGA Tour qualifiers or the number closest to 50. After the 46 players who qualified for full Nationwide status, there were 11 more at three under, meaning those at that number received only conditional status. For players like Patrick Damron and Scott Ford, hanging on to full Nationwide status at four under was important. For Hiroshi Matsuo, missing out by three shots after a final-round 72 also was important because it meant he wouldn't get into all the tournaments he wanted to play in early in the year.

"I'll still have a decent number," he said. "I just have to take advantage when I get a chance."

Nine players had come from outside the number on the final day to get their cards. Alex Aragon's 65, moving him from a tie for 65th to a tie for 18th, was the most dramatic. No one else had come from more than two shots outside the number to make the PGA Tour. The two players who took the biggest tumbles were Johnson Wagner and Joe Alfieri, who both shot 78 the last day. Alfieri bravely hung around the scoreboard for a while watching the late numbers go up. He forced a smile when people asked him how he had done and said simply, "Didn't play well today."

The worst back-nine collapse belonged to Grant Waite, who shot 32–42 to miss reclaiming full-fledged tour status by one shot, going from a tie for seventh place with nine holes to play to a tie for 33rd at the end of the day. A four-putt double bogey on the 10th hole had started his slide, and unlike at Lake Jovita, where he had been able to turn things around on the back nine, he couldn't regain control of his swing or his game.

Scott Sajtinac, who caddied on tour for Paul Goydos, was working for Waite at Q School and looked as shaken as his player walking off the 18th green. "I'm not sure I've ever seen a good player go through anything like that in all my years in golf," he said. "I don't know who felt more helpless out there, Grant or me."

Three Walker Cuppers playing their first Q School had won their cards, led by John Holmes, who never shot higher than 69 all week. He was the only player with six rounds in the 60s, and his last-day 69 wrapped up first place by three shots over veteran Alex Cejka. Nick Thompson, tied with D. A. Points for third place another two shots back. Jeff Overton, who had started the day one shot outside the number, came through with a 69 that jumped him past eighteen players into a tie for 13th place.

Holmes, Thompson, and Overton were three of the ten players who pulled off the unlikely feat of making it through all three stages. A total of 973 players had teed it up at the twelve first-stage sites in October. Ten would be members of the PGA Tour in 2006. In addition to those three, they were Ron Whittaker, John Engler, Alex Aragon, Henrik Bjornstad, Matt Hansen, Michael Connell, and B. J. Staten.

In October 2006, those ten names would give hope and inspiration to everyone playing at first-stage sites or even at the preliminary-round sites that Steve Carman promised would be in place for the 2006 Q School.

BOB HEINTZ KEPT HIS PROMISE, lingering by the scoreboard while the late numbers were being posted. As at Lake Jovita, he knew his only hope was that someone in one of the late groups had suffered the kind of monumental collapse that had afflicted Colby Beckstrom.

"Almost everyone playing late is an experienced player, except for Holmes and Thompson," he said. "They'd both have to shoot close to 80 to give the 10 unders a chance, and I don't see that happening."

He was right. Several players did what Bill Haas had done, birdieing the 18th to get to 11 under, including veterans Frank Lickliter and Mathias Gronberg. Mike Sposa, another ex–tour player trying to return there, eagled the last hole to jump from 10 under to 12 under. As soon as the final scores went up, Heintz headed for his car.

"There are a lot of guys I'm really happy for," he said. "But right now, hanging around to watch people celebrate isn't going to work too well for me."

The scene around the clubhouse had turned into a late-afternoon party. Players who had been living something approaching a monastic life for nine days were letting loose. It was unlikely that anyone would top the David Feherty record for celebration, however. In 1993 Feherty had made it through Q School in Palm Springs and had passed out in the back row, stretched across several chairs the next morning while enduring a media orientation session.

Still, there were a lot of happy people inside the dining room and on the back patio next to the scoreboard. Most of the players who had made the PGA Tour were celebrating, as were a handful of players for whom full status on the Nationwide was a victory.

Daisuke Maruyama, a thirty-four-year-old Japanese player who had finished tied for seventh in his first attempt to make it to the PGA Tour, stood in front of his name and score having his picture taken repeatedly by Japanese photographers.

Mac Fritz sat inside at a table with friends accepting congratulations from people who knew how important it was to him to have Bill Haas on the PGA Tour. One player after another paraded over to the Golf Channel to talk about how thrilled he was to be going to the PGA Tour.

"It's an interesting dichotomy," said Marty Caffey, who had been on hand for many Q School finales. "You will see more happy people — really, truly happy people — on the last day of Q School than at any other tournament all year. Where else do you break out champagne for finishing in a tie for 26th?

"But you also see more sad people—truly sad people—than [on] any other day of the year, because there are always those guys who have put in heart and soul and have come up one or two strokes short, who have to live with one missed putt or one bad swing for an entire year, or longer, because there's no guarantee that you'll make it next year or the year after."

Ten players had missed the tour by one shot. No one was more of a hard-luck case than Briny Baird, who was at Q School only because of Jason Gore's sudden success. He missed his card by one shot. So did Heintz, Waite, and Forsman—each in a different way, each as brokenhearted. Tomasulo and Tolles would each look back at one bad swing that had produced a backbreaking double bogey—Tomasulo at the 17th, Tolles at the ninth. Johnson Wagner and Joe Alfieri would go home and wonder why their games had fallen apart on the last day.

For those who had made it, the celebration would continue that night at a party thrown by the tour to welcome them—or welcome them back—to the land of courtesy cars, free telephones, and first-class plane tickets. One player who would not be going to that party was Jeff Martin. It didn't matter. He walked out of the clubhouse with some friends shortly after five o'clock with a bottle of champagne in each hand. Martin had finished 152nd among the 154 players who had completed all six rounds.

That was just fine with him. He was a club pro who had surprised himself by getting through second stage. He had shared a range with Larry Mize, and he had competed solidly for six days. After a second-round 79, he had shot 75 each of the last four days. He wouldn't be going to the PGA Tour, but he was justifiably proud of what he had accomplished.

"Greatest week of my life," he said, holding up a champagne bottle. "I'll never forget it."

In one sense, he spoke for everyone in the field. No one who plays Q School ever forgets the experience, but only a few get to savor it. In 2005 there were thirty-three players who would relish the memories of their week at Orange County National: the thirty-two who left the premises with PGA Tour cards in their hands, and the one who left with two bottles of champagne in his.

EPILOGUE: DECEMBER 2006

ONE YEAR LATER, nine members of the Q School Class of 2005 were home relaxing when Q School began again. Two of them—John Holmes, rechristened J. B. Holmes, and Brett Wetterich—had won on the PGA Tour and earned exemptions at least through 2008. Wetterich, after making it through the '05 finals on the qualifying number, had one of those dream years that all players believe is within their grasp. He finished 10th on the money list with slightly more than $3 million in earnings and made the Ryder Cup team. To go from Q School in December to playing in the Ryder Cup the following September is an almost unheard-of feat.

It is stories like Wetterich's that keep players coming back to Q School year after year. Frank Lickliter, the forty-two-year-old tour veteran who had to make a five-foot birdie putt on the last hole on the last day at Orange County National to get his playing privileges back, ended up making $1,655,678 in '06—good for 44th place on the money list. Bill Haas, who kept his father and Mac Fritz of Titleist in so much suspense until he made *his* last birdie putt, made more than $887,000 to finish 99th on the money list, keeping him comfortably clear of a return trip to Q School.

In addition to Wetterich, Holmes, Lickliter, and Haas, five other players kept their cards for 2007: Nick Watney, Hunter

Mahan, Daisuke Maruyama, Will Mackenzie, and Mathias Gronberg, who squeezed in by finishing 124th on the money list. Six other members of the class of '05 finished in the 126th to 150th category, led by Bubba Dickerson (who missed the top 125 by $10,000), Brian Bateman, Jeff Overton, Marco Dawson, Robert Garrigus, and Alex Cejka. All but Dickerson and Overton made it successfully through the '06 finals, improving their '07 status.

Seventeen of the thirty-two players who celebrated on Q School graduation day in '05 found themselves back at second stage in '06 after failing to make the top 150 on the money list. Michael Allen, the man who plans his winter vacations around the finals, made it to his thirteenth finals and then survived there again, finishing tied for 25th, giving him yet another chance to play the tour since he would have exempt status in 2007. Other second-stage returnees weren't as fortunate. Ron Whittaker, now a father, finished 174th on the money list, then missed at second stage by one shot for the fifth time in his career. B. J. Staten, after finishing 182nd on the money list, also failed to make it through second stage. Fortunately for both, they had already guaranteed themselves full status on the Nationwide Tour for '07 by finishing in the top 200 on the PGA Tour money list. So missing at second stage wasn't quite as painful as in the past, when it left them with no status at all. The same was true of Nick Thompson, who finished 180th on the money list and didn't survive second stage. Tom Byrum, like Allen a finals veteran, did make it back there for the tenth time but fell one stroke short of getting his card back. He would play 2007 on past champions status.

The best story from the Q School Class of 2005 was about someone who failed to get his card. Steve Stricker rallied late at Orange County National but came up two shots outside the cut number. As disappointed as he was, he went home believing he had found something in his swing that would benefit him when he got into events during '06 as a past champion. Like other good players who had lost fully exempt status, he wrote letters to tournament directors asking them to consider him for sponsor exemptions. "I was thinking between my [past champions] number and a few exemptions I might get to play twenty times," he said.

As it turned out, he played in seventeen tournaments in 2006, but that was plenty. He started the year well by finishing tied for 14th at the AT&T Pebble Beach National Pro-Am. He then got a sponsor exemption into Houston in April, played well the first three rounds, and then shot 66 on the last day to zoom past most of the field and finish third. The $374,000 he earned put him well along the road to avoiding a repeat trip to Q School. By the time June was over, Q School was nothing more than an unpleasant memory. Stricker successfully qualified for the U.S. Open, then led after two rounds before finishing sixth, which added another $174,000 to his earnings. A week later, he finished tied for second at the Booz-Allen Classic outside Washington and went over the $1 million mark for the year after cashing a check for $330,000.

"It's nice to know that my game was there; it was just a matter of finding my confidence again," he said, relaxing in the clubhouse during a rain delay at the Booz-Allen. "It's amazing how playing well in one tournament can remind you that you're a good player again. I'll always be grateful to the people in Houston for giving me the sponsor's spot. That tournament jump-started my career again."

Stricker's story is not an unfamiliar one: a good player falls on hard times, keeps grinding, and then finds something again. What is frightening is how quickly it can come and go, even for an elite player. During the 2006 season, Lee Janzen was where

Stricker had been in 2004 and 2005. The two-time U.S. Open champion was exempt only because, being in the top 50 in career earnings, he was able to use a one-time one-year exemption. Most of the year he struggled to make cuts, before a late rally in the fall vaulted him to 132nd on the money list. He decided to endure Q School again, trying to improve his status for 2007. But he could do no better than finish 90th at Q School and would go into the new year depending on the kindness of strangers — tournament directors — who he hoped would look at him as a two-time U.S. Open champion, not as a struggling Q Schooler.

Several players who had failed at Q School in 2005 had much better luck in 2006. Most notable in that group was George McNeill. In '05 at the TPC Tampa Bay, McNeill had bogeyed three of the last five holes — including the 18th — to miss making it to second stage by one shot. His par putt on 18 swerved about two inches wide of the hole, leaving him wondering if it was time to stop chasing the dream.

"I had to at least think about it," he said. "I was getting married and closing in on thirty and the best I had been able to do was make it to the finals once and then I did nothing on the Nationwide the next year. I had no status anywhere. I really didn't want to go back to grinding in mini-tour events trying to break even or make a little money if I was lucky."

Thinking about his future, McNeill accepted a job as an assistant pro at a club in Naples, Florida. He wasn't sure if being a club pro was what he wanted to do long term, but in the short term he figured it would give him time to decide what his next move might be and to perhaps find out if he would enjoy teaching and trying to run a business.

By early spring he was pretty convinced club pro life wasn't for him. "As soon as I got back to the range and began practicing, I knew the bug was still there," he said. "Of course, there's a big difference between having the bug and having the talent. But I knew I wanted to keep trying—at least one more time."

In June, McNeill qualified for the U.S. Open at Winged Foot. That was a confidence builder, although he had qualified for the Open before. He missed the cut but felt he had played pretty good golf on a very difficult golf course—one on which the winning score on Sunday was five over par. He arrived at Q School thinking his game was in better shape than it had been in several years, but knowing if he didn't get out of first stage, he would have to think seriously about leaving competitive golf behind. He breezed through the first two stages—fourth at TPC Tampa Bay, third at Lake Jovita—and arrived at PGA West for the finals brimming with confidence. He started well—an opening 67—and went from there. He went into the last day with a two-shot lead and proceeded to shoot a 30 on the front nine to blow the rest of the field away. Even with a back-nine bogey, he still finished 23 under par, which put him five shots clear of runner-up Robert Garrigus. Not only was he on the PGA Tour for the first time, but with card number 1 from Q School he would be able to plan his schedule in advance, not wait to see if his number came up—especially on the West Coast.

"It's the most unbelievable feeling I've ever had in golf," he said. "Now I just have to carry this over to playing the tour. My goal now is to *not* have a chance to defend my title."

Almost as happy as McNeill was Steve Wheatcroft, the young pro who had surprised himself in '05 by making it through second stage at Lake Jovita, then had a chance to go low on the third day at the finals before a late collapse dropped him way back—a lapse that he never recovered from. Wheatcroft played reasonably well on the Nationwide Tour with partially exempt status (he finished 85th on the money list), but the experience of playing at that level week after week clearly paid off when he got back to Q School. This time, he easily made it through second stage, and then he played six steady days of golf at the finals to finish all alone in seventh place. He had come a long way from pulling his clubs around Lake Jovita back in November of 2005. Needless to say, he instantly became very popular with caddies, agents, and equipment reps—his new best friends.

Bob Heintz already knew caddies, agents, and equipment reps. He had slogged back to the Nationwide Tour in '06 after missing getting his PGA Tour card back by one shot at Orange County National. He played decently but not as well as he had hoped, finishing 43rd on the Nationwide money list, meaning he had to make the trek back to second stage again. He made it through second stage and during finals was never in serious danger of falling out of the top 30. He wound up in 13th place, sending him back to the PGA Tour for a third time—hoping that the third time would be the charm and he would spend the following November home with his family rather than wondering one more time if he was putting his Yale degree to its best possible use.

McNeill wasn't the only player who had failed to get out of first stage in '05 whose fortunes improved in '06. Stephen Gangluff, who had gone from full status on the PGA Tour in 2002 to starting 2005 working as a cart boy at a club in Ponte Vedra Beach in order to have the chance to practice, ended 2005 wondering if he would ever find his game after not even coming close to getting through first stage at TPC Tampa Bay.

He had played reasonably well on the Canadian Tour in '05, so he decided to go back there and try again in '06. His year began to turn around in June when he not only qualified for the U.S. Open but made the cut and finished in a tie for 40th place after shooting one of the lowest rounds of the last day—a one-over-par 71. Suddenly, the demons that had been following him around golf courses for two years were nowhere to be found. He played well during the summer, then made it through first stage and second stage for the first time in four years. He ended up 48th at the finals, but having status back on the Nationwide Tour was a huge step in the right direction after two years of complete frustration.

As happy as Gangluff was to be back on the Nationwide, he could not have been any happier than Marc Turnesa. Having missed getting through first stage for a fifth straight year in '05, Turnesa had expressed the doubts many players express when it begins to look like they might be fooling themselves into believing they have the game to play on the tour. His comment about those who consistently missed at first stage: "When you can't get out of first stage, you can't claim that you're close to being good enough because the evidence shows that you aren't"—holds true for a lot of players.

In 2006, Turnesa could finally lay claim to being close. For the first time in six years as a pro, he made it through first stage. Then, as if to prove it wasn't a fluke, he made it through second stage, guaranteeing himself some status on the Nationwide Tour in '07. He arrived at the finals and promptly freaked out—shooting 83—the first day. Most players would have been convinced after such a round that they were overmatched. Turnesa put his head down and played his way back into the tournament, shooting 16 under par for the last five rounds to finish at five under for the week. That left him three shots outside the cut line for the PGA Tour but with full status on the Nationwide.

He wasn't on the big tour, but he could go home at night, look in the mirror, and tell himself that—at last—he was close. Very close.

Not everyone had a happy story to tell at the end of '06. Tommy Tolles never completely recovered from the recurring nightmare of his last tee shot at Orange County National. He failed to make a cut during the first three months of the Nationwide season and never got anything serious going all year, finishing 85th on the money list. That sent him back to second stage, where he had been so dominant a year earlier. This time, he failed to make it back to the finals, leaving him playing the "what-if" game that so many golfers play: what if that tee shot had found the fairway and he had spent 2006 back on the PGA Tour?

Garrett Frank was also doing a lot of wondering by the end of 2006. He had decided to give it one more try on the mini-tours and hope that his seventh try at Q School would be the lucky one. Instead, his Groundhog Day experiences continued. He made it through first stage for the seventh time, then flunked second — for the seventh time — finishing tied for 39th place, five shots outside the cut line. He would turn thirty-five during 2007.

David Sutherland would turn forty-one during '07, but he wasn't playing any more "what-if" games. He had played well during the second half of the Nationwide season, well enough to convince himself that it was worth the entry fee to try Q School one more time. This time, though, he couldn't get through second stage, and he knew it was time, once and for all, to find his second act. Jason Buha was considerably younger than Sutherland but also at a point where he had to think about putting his college degree to good use. After finishing 122nd on the Nationwide money list, he failed to make it through second stage, leaving his golf future in doubt.

At twenty-two, Ty Tryon wasn't close to thinking that way, but he had to be discouraged after finishing dead last — at 17 over par — at the second stage in Lake Jovita. The kid who couldn't be stopped at the age of seventeen appeared to be confused and discouraged at twenty-two. He could hardly be blamed. David Gossett's struggles also continued. He got into seven tournaments on tour in 2006 but made only one cut and then failed once again at second stage.

A number of players who didn't make it onto the PGA Tour

through Q School in 2005 played well enough on the Nation-wide in 2006 to avoid a return to Q School. Ken Duke, who had double-bogeyed the last hole at Lake Jovita from the middle of the fairway, was the tour's leading money winner (with $382,443, which would have been good for 167th place on the PGA Tour money list), thus ensuring himself a return to the big tour in 2007 and a spot in the Players Championship, the extra perk of finishing first on the Nationwide list.

Johnson Wagner, the kid from New York who had blown to a 78 on the last day at Orange County National, played almost as well as Duke and finished in second place, $10,000 behind him on the money list, meaning he would be a PGA Tour rookie in 2007. Peter Tomasulo, who had been so close to his card in '05, spent most of '06 running in place, never able to piece together a big enough week to jump-start his year. He finished 47th on the Nationwide list, meaning he had to return to second stage. He didn't make it to the finals and headed back to the Nationwide for at least one more year.

A number of fortysomething players also failed to get past second stage, including Brian Henninger, Mike Hulbert, and Grant Waite. Donnie Hammond finished 233rd on the PGA Tour money list in eleven starts but had his fiftieth birthday in 2007 to look forward to. Briny Baird, who had been hit with the double whammy in 2005 (finishing 126th on the money list be-cause of Jason Gore's battlefield promotion, then missing at Q School by one shot), was able to take advantage of his partial status to win more than $844,000. That put him 102nd on the money list and got him back to the tour without a stop at Q School. Guy Boros played well enough to make it back to the finals, but he couldn't hold his game together for six rounds. In all, forty players received cards at the finals, with thirteen play-ers tying for 28th place.

One of those who tied for 28th was Bob May. More than six years after his epic duel with Tiger Woods at the PGA Championship and more than three years after injuring his back so severely that he wondered if he would ever swing a golf club again, May played well enough in twenty-one starts on tour in 2006 to finish 142nd on the money list. But he wanted to be able to plan his entire year in advance in 2007, and he made that happen by slogging through six rounds at Q School. It was the continuation of a remarkable comeback story.

Q School is all about stories. Some have happy endings, some sad, some bizarre. But they are all stories about people who know why Greg Norman always says, "Golf is a four-letter word."

Nowhere is that more true than at Q School. Those who go there will frequently curse their fate, even those who survive and go on to have years like Brett Wetterich did in 2006. Nothing is easy at Q School. In a sense, those fans who told Larry Mize that he didn't deserve to be back at Q School were right. It isn't fun for anyone, young or old. But Q School is also a rite of passage for 99 percent of those who play professional golf. It is something they will never forget, something they will tell you they were glad they went through — though none of them ever want to go through it again.

It is like no other golf tournament. And for that, the players are very thankful.

AFTERWORD: 2007

THE PGA TOUR made Q School even tougher in 2007 than in the past by limiting the number of players who would make it to the tour out of the finals to 25 and ties instead of 30 and ties. Those last five spots that had gone to Q Schoolers in the past went to the Nationwide Tour, meaning the top 25 players automatically graduated to the PGA Tour.

This was part of a continuing trend and a desire on the part of the tour to continue to ratchet up the importance of the Nationwide Tour—something many players wanted, especially those who had been on the PGA Tour in the past or had been on the Nationwide for a number of years. In eighteen years the Nationwide has gone from sending five players to the tour to twenty-five, while Q School has dropped from 50 and ties to 25 and ties.

The thinking was that a full year of play is more of a test than fourteen rounds of golf, no matter how pressure-packed those fourteen rounds might be. Those who were exempt to second stage or the finals had earned those exemptions with their play during the year, so one could make the case that they had to pass two tests: one to get a first- or second-stage exemption, the second to get back to the tour.

Lost in all the pumping-up of the Nationwide was the fact that Q School remains the place where truly fresh faces can break in and where players who have had a lost year for one reason or another — often a crisis in someone's personal life sends him back to Q School — or old pros can find it again.

What's more, the case can certainly be made that Q School is a tougher test than the Nationwide. There's no margin for error. On the Nationwide, bad weeks can be overcome. If you play really well for two or three weeks and win or finish second a couple times, you can afford a dozen bad weeks along the way. At Q School one bad day, especially in the first two stages, can be the end of the dream. The one thing that is fair to say is this: bad players don't make it to the PGA Tour, whether they get there off the Nationwide or through Q School.

In all, twenty-six players made it through Q School in 2007. They ranged from forty-five-year-old Duffy Waldorf, a four-time winner on tour; to twenty-three-year-old Dustin Johnson, fresh out of Coastal Carolina University; and David Lutterus, a twenty-two-year-old Australian who had played the Nationwide in '07.

The medalist was thirty-eight-year-old Frank Lickliter, who in many ways defines the vagaries of life on tour. In 2003, Lickliter won for the second time in his career, made well over $1 million, and finished 49th on the money list. Two years later, he was back at Q School, where he had to make a four-foot birdie putt on the last hole to make it back to the tour on the number. In 2006, he earned more than $1.6 million, finished 44th on the money list, and put his career back on track. Then, in 2007, he went south again, finished 139th on the money list, and landed back at Q School...again.

Lickliter was one of a number of past winners on tour who found themselves grinding their way through Q School in 2007. The group included Waldorf and Carlos Franco, another four-time winner, and forty-two-year-old Jim McGovern, who had won in 1993 and had been a full-time tour player from 1991 to 1999. He had spent the previous eight years playing occasionally on the big tour when his past-champion status got him into an event, but had been, for the most part, on the Nationwide during that time. Each year he would enter Q School and each year he would come up short.

But he never gave up, and in '07, with the finals back at Orange County National, he started fast, getting to 14 under par after three rounds, and then hung on for dear life, finishing 15 under, which was good enough to tie for 19th place. Thus he earned a second life on the PGA Tour.

There were, as always, numerous intriguing stories among the qualifiers. Todd Demsey, who finished alone in eighth place, was thirty-five and was returning to the tour after surviving a brain tumor. John Merrick, Peter Tomasulo's pal from Long Beach, had the distinction of playing in thirty PGA Tour events in 2007 as a rookie and only *once* played in the same event as Tiger Woods. If nothing else, that showed the difference between superstar and newcomer: Woods played in a total of three full-field tour events during the year (San Diego, the Players, and Charlotte). Merrick's tour number didn't get him into the Players or Charlotte, so the only time he shared a locker room with the great man was in San Diego.

Woods won the PGA Championship and was player of the year for the eighth time in nine years. Merrick ended up back at Q School. He managed to get through the finals right on the number (14 under par) and earn back his privileges for 2008. If he is fortunate, he may get to tee it up in the same tournament as Woods more than once.

LICKLITER, WALDORF, FRANCO, and McGovern were the four former tour winners who made it back to the tour for '08. They were not — by any stretch — the only past champions in the field.

Among those who would play '08 with partially exempt status after not making it through the finals were Notah Begay (four-time champion), Steve Lowery, Steve Pate, Dicky Pride, Robert Gamez, Grant Waite, Ian Leggatt, and Peter Jordan. The most frustrated ex-champion had to be Ted Purdy, who dropped out of the top 125 (to 127th) during the last week of the season and then couldn't make it through Q School, meaning he would play on 126–150 status in '08.

Tommy Tolles, who had failed to make it back to the finals in 2006 after his nightmarish ending in 2005, did make the finals in 2007 — but never contended all week and headed back to the Nationwide Tour for another year. The same was true for B. J. Staten, who had a good year on the Nationwide, making more than $193,000 and finishing 28th on the money list. But he wasn't as fortunate at Q School in '07 as he had been in '05, finishing at 12 under par, two shots outside the number, meaning he too would be back on the Nationwide.

So would Peter Tomasulo. He never got his year in gear on the Nationwide, finishing 48th on the money list — one spot lower than a year earlier. He was right there throughout the six days, but needed one more birdie down the stretch — and never got it. He walked off the final green with the same exhausted look he had on his face two years earlier.

Marty Caffey, the Nationwide's player liaison who had become friends with Tomasulo the previous three years, saw him walking off 18 and felt awful for him. "Normally Peter's the friendliest guy out there," Caffey said. "When he walked by me coming off 18 I don't think he even saw me. He was completely drained. I honestly think '08 will be his year to get to the tour."

What's more, even though Tomasulo probably felt about a hundred walking off that final green, he was still only twenty-five.

The Nationwide Tour was much kinder to a number of other players who had failed Q School in 2005 and 2006. One was Marc Turnesa, who had been close to packing it in after his fifth first-stage failure in '05. He had made it to the finals in '06, which got him onto the Nationwide. Turnesa started well, lead-ing the season-opening tournament in Panama for three rounds before dropping to a tie for fifth after a tough Sunday.

He struggled for much of the summer but found his game again with two weeks left in the season, winning the Miccosu-kee Classic in Miami. That vaulted him from 43rd to 13th on the money list and clinched his spot on tour for 2008. He ended up 16th on the Nationwide money list, meaning that two years after he wondered if he needed to think about going home and finding a job, he would spend 2008 in the land of courtesy cars, free food, and $5 million tournaments — at least — week in and week out.

"It's a long way from mini-tour life," he said. "I just hope I can play well enough to stay out there."

Spoken like a true Q Schooler. Everyone knows that getting to the tour is only the first step — as difficult a step as it is to take. As Kevin Sutherland said to David Sutherland the first time the two of them made it through Q School, "We haven't done anything yet."

That's really not true, because you have to play a lot of good golf just to get the chance to play good golf for a lot of money. It's not easy to get there and it isn't easy to stay there — as all the former tour winners and players who have been back to Q School after playing on the tour can attest.

Turnesa wasn't the only 2005 Q Schooler to make it back to the tour for '08 off the Nationwide list. Nicholas Thompson won the second tournament of the year in New Zealand, was near the top of the money list all year long, and finished sixth at year's end, clearly benefiting from having spent 2006 on the big tour. He went back to play with the big boys feeling as if the ex-perience he'd had on both tours would leave him much better pre-pared to succeed than he had been after getting there in 2006.

Ron Whittaker also made it back to the tour. He won in Chat-tanooga in October on the Nationwide and jumped to 11th on the money list. He finished the year with more than $271,000 in earnings and headed back to the tour hoping that the third time — at the age of thirty-six — would be the charm. He would be joined by Brad Elder, who had first arrived on tour with the label of a future star nine years earlier but would now return off his play in the Nationwide (he finished 17th on the money list) hoping simply to find permanent employment there.

Some players were delighted to be on the Nationwide Tour in 2008. Pat Bates, after his withdrawal from the finals and his injury-ridden 2006, was happy to make it back to the finals in 2007 — without any issues — and, even though he didn't come close to making it back to the big tour, he did secure a place on the Nationwide. On his sixth try, Josh McCumber finally made it through second stage to the finals. Even though he didn't get his tour card (he finished tied for 85th place, eight shots outside the number), he did make it to the Nationwide at the age of thirty-one, which was a major step in the right direction.

Bob Heintz was nearly as happy with the way his year ended. Throughout the fall he was one good finish from clinching a spot in the top 125 and a second straight year on the big tour. It never came though and he finished 136th on the money list, meaning he had to slog back to Q School — again. This time he didn't make it through, shooting 11 under par to finish in a tie for 42nd place, leaving him with partial status on the PGA Tour and full status on the Nationwide for 2008.

"I'm hoping between my number and a few sponsor exemptions I can get 15 to 20 stars on the tour," he said. "The rest of the time I'll play the Nationwide."

Not ideal, but far from terrible. Heintz made more than $649,000 on the golf course in 2007, which is not a bad living by any stretch of the imagination. Richard Johnson, who led the Nationwide Tour money list, made $445,421, which is also a decent wage. In all, sixty players made more than $100,000 on the

Nationwide Tour. That was nothing compared to the ninety-nine players who made more than $1 million on the PGA Tour (216 made at least $100,000), which is why everyone wants so much to be out there. Matthias Gronberg, who finished 125th on the PGA Tour money list, barely keeping his card, made a little more than $785,000. The big tour is clearly the place players want to be, as it always has been. But there is a living to be made if you can make it to the Triple-A level in professional golf.

As long as they can carve out a living of some kind, players will keep coming back year after year. They will do it because golf is what they do and they don't want to give up playing a game they love to go and work someplace.

Beyond that, they come back because of people like Marc Turnesa, who went from zero-for-five at first stage to the tour in two years. They come back because of Jim McGovern and guys like Ron Whittaker and Brad Adamonis, who was a PGA Tour rookie in 2008 at the age of thirty-four.

But it may well be that their real inspiration in coming back year after year is Steve Stricker. From 2003 to 2005, Stricker never finished in the top 150 on tour. He struggled to find fairways, he wondered if he would ever be a good player again. At Q School in 2005, he struggled to keep the ball on the planet for most of the week. Only his experience and his ability to putt kept him in contention before he fell two shots short.

At the age of thirty-nine, he found himself playing in 2006 only on his status as a past champion and a good guy. He was able to use those two things to get into seventeen tournaments and finish 34th on the money list. He was voted the comeback player of the year, having jumped 128 places on the money list in spite of a limited schedule.

An inspiring story for all struggling golfers.

Except that Stricker was just getting started. In 2007, with the tour more or less reinvented with the FedEx Cup and "the play-offs," Stricker played even better than he had in 2006. He went into the play-offs ranked 12th in the new points standings, and as if to prove it wasn't a fluke, he *won* the first-ever play-off event at Westchester, vaulting himself into second place on the points list behind you-know-who. He then played well enough during the remaining three weeks of the play-offs to stay in second place. Woods won the last two tournaments to win the first FedEx Cup (not a major in spite of the tour's relentless hype).

Stricker finished second—first in the mere-mortals division. His winnings for 2007 were $4,663,077, meaning he finished fourth on the money list. (Which is slightly different from the FedEx points list, something about twelve people on earth understand or care about.) He was *again* voted comeback player of the year, something that is just about impossible to do—win that award two years in a row.

At the age of forty, Stricker was a star again. He had an exemption through 2009 and found himself in commercial demand—two years after he honestly didn't know how much longer he would be able to keep playing golf.

On one hand, the case can be made that Stricker's story is a once-in-a-lifetime airy-fairy tale. On the other hand, the case can be made that it does happen. Tom Lehman went from nowhere at twenty-nine to a start in his thirties and forties. It may not happen often, but it *does* happen. Players go from almost done to all the way back, just as they go from stardom to Q School almost overnight.

That's the nature of golf. It is why the game can be so gratifying and so damning—sometimes in the same week, sometimes in the same day. It is the toughest game there is to play mentally and it is the most unforgiving when your skills fail you at all.

But it is also a game in which there is always hope.

Steve Stricker's story is about hope.

So is Q School. Every single year.

ACKNOWLEDGMENTS

THE LIST OF PEOPLE who get a kick out of making fun of my lengthy acknowledgments is almost as long as the acknowledgments themselves. So to ensure that those people will continue to have the opportunity to joke about my tendency to go on...and on...buckle up.

I begin, as always, with the people who are the subject of the book: in this case, the golfers who took the time to talk to me before, during, and after the 2005 Qualifying School, along with those who shared stories about Q School experiences from the past.

They include Casey Martin, Tommy Tolles, B. J. Staten, Peter Tomasulo, Dan Forsman, Larry Mize, Jaxon Brigman (who was remarkably gracious telling the story of his scorecard at Doral for the one millionth time), Marc Turnesa, Josh McCumber, Stephen Gangluff, Garrett Frank, Toddy Brown, Kelly Gibson, Donnie Hammond, Mike Hulbert, Guy Boros, Blaine McCallister, Chad Wilfong, Ty Tryon, Bob Heintz, Colby Beckstrom, Rick Fehr, Nick Thompson, Tom Byrum, Michael Allen, Ron Whittaker, Bill Glasson, Brett Wetterich, Bill Haas, Grant and Lea Waite, David Sutherland, Steve Stricker, Joe Alfieri, Johnson Wagner, Jason Buha, Patrick Damron, David Peoples, Hiroshi Matsuo, Nick Malinowski, Bob May, Patrick Bates,

Steve Wheatcroft, Bubba Dickerson, Barry Cheesman, Skip Kendall, Brad Klapprott, Brad Lardon, and Jeff Mitchell. All of the above took part in Q School '05.

Others who were generous with their time and stories: Jeff Sluman, Peter Jacobsen, Tom Watson, Joe Ogilvie, Shaun Micheel, Jim Furyk, David Duval, Jay Haas, Labron Harris, Jerry Foltz, Kevin Sutherland, Billy Andrade, Brad Faxon, and Davis Love III. Special thanks as always to my longtime friends Brian Henninger, Jeff Cook, and the immortal worst player in history Paul Goydos.

Through the years, the tour's rules officials have always gone way out of their way to make my life easier and try to help me get things right. That was never more true than in this book. Steve Carman, who works hard to make Q School as painless an experience as possible for the players, was remarkably patient with all my questions and requests. Jon Brendle was, as always, the best there is. Dillard Pruitt and Steve Rintoul helped make my life much easier at the early stages—even though Rintoul was undoubtedly responsible for my lost wallet at Lake Jovita—and Mark Russell was, as always, Mark Russell. Enough said. Thanks also to Laura and Alex Russell for putting up with the token liberal in their lives. Slugger White, though always wrong, is always there to help, as are Mike Shea, George Boutell, and, particularly during Q School, John Lillvis. Brian Claar provided me with the perspective of both a recent Q Schooler and a current rules guy.

At the PGA Tour, I received ample help from Tim Finchem and his remarkable assistant, Cathie Hurlburt. Thanks also to Todd Budnick, Joan vT Alexander, Joel Schuchmann, John Bush, Joe Chemycz, James Cramer, Dave Lancer, Denise Taylor, Don Wallace, Chris Smith, and, of course, the king of all golf—at least in his mind—Henry Hughes.

I thank Sid Wilson for his friendship, if not his taste in Mexican restaurants. A special nod must go to Marty Caffey, who has dealt with just about every player who has been through Q School in recent years and spent large chunks of his time helping me chase players and other people down. This book doesn't happen without Marty.

Esther Newberg has been my agent for twenty-one books and is somehow just as enthusiastic and encouraging now as she was in 1986. She is still the world's worst sport and always will be. Michael Pietsch has now edited thirteen of those books and has lived to tell about it. His two most recent assistants, Stacey Brody and Zainab Zakari, have been remarkable resources for me — and, no doubt, for Michael. His new assistant, Vanessa Hartmann, has already shown exemplary patience. Heather Fain displayed great patience in doing public relations for ten books, and her latest assistant, Katherine Molina, has somehow survived the "Curse of Heather." Thanks, as always, to Heather Rizzo, Marlena Bittner, and, in absentia, Holly Wilkinson.

Chris Bauch and Kari Stuart, Esther's two assistants, deserve special mention because they have a boss who simply won't deal with whiny clients, so *they* deal with whiny clients — notably me.

My friends and family never get enough credit, but that's especially true at the end of this book and this year. My father's death was, as it is for anyone losing a parent, a traumatic event in my life, and I got through it only because of the amazing support I had from so many people. Just mentioning them here isn't nearly enough, but, for the moment, it is the best I can do, so here goes:

Keith and Barbie Drum; Bob and Anne DeStefano; David and Linda Maraniss; Jackson Diehl and Jean Halperin; Lexie Verdon and Steve Barr; Jill and Holland Mickle; Shelley Crist; Bill and Jane Brill; Terry and Patti Hanson; Mary Carillo; Bud Collins and Anita Klaussen; Doug and Beth Doughty; David

Teel; Beth (Shumway) Brown; Beth Sherry-Downes; Erin Laissen; Bob Socci; Pete Van Poppel; Omar Nelson (okay, Omar?); Frank DaVinney; Eric Ruden; Scott Strasemeier and Chet Gladchuk (who proved definitively last year he is anything but a fairweather friend); Billy Stone; Mike Werteen; Chris Knoche; Andrew Thompson; Joe Speed; Jack Hecker; my hero, Dick Hall; Steve (Moose) Stirling; Jim, Tiffany, and James Cantelupe Jr.; Derek and Christina Klein; Anthony and Kristen Noto; Pete Teeley; Bob Zurfluh; Vivian Thompson; Phil Hochberg; Al Hunt; Bob Novak; Wayne Zell; Mike and David Sanders; Bob Whitmore; Andy Dolich; Mr. Monday Night, Tony Kornheiser; Mike Wilbon; Mark Maske; Ken Denlinger; Matt Rennie; Jim Rome; Travis Rodgers; Jason Stewart; Mike Purkey; Bob Edwards; Tom and Jane Goldman; Jeffrey Katz; Mark Schramm; Kenny and Christina Lewis; Dick (Hoops) Weiss and Joanie Weiss; Jim O'Connell; Bob Ryan; L. Sandy Genelius; Jennifer Proud-Mearns; David Fay; Frank Hannigan; Mike Butz; Mike Davis; the fabulous Mary Lopuszynski; Jerry Tarde; Mike O'Malley; Larry Dorman; Marsha Edwards; Jay and Natalie Edwards; Len and Gwyn Edwards-Dieterle; Chris Edwards and John Cutcher; Joe Valerio; Dennis Satyshur; Mike Muehr; Andy North; Joe Durant; Bob Low; and John Cook.

Norbert Doyle has set more Q School records than anyone.

Basketball friends: Mike Krzyzewski, Gary Williams, Roy Williams, Rick Barnes, Mike Brey, Karl Hobbs, Phil Martelli, Jim Calhoun, Jim Boeheim, Fran Dunphy, Thad Matta, Jay Bilas, Tom Brennan, Frank Sullivan, Jay Wright, Dave Odom, Jim Larranaga, Jimmy Patsos, Tim Frank, and everyone in the Patriot League. Thanks again to the orthopods: Eddie McDevitt, Bob Arciero, Gus Mazzocca, and Dean Taylor.

Howard Garfinkel is the closest thing to a true Damon Runyon character I have had the chance to know, and Tom Konchalski will always be the only honest man in the gym.

The swimmers: Jeff Roddin; Jason Crist; the FWRH trio of Clay F. Britt, Wally Dicks, and Mike Fell; Erik (Dr. Post— occasionally a split second too soon) Osborne; John Craig; Mark Pugliese; Doug Chestnut; Peter Ward (my once and future coach); Penny Bates; Carole Kammel; Margot Pettijohn; Tom Denes; A. J. Block; Susan (where have you gone?) Williams; Danny Pick; Amy Weiss; Warren Friedland; Marshall Greer; Paul Doremus; Bob Hansen; and, as always, Mary Dowling.

The China Doll/Shanghai Village Gang: Morgan Wootten, Aubre Jones, Sam Jones, Rob Ades, Jack Kvancz, Joe McKeown, Stanley Copeland, Reid Collins, Arnie Heft, Bob Campbell, Pete Dowling (in absentia), Chris (the Rookie) Wallace, Stanley Walker, Harry Huang, Herman Greenberg, Joe Greenberg, Bob Ferry, and the professor, George Solomon. Red, Zang, and Hymie's voices can still be heard loud and clear.

The Rio Gang; Tate Armstrong, Mark Alarie, Clay (LB) Buckley, and the official secretary, Terry Chili.

The Feinstein Advisory Board: Keith Drum, Frank Mastrandrea, Wes Seeley, Dave Kindred, and Bill Brill.

Last, but not least, family: Jim and Arlene; Kacky, Stan, and Ann; Annie, Gregg, Rudy, Gus, and Harry; Jimmy and Brendan; Margaret, David, Ethan, and Ben; Bobby, Jennifer, Matthew, and Brian. Marcia made the last eleven years of my father's life joyful, and for that I will be forever in her debt. Mary Clare Gibbons put up with a lot the past nineteen years, and I am thrilled (almost always) to be known to most people as "Danny and Brigid's dad." It is the nicest thing anyone has ever called me.

John Feinstein
Shelter Island, New York

INDEX

ABOUT THE AUTHOR

John Feinstein's bestselling books include books on golf (*A Good Walk Spoiled, The Majors, Open, Caddy for Life,* and *Tales from Q School*), basketball (*A Season on the Brink, A March to Madness, The Last Amateurs, The Punch, Let Me Tell You a Story,* and *Last Dance*), football (*A Civil War* and *Next Man Up*), baseball (*Play Ball* and *Living on the Black*), and tennis (*Hard Courts*). He is also the author of three young-adult mysteries: *Last Shot,* which won the 2006 Edgar Allan Poe Award in the young-adult category; *Vanishing Act;* and *Cover-up.* He writes for the *Washington Post, Golf Digest,* and America Online, and is a regular commentator on National Public Radio, Washington Post Radio, and ESPN's *The Sports Reporters.*